EUROPE

BY COUNT HERMANN KEYSERLING

TRAVEL DIARY OF A PHILOSOPHER
THE BOOK OF MARRIAGE (A SYMPOSIUM)
THE WORLD IN THE MAKING

EUROPE

✦

BY
COUNT HERMANN KEYSERLING

✦

TRANSLATED BY
MAURICE SAMUEL

For all have sinned and come short
of the glory of God.—Rom. 3 : 23.

NEW YORK
HARCOURT, BRACE & COMPANY

Published in Germany as "Das Spektrum Europas"

❧ CONTENTS ❧

INTRODUCTION

INTRODUCTION

ALL NATIONS are of course thoroughly unpleasant things. Man, as such, is a dubious enough sort of creature; only in exceptional cases does a sample of the genus achieve the standards which every one instinctively imposes on every one else. And the moment he emerges as a collectivity the objectionable side of him increases in direct proportion as the pleasant side of him dwindles. The fact is that nearly every one has a special affection for his own failings. And as nature gives the preference to the defective rather than to the perfect, there are very few who do not take a particular delight in those qualities which others find distasteful—from smells to national prejudices. Toward foreigners most people feel all the more intolerant. The closer and more enduring their contact with other nations, the more clearly do they perceive their objectionable qualities: hence the general phenomenon of foreigner-hatred. I know of only two typical exceptions to this rule. Of these the first is constituted of the authentic ruling races, in the judgment of those whom they have not personally subjected; the second is constituted of the innately courteous. But these exceptions only prove the rule. In both cases the essential element is the maintenance of a certain distance; on both sides the mutual knowledge remains superficial.

These brief reflections should, in my opinion, suffice to demonstrate the absurdity of all national self-glorification. Of course every man should be proud of his nation, and should prove it in his actions: not in the sense that he believes his nation to enjoy special privileges as the result of special virtues, but in the sense that he feels himself to belong to it personally, and that he associates it with his self-respect. The early Roman understood it thus: his *civis Romanus sum,* his relationship to Rome, awoke in him as an individual a profound sense of self-discipline and of obligation. This, again, inevitably resulted in a tremendous power of attraction. But the man who

3

attempts to deduce his own worth from the fact that he is a member of a particular group is thinking askew, and, besides presenting an absurd spectacle, gets himself disliked. This explains the hatefulness of modern nationalism. The first thing, then, to be noted concerning nations as nations is that they are devoid of value. In not a single nation is the national element, as such, bound up with anything of worth. The individual who plays off any one nation against the others, who considers any one nation infinitely superior and the others inferior, should be forgiven only if he knows not what he is doing. For all of us have sinned and come short of the glory of God; we are altogether too narrow. It is only when the nations are taken in the lump that we get a tolerably satisfactory image of human gifts. The gifts of every nation are balanced by complementary defects. No; the only value in the national spirit is that it may serve as the basic material, as the principle of form, as the guide for the individual. It is for this very reason that every nation instinctively measures its standing by the number and the calibre of world-important figures which it has produced. And obviously there can be no question of worth among nations except as it derives from and leads back to the individual, for the one and only exponent of all values is the unique individuality.* Something further follows from this; namely, that the individual and the unique are more than the nation, be it one's own or another. Value and mass have absolutely nothing to do with each other. Christ preached love of one's neighbour just because he did not have in mind philanthropy and democracy. Accordingly every individual, as an individual, naturally possesses the right to sit in judgment over entire peoples. The value of his judgment depends solely upon his personal worth. In this connection his worth is measured by his ability to understand the material which a nation offers— and a nation offers nothing more—as a means of sense-realiza-

---

* Cf. the development of this train of thought in the last five chapters of my *Wiedergeburt*.

tion and spirit-realization in his individual manner and style. This, again, has nothing whatsoever to do with so-called "information." Whatever there is, is there, no matter whence it comes; it is to be seized immediately, directly, or not at all. A person can infer the national characteristic from a few representative individuals—or else never seize it at all. Understanding is something altogether different from knowing: it is a direct grasping of the sense or meaning, just as the art of painting, as distinguished from the labour of the copyist, is a direct grasping of the meaning of the visible in its total relationship.

As regards the meaning and the purpose of my critique of the nations, the following must be borne in mind. There is a fundamental distinction between that which a person means to himself, to others, and before eternity. And here we may already perceive the significance of one of the most tragic aspects of the "I-and-You" relationship: no man is ever really loved or honoured for his own sake—and he never can be, for it is impossible for the "I" to see the "You" otherwise than in relation to itself. The significance of historic personalities lies altogether outside of their intrinsic character: their personality serves only as the exponent and representative; and frequently the distortion between the personality as such and its significance "for others" goes so far that the living individual sees all the importance attached to something which to him mattered least of all. And every religion teaches that before eternity, all the standards derived both from the "I" and the "You" disappear.

That which holds for interpersonal relations also holds for international relations. This question, too—what a nation means to itself, to other nations, and before God—calls for three fundamentally different answers, which can never be reduced to a common denominator. In a certain sense the Jews are demonstrably the chosen people; but this in no way affects the negative judgment which, both from the personal and from the national viewpoint, it frequently merits. But as applied to nations, the question of evaluation in the light of eternity, in the full sense of that word, falls to the ground. No people as such has eternal worth, for it is only the unique individual subject which stands in direct relation to the absolute; for a nation to credit itself with the eternal worth of its greatest sons is nothing more nor less than to beg the question. As against this, however, it is possible for nations working through and beyond their historic significance, to achieve a higher degree of significance for humanity than any individual can—the very highest individuals alone excepted. This may be explained as follows: human significance is obtained through the symbolic treatment of the human theme; and if a nation is fundamentally so predestined, it may present the human theme not in one, but in many variations. Thus, from the point of view of humanity, German music as a whole means more than the music of any single German composer. But this particular circumstance leads only to one result: it reveals in a new, tragic light the irreducible difference in the relation between the One, the Many, and the Whole. A nation can achieve significance for humanity only in certain respects; namely, in those wherein its special aptitudes fit it to become the appointed organ for all humanity. Against this cosmic truth it is useless to invoke abstract considerations of justice—be they the grossly material claims of "a place in the sun," or the very sublimest which issue from the infinite worth of every human soul. And this cosmic truth constitutes the final cosmic court of appeal. In its presence, humanity, as distinguished from the individual and the nation, stands for the primary as well as for the higher reality.

It is my nature to see the one in its relation to the whole within which it belongs. And so, in this book, I examine the individual nations from the point of view of Europe as a whole; the question as to what these nations may mean to themselves I ignore almost completely. By and large I am convinced I have dealt justly with the nations in question. But I must concede from the outset that the reader can agree with me only if his world, like mine, is a purely dynamic world —if he believes the state of contentment to be a goal unworthy of man; if he judges all things solely as functions of inner progress, whether actual or potential; and, finally, if human life means for him nothing more nor less than the means of spiritual growth. Personally I have no views concerning a life after death, since I do not know. But if I examine my profoundest convictions, I must say this: I believe that the nations are nothing else than various embodiments which the soul chooses in accordance with its special character. In the last analysis, all mass phenomena, all historic effects, exist solely for the benefit of the single individual. To the extent that there are various stages, there must also be, if I am right, peoples of a higher and of a lower level. I believe also in a hierarchy of human values. Strength and beauty are higher, in the absolute sense, than weakness and ugliness; superiority is higher, too, in the absolute sense, than inferiority, and the aristocratic is higher than the plebeian. In the same way I believe that by the law of correspondence between meaning and expression, beauty and ugliness are always symbolic; for which reason I consider it a misunderstanding to make comparisons between different orders of values. And yet I am not a pagan in the classic sense, but a Christian; first, to the extent that I consider only the inadequate to be productive; second, to the extent that I consider every state of being, such as it is, capable of becoming ultimately a means of expression for the highest values. All this, of course, in different senses and on different levels. Small and low things, too, can become perfect—but precisely in the form proper to the small and the low alone. Again, it is metaphysically significant to the man himself whether he achieves perfection in the form of greatness or of smallness.

Thus I assuredly write—I do not believe myself to be mistaken in this—freely, without embarrassment or prejudice, yet not without a certain tacit premise. For me, dynamic as I am, such a premise is naturally, in addition, a specific goal in the scheme of development. That goal is a better Europe, peopled by finer nations: finer, that is, to the extent that this unchangeable natural human material, once it is thoroughly understood, can be made to embody a loftier meaning. Indeed, freedom can make of the thing that is, be it ever so ugly, something more beautiful. But for me another premise is also the unity of Europe today. Hence the title of this book.* The title only occurred to me afterward, when I perceived that what I had undertaken was actually a spectroanalysis of Europe. But the very fact that I could undertake such a task does presuppose that for me Europe is essentially a unity, built up of specific and mutually complementary component parts.

A few words, in closing, on the particular character and origin of this book. It is, as I believe, essentially different from all those that I have written hitherto. Fundamentally it expresses the same psychological state as that which resulted in the *Travel Diary:* since 1925 the focal centre of activity in my nature has again shifted, in accordance with the special periodicity of my life, toward vision and experience. But since life never repeats itself, the return of that psychological adjustment peculiar to the time of the *Diary* has resulted in new formations. This introduction, written *post festum,* may create the impression that some abstract plan originally underlay the schematic writing of this book: actually these portraits of the nations are the spontaneous formations of my unconscious; the processes of my thinking have had less to say in these than even in the case of the *Travel Diary.* The one thing I was conscious of while I wrote was the urge toward the concrete, the specific, the plastic—and then there was the need to let the ironic and satiric side of my nature live itself out for once. In giving free

* In German: *Das Spektrum Europas* ("The Spectroanalysis of Europe"). —*Translator's note.*

rein, during the years of work on this book, to certain forces within me which had not yet worked themselves out, I experienced a wonderful inner liberation. Logically, then, this book should produce the same liberating effect in others. Will it do this? That depends wholly on the sense of humour and the superiority of my readers. The only help I can offer them is the following piece of advice. Let the reader bear in mind, at every step, that the title-page motto, "For all have sinned and come short of the glory of God," bespeaks the true soul of the book, and that whosoever takes offence at one or another piece of banter is simply not playing the game. For some solemn spirits this observation may not suffice; they may still be unable to pass off with a smile whatever hurts their sensibilities: these I would advise to ponder à la Coué the fact that I have treated my own people no differently from the others: if they are able to rise, in the slightest degree, above their "I," a little reflection will enable them either to laugh with me, or else to think of ways of improving the national fault.

But there are some who will have for this book nothing but resentment. I think it well to state, then, that far from regretting this fact, I really hope for it. I hope that all Pharisees, all Philistines, all nitwits, the bourgeois, the humourless, the thick-witted, will be deeply, thoroughly hurt. Whosoever is untouched by the divine grace of self-irony, with him I can and will have nothing in common. I can have nothing to do with those who are in deathly earnest, who are unapt for laughter, with those, altogether too numerous, who are at once both profound and stupid. They are the ones who are really incapable of true psychological seriousness. No God can help them, and all intercourse with them is labour lost. It was of them that the great William Blake wrote: "The fool shall never enter into heaven, be he ever so holy." The ponderous of spirit are the enemies of the wise.

ENGLAND

ENGLAND

To the continental european the natives of the British Isles are altogether incomprehensible. This, more than anything else, explains the phenomenon of Anglomania. No people ever loves another than itself; and least of all for its own sake. The most primitive self-seeking so exclusively possesses this field that the Italian people, the most naïve of all peoples in matters of politics, promptly translated the national egotism into something divine. Thus, for me, the most gratifying feature in post-war international relations lies in the fact that henceforth every people believes in itself alone. There are external disadvantages, of which the most obvious is the desire of every people—including the Swiss German provincial—to speak its own language at home, even in the presence of strangers; but these disadvantages are more than compensated for by the circumstance that from now on, the relations between people and people rest for the first time on a secure foundation: we readily betray those whom we love—ourselves never.

On what foundation, then, does the apparent love of one nation for another rest? Where it is not a case of plain cupboard love, but an actual, undeniable, and disinterested attraction and admiration, the reason can be none other than this: that one nation sees itself mirrored in the other, not as it is, but as it would like to be; just as, during the World War, every nation attributed to its enemy the worst features of its own unconscious. Outside of France no one ever loved the French as individuals, in spite of their demonstrable virtues. In the folk concept of the Germans they are conceited and shallow; in that of the Russians, insincere and excitable; the Spaniard calls them undignified, the Italian arrogant, while the English simply call them apes. But for two hundred years the supremacy of France in the field of the mind, and of the forms of life, remained unchallenged; for every European involuntarily

13

saw in the French synthesis of form and meaning, in French
depth of content allied to external grace, an absolute model.
So every man who aspired to culture, whatever his personal
feeling in regard to Frenchmen, imitated France for the sake
of self-perfection; the position of power which France thus
indirectly achieved stood her in good stead—frequently to the
considerable astonishment of the others, who did not think
their high regard for the French spirit and the French language
the slightest reason for respecting the Frenchman as a superior
person. The same phenomenon, in its extremest form, is to
be observed today with regard to Anglomania. It is not because of the Englishman, but because of himself, that the
Continental is an Anglomaniac. Here is that absolute ideal
which deserves all honor and emulation, that English self-
control which involuntarily leads to a superior position, and,
radiating outward, to world-mastery. But if the British power
of attraction outrivals any which, as far as I know, has ever
existed, it is due to what I mentioned at the beginning; namely,
that the British are absolutely incomprehensible to the continental European. Thus nothing prevents him from regarding
them as pure ideals and ideological symbols. Every one gladly
offers himself on the altar of an ideal: he is not merely "pulling
some one else's chestnuts out of the fire." Nor are men inclined to be too hard on an ideal simply because the particular
embodiment of it is defective. Just as actual conditions in
Russia do not discourage the Bolshevist devotee, so we are
ready to forget England's disreputable actions. That the
most important source of Anglomania is to be found in lack of
understanding is definitely proved by the counter-type to the
approved Anglomaniac. Let European Continentals speak all
the English they want, affect English clothes and the English
way of life—they never bear the slightest resemblance to the
authentic Briton.

W HAT is it that is incomprehensible about these islanders? It is the particular adjustment of their psyche—the only one of its kind in Europe. With them the emphasis lies not on the conscious, but on the unconscious. It is not intelligence, but instinct—rising at its highest to intuition—which determines the course of their lives. But to the intelligence they appear to be sensitive extraverts, i.e. men whose being is essentially directed outward, so that psychically they have the same direct contact with the surrounding world as every one else has physically—an arrangement obviously different from that of all other Europeans. If the Frenchman or the German —I mean of course of the thinking type—is to find an intelligent approach to them, he can do so only by comparison with the animal world. When Field-Marshal Lord Roberts died, one obituary contained the following appraisal: Roberts had two great virtues: first, his instinct; second, his belief in his instinct. What Frenchman or German would ever pass the same judgment on a Foch or a Von Moltke? It is the custom, on the Continent, to apply such phrases to pedigreed hunting-dogs. To the thoughtful Continental this English character seems eminently proper for hunting-dogs rather than for human beings. Actually the average Britisher never reflects. When he does, the effect is generally devastating; and when, as an exception, this is not the case, we involuntarily get the feeling which Rivarol once expressed: *Si un homme, connu pour bête, dit un mot d'esprit, cela a quelque chose de scandaleux, comme un cheval de fiacre au galop.* If ever the proverb applied that the exception proves the rule, it certainly applies in the case of the exquisitely fine minds of England. The whole nation, as such, has an unconquerable prejudice against thinking, and, above all, against any insistence on intellectual problems. I could never understand why it was precisely the English critics who reproached me with "a lack of a sense of humour" until I perceived that this was their way of getting rid of something which made them uncomfortable. On their side of the Channel a social reformer can be put outside the pale (or could until recently) by the simple observation that "he sneers at the King"; in the same way the danger of somewhat profounder thought is avoided by the simple insinuation that it betrays a lack of humour in "its lack of a sense of proportion." And it really is a fact that a profound, clearly-formulated thought does not fit into the normal framework of English life. Already in the time of Queen Elizabeth, the German spirit (which, it is acknowledged, produced the Reformation with its demand for independent individual thought) was to the respectable Britisher a horrid spectre; even then intelligence as such was already regarded as an unhealthy product made in Germany. And not without some justice: in the modern world it is altogether impossible, as a philosopher, not to be wholly un-English and essentially German: just as in Roman days every philosopher was essentially Greek.

Yet the same Englishman whose distaste for intellectual problems borders on disgust is often capable of uttering surer judgments in the intellectual field than any but the most gifted Continentals: but on one condition; the problem in question must be of inmost concern to him. If, on the other hand, he is not thus concerned, he passes no judgment. Again we perceive the advantage of this animal psyche: animal instinct is unerring; but it only comes into play where the life of the animal makes it proper and necessary; whatever does not affect it just does not exist; it is outside its world of perception. Here we may find the creative significance of the oft-observed fact that for the Englishman the deed is the all in all; young people "do" something together; they hardly speak, or, if they do, it is to utter either an obvious triviality or a piece of nonsense; the rising to emergencies is typical for all of them; when the moment comes for a practical decision, for effective action, the decision comes and the action follows; and all of them see more sense in panting after a ball than in the perusal of good books, unless these mean preparation for some practical end. It further becomes clear, at this point, to what extent the strong-willed Englishman, with whom self-control is a national ideal, is no man of will at all: the ideal of self-control has sense only as an unfaltering, instinctive preparedness for action; the mechanism of inhibition, which really wakes the will, comes into play only on reflection; but, as in the animal world, the English live only through the spontaneous unconscious, and consequently the basic function through which they achieve their goal is, in strict accordance with Coué's teachings, the imagination. Finally we shall find in this animal character the explanation of their exceptional hardness and ruthlessness. We have yet to hear of the lion or the wolf who, while still hungry, was amenable to human considerations; beasts of prey follow their instincts frankly and freely. The moment they are sated they are again as harmless as dogs. At the time when the British and French disputed the mastery in North America, almost all the Indians were friendly to the latter; it was easier to deal with them. And that was why they lost.

Yes; the Englishman lives through different functions than ours. He is the animal-man. At the lowest end of the scale he is the horse-man, with corresponding equine features; in general he is, to use the physiognomic terminology of Huter, the mobile type, so that the prettiest miss frequently resembles, through sheer lack of inner content, a tennis-racket—how can a woman develop sensual charm when she is fundamentally known as "old girl," and when the highest praise she can win is that she is "a good sport"? However charming she may be in her youth, how can she help carrying in her knapsack—as the Napoleonic soldier carried the field-marshal's baton in his—the weather-beaten spinster with long teeth rather than the sweetheart and the mother?—If all this be true at the lowest end of the scale, then at the highest end the Englishman is the ideal model of the political animal. In political matters, therefore, he is as much at home as the setter among partridges. But it is exactly thus that he understands politics, and not as a thinking person. For the most part he gives no thought at all to the matter in hand. If those Englishmen who are capable of thinking, in the European sense—and there certainly are such Englishmen—are all agreed that "to muddle through" is the normal English method of advance, and that the British Empire simply grew up, with no intention on anybody's part, they assuredly know what they are saying. In any case the ablest English colonial administrator, responsible for the most far-sighted measures, rarely thinks of anything but food, drink, sport, and, if he is young, flirtations.

But now England no longer lives for herself alone; she must now behave as though her natives were just like other people. The most astonishing situations have resulted. English statesmen have taken to explaining themselves, as if they were Frenchmen; they confess to programs and ideals, like Germans. But the explanations will seldom stand the slightest scrutiny, the programs change with every wind, and as for their ideals—no practice whatsoever has ever been found, by any Englishman, to be in contradiction to these. The naïve Continental naturally gets an impression of complete dishonesty, perfidy, and characterlessness. But the results of this so-called imposture, and of this so-called faithlessness, prove that the impression cannot be right. In spite of all her proven hypocrisy, England always recaptures the confidence of others; in spite of all her proven faithlessness she not only does not lose her honour; she actually advances it! During the Napoleonic wars a Spanish general once demanded of a hard-pressed English officer, who had come to him for help, that he fall on his knees before him. The latter recounted the story at home, over the port: "Down I went, of course. . . ." Everybody in England understood. Thanks to this action, he conquered. All's fair in love and war. It is precisely where ideologies and similar things are involved that the Englishman makes expediency his watchword. How should the average Continental

understand this? The greatest and most important part of that
which primarily occupies his attention, giving it content and
direction, is of secondary importance to the Englishman. The
latter, too, has his high ideals, but scrutinized closely, they are
seen to be what the European would call rules of the game: and
that in a sense which has been abundantly made clear in Galsworthy's *Loyalties*. Loyalty to one's land, one's party, one's
class, one's prejudices, is the first law. The question of absolute
value is beside the point. If our ideals occasionally coincide with
those of the English—as, in private life, they do frequently
enough—it is sheer coincidence; in spite of this resemblance,
the psychological roots remain different. The Britisher lives
through instinct, through intuition, and uses his intelligence to
smooth the way for these, and primarily to gain time. The
German is fundamentally incapable of understanding this; for
him, abstract considerations are ruling realities. For all these
reasons, most of what is written in Germany about the Englishman is false; and equally false are the views of the French, who
so closely resemble the Germans in their objective intelligence.
They always were false. Did such a thing as the famous
English "spleen" ever exist? It is certain that the English
people have passed through a greater number of transforma-
tions than any other. Because of its immediate psychic contact
with the surrounding world it always undergoes an involuntary
transformation in conformity with the influence of the times.
It is self-understood that when new circumstances are created,
England will not cling to the old. New intellectual and spiritual
impulses penetrate much more deeply with the Englishman, for
the most part without his being conscious of them; they penetrate every part of his psyche, and produce changes which in
other peoples, more self-conscious, and therefore more faithful to principles, must work themselves out, if at all, over a
longer period of time. By this token it is precisely that British
empiricism, so repugnant to the French, which enables the English successfully to anticipate the crises precipitated by the spirit

of the times. The same quality accounts also for their happy lack of sentimentality, their mobility, their ready abandonment of an impossible position: those elements which the conscious type of mind retains simply as a memory, the Englishman uses and absorbs in the new adjustment. The English of the Norman period resembled, more than any one else, Baltic barons; those of the Elizabethan period differed little from the Flemings of the War of Independence; if Shakespeare was an Englishman, so could Rubens have been, too. The Puritan and the Methodist were in their time something altogether new; similarly the War affected England, in a physiological way, more deeply than any one else; today the twentieth-century Briton is more closely related to the Bolshevik than to his Victorian grandfather. Thus, today, the English miss is as free and unembarrassed, when she speaks of her sexual complexes, as she was in the days of her Victorian innocence. But I doubt, again, whether there ever was such a thing as the English "spleen." The situation is really as follows: the continental blockade had simply served temporarily to intensify the insular character of the natives of the British Isles. They consequently became more incomprehensible than ever. In the first place, when the blockade was lifted, they emerged as extraordinary eccentrics, in dress (the operettas of my boyhood days still carried the echoes) as in everything else. One of the first lords to cross the Channel and to reach Paris would have a lackey, carrying a parrot, precede him wherever he went. Outwardly this seems to resemble the habit of the poet Gérard de Nerval, who used to stroll along the boulevards accompanied by a tame lobster. Inwardly it meant something else. In the case of the Frenchman it was the self-advertisement of a poet on the hunt for readers; in the case of the Englishman it was frank and unfettered individualism.

EXAMINED psychologically, the Englishman undoubtedly stands closer to the animal than to the intellectualized European. Only he who perceives this can do him justice. He is accused of hypocrisy: no one plays the hypocrite less than he—and this is truest when he is ruthlessly pursuing his own ends under cover of an ideal. For to a certain extent he *does* consciously believe in his ideals, just as he believes in his religion; he is only completely ignorant of the driving shaft of the unconscious. This is exactly why he seldom produces the impression of moral ugliness. That impression is produced only when the self-seeker is conscious of the significance of his actions. This holds true particularly of the German; he is never forgiven, for every one feels that he can and should know better. If, in the shifty political game, he at least had that naïve good conscience while doing evil which is characteristic of the Italian, he too would produce an innocent effect. But of the German we know that he may be credited with all the conscience in the world. Everything, literally everything, is forgiven the Englishman because, judged from the degree of his thoughtfulness, he is an animal. His instinct for power works in him with the unconscious force of the animal. It never occurs to him not to follow that instinct. Such superb innocence and frankness is just the thing to achieve what would otherwise be impossible in these days of over-consciousness. Let England break all the treaties she wants—it arouses resentment, but not an ugly resentment. There is no doubt that England did Germany more harm than France did; yet German hatred of England is a thing of the past. Not a single one of her pre-war or post-war promises to India has England kept—yet she has not wholly lost the confidence of most Indians. It is astounding to observe how well the animal instinct for power understands the art of using the materials of the human spirit for the furtherance of its own ends. This applies to the spoken word before all else. The word that has been uttered is, at the proper moment, factually and simply forgotten. It is fundamental never to say whatever it is to the purpose to pass over in silence. More than one colonial possession has passed into British hands via the assault of a private buccaneer on the property of a foreigner. Should the outraged foreigner make representations, England turns a deaf ear. Deaf as she was to all reason and to all objections, England has never failed to come to the protection of the British subject when the foreigner tried to help himself again to his own property. A certain German of my acquaintance recently succeeded in obtaining the release of his confiscated property, the case being clearly in his favour. The administrator, however, failed to turn it over. He simply did not reply; and so England will keep the money, for the only recourse lies in a process of law which would be altogether too expensive. It is quite certain that the trustee in question feels perfectly honest about it. Animals simply do not reflect. They are innocently devoid of conscience. Thus the complaints of the Hindoos against the unparalleled depredations of the East India Company fell on ears quite honestly deaf just as long as the English instinct for power did not feel itself engaged. And today, in spite of all the enormous blunders they commit, English officials in India still remain, in their own eyes, in the right, because as a matter of self-preservation it is impossible for them to be in the wrong. The same childlike innocence characterizes the English attitude toward Ireland.

But that same instinct for power also teaches the Englishman how to back out at the right moment, and in this case too he acts with such transparent honesty that the question of conscious faithlessness does not occur to others, any more than the question of guilt occurs in the previous cases. It is impossible for animals to be inconsistent. And something else should be added at this point: involuntarily we think of the age before the Fall, before the apple was eaten, as of the happier age. The innocence of the English has in it something of the same effect. God knows what fearful evils Adam and Eve may not have committed before they ate from the Tree of Knowledge; in any case it was not written down against them. Let every philosopher and every moralist ponder these facts:

they seem to prove, and, as I think, conclusively, that everything is permitted to a man, as long as he acts in accordance
with the laws of his being, and as long as he acts in all
innocence.

B UT in defining the English as creatures of the animal type
we have naturally not exhausted the subject. Their claims
to racial superiority over all Europeans, as well as over the Chinese and Hindoos, are of course ludicrous. They are superior
only as political animals, and one may very well ask oneself
whether the Aristotelian definition should not be taken to
mean that political ability still belongs to the animal stage.
But the British have other immense advantages. If they are
intellectually inferior, they are all the more gifted psychologically. Their skill in handling human material is extraordinary. This implies that, over and above their animal gifts,
and apart from the intellectual aspect, they must possess very
noble attributes of a purely human order. And precisely because of his lack of intellectuality, the Englishman far out-
ranks any other European in his ability to establish direct contacts with the human element in others. He is the man who,
first and last, sees into and understands his fellow-man. He
does this even with those whom he is actually oppressing. He
never behaves as though they were not human beings; he is
always ready to recognize, as a fundamental human right,
their particular character; and he never awakens in others the
feeling that to him the thing matters more than the person. It
is for this reason that he is respected even by those whom
he oppresses. We find it quite natural that one man should
subjugate another and take personal advantage of the conquest; the one thing that we cannot forgive is a denial of the
loser's right to be what he is. In this respect, then, the Englishman is the most human of men. He allows every one his full
quota of prejudices. All customs are permitted to stand, as long

as they are considered "fairly harmless" (in India the burning of widows was thought to lie outside the limit). This respect is so deep-rooted that it finds expression in every phrase uttered. No one, unless it be an immediate subordinate, is ever commanded to do this or to do that. It is always: "May we suggest to you that you may perhaps wish to do such and such a thing?" On no account must the convention be broken that, in the last analysis, it is up to the man himself. Never is a phrase turned so sharply that the opinion expressed may provoke an opposite point of view. Is it the weather that is under discussion? Then it is: "I think I may say without fear of contradiction—at least, it seems so to me and I should not wish for anything to hurt any one's feelings—that the weather today may be safely called not really bad, that would perhaps be saying too much, but somewhat less satisfactory than yesterday's weather. Don't you think so too?" If the answer has to be in the negative, then, wherever possible, silence is observed; an uncomfortable subject is essentially taboo—and if it must be mentioned, this is done with the utmost delicacy. Judged from the practical point of view this attitude is, under all circumstances, one of absolute wisdom. For in this respect every human being approaches the animal. It is only the unpleasant *impression* that rouses his resentment. It is only the exceptional person who is angered by something on which he has to put an unpleasant construction on second thought. Thus all the resentment of the Russians, after 1905, was directed against those landowners who had been *observed* taking a part in the punitive expeditions. It is possible in this way to induce people to do anything—if only they are permitted to make up their own minds to do what is wanted of them; it does not matter if this freedom consists of nothing better than making a choice, before the politely offered alternative of one's money or one's life, in favour of the latter. In this and in no other way have clever women always ruled the world of men.

On this method, which always reckons first with the free

will of others, and never even thinks of breaking that will, is based the very possibility of the British Empire. The ruler has two methods to choose from: force and authority. Force is of no avail in the long run; its appeal, first and last, is to material power, and the ruler is always in the minority. It is not only the experienced ruler of men: every fairly capable animal-trainer knows that, once he has established the mastery by sheer force, he must operate, not primarily with force, but with sympathy and respect, and with the authority which derives from these. Permanent power belongs only to the man who has at his command the means of compulsion, but who has to use them and does use them only in extreme cases; for he alone has at his command the natural force contained in the free will of those whom he rules. And it is universally known that not only English politics, but also English education of the young, is based on the methods outlined above.

W HAT does this extraordinary gift spring from? It is in part the product of that Germanic world of freemen which has survived in its purest form in the British Isles. The Germanic freeman has always been such a self-willed individu-alist that early in his history he had already evolved those forms which made possible a group life without danger to his independence. But that gift is based primarily, again, on the animal nature of English psychology. Only he can become a good psychiatrist whose first problem is whether he ought to enter the lunatic asylum as a doctor or as a patient; only he promises to become a skilful animal-trainer who has in himself much of the soul of a wild beast—which itself explains his affection for his charges: in the same way only he who is fundamentally, that is, by his very nature, capable of reckon-ing with his own basic instincts, can respond to the basic in-stincts of others with such accuracy. The English way of doing things is to take only these instincts into account. And this is none the less true if, on the other hand, the Englishman always keeps his weather eye open, not to primitive matters, but to the pickings: this is the real relationship between the conscious and subconscious selves. The primitive in us is the deciding factor: but other motives are at work in the conscious mind. This is the correct order, and most misinterpretations of Freudian psychoanalysis result from the attempt to invert this natural order. But from the political point of view it is the primitive side which makes the ultimate decision. This is proved conclusively by the mere existence of the British Empire and by the tremendous attractive force of British forms. Even colloquial English is, at bottom, hardly different in its essential nature from the language which the elephant driver uses to his beast. A few stereotyped phrases. Infinitives. Sentences of very simple grammatical structure. A large number of cheerful ejaculations. Apologies. The subject matter must be entirely obvious, and must under no circumstances contain anything which might be personally painful to any one. In addition, the thing that is meant is hinted at, not, in the French sense, clearly and explicitly stated: in this way every one can think exactly as he wants to, without ever betraying his personal secret.

But the definition of the animal quality is not the last word even on this subject. The decisive element is the primarily *social* character of English self-consciousness. It is self-evident that this embraces, before all else, the English race and nation, for we are concerned here with something which is instinctive, and not with a product of moral considerations. Within the common body of the people as a whole, the English self-consciousness takes as its basis the "I-and-You" relationship; it therefore knows nothing of that complex of problems which the unsocial German perceives in his individual relationships of "I" and "You." Good relations with his fellow-men are more important to the Britisher than anything else. If the problems of English novels, with their norms of good behaviour, right action, courage, and consideration for others, read to Continentals like the problems of children, this is explained by the fact that in this regard English life is actually a sort of child-life. When Galsworthy once admonished Shaw that if he went on behaving as he did, he would soon be left without friends, the latter retorted, "And if you keep on as you are doing, you will soon be without a single enemy." This is the ideal of children. For children there is nothing higher than living nicely together. Only in this domain children are wiser than grown-ups; a good group life depends, in fact, on obedience to its accepted norms. Thus the finest blossom of English social life takes its roots in the primitive. For the Englishman, "Live and let live" is a self-evident maxim. He accepts it as a matter of course that his opponent, too, belongs within the commonalty. Among highly individualized persons this commonalty cannot possibly be based on "like-mindedness," as the German would have it (whereby he already betrays his complete social incapacity), but on the maxim "Let's agree to differ." It is this that makes possible a creative parliamentary life in England, in contrast with Germany: for in the last analysis the Englishman sees in his opponent, in the man who disagrees with him, some one who belongs to him. This explains the absence of bitterness and hatred from the social struggle in England. The struggle may, from time to time, be just as obstinate as anywhere else, but it is regarded as a struggle between combatants with equal rights. Every Conservative regards it as natural that the Labor Party should also want its day in court, and he does not begrudge it the right. At the time of the general strike of 1926 the Prince of Wales made a personal contribution to the strikers' relief fund, and at stated hours strikers and police joined in a friendly game of football. It is for this very reason that caste distinctions can flourish in England in a way no longer known to any other part of the Continent. That which produces an effect of intolerable "haughtiness" toward the "foreigner" and the "native," because of the fact that the basic common consciousness of the British is confined to their own people, does not, within the country, strike one as haughtiness at all, but as the frank affirmation of a reality. The various classes are, as a matter of fact, different from each other; but when no man is denied, on his own level, the full recognition of his human worth, even the lowliest has no occasion to pretend to be what he is not. The private life of a good butler is strictly his own affair; he participates in the life of his own employer only to the extent demanded by his duties, and takes it almost as an affront that the latter should investigate his private affairs—even to the extent of inquiring after his health: it is none of his employer's business. Thus I know of one case in which a conservative peer came to the assistance of his sister when, having been jailed as a suffragette, she went on a hunger strike; her ideas, her actions, were *her* business; she was somebody different from himself. But whatever she did, she did in accordance with the same moral norms which he recognized, and that put the matter straight. In England the diametrical relationship of "I" and "You" is recognized and sustained throughout. Let every man think and act as he wishes. In Hyde Park, London, the most incredible speeches obtain a respectful hearing. No one stops on the street to gape at an unusual spectacle. I remember once meeting in London a poet who had made it a principle to appear in society in evening dress and bare feet. After all, it was his own affair. As long as he differed from the average in a pleasant sort of way, and did not overstep certain bounds of decency, there was no occasion to turn him down.

But, by the law of compensation, this universally acknowledged right of every individual to be himself is balanced by a public life which is all the stricter in its forms. And this, too, is an expression of a *correct* evaluation of the polar relationship of the "I" and the "You." Thus it is that English conventionality and the English sport spirit spring from the same roots as the English feeling of individuality. Since all group life premises a renunciation of the personal element, that life must be all the more frictionless in proportion as the renunciation is universally observed as an impersonal rule of the game. The fundamental effect of this realization is to obviate personal conflicts. It is, moreover, precisely this practice which safeguards the private rights of the individual. English convention makes it taboo to inquire after personal matters unless they are spontaneously disclosed. And on the other hand personal matters should hardly ever be disclosed: one does not divulge one's emotions. Contrariwise, the forms of the group life should be wholly adjusted to the needs of one's private emotions. This leads to a fundamentally complete satisfaction of the two polar extremes of life—the private and the group life. And this complete satisfaction suffices to explain why one meets so little of the ugly in England: no envy, no rudeness, no indiscretions, no mob spirit—and yet no intrusive individualism. It is quite true that this satisfaction is complete only from the *English* point of view: the Englishman being the primarily social being—in many respects animal, and almost totally devoid of reflection. But this limitation applies to every form of life. Every form of life is subject to the law of uniqueness.

For all that, the English solution of the problem also has absolute defects, which, as symbols, are no less important than the virtues. These defects begin with the exaggeration of the virtues. The exaggeration of the private character of one's outlook results in that view of loyalty which Galsworthy has exposed so finely in his play of that name: loyalty means nothing more nor less than the unconditional defence of everything that one is part of—if necessary, at the expense of honesty, of truth, and of morality. On the other hand this practice of keeping as distant as possible from others unconsciously results in one's keeping equally distant from oneself. And the latter effect is even deliberately insisted on: did not a well-known critic, writing in one of the foremost English periodicals, declare, with regard to my *Travel Diary*, that the author lived "in positively indecent intimacy with himself"? Occupation with oneself—the primal source of all inner growth, of all true progress—is regarded with disgust. The consequence is bound to be that primitiveness which produces so childish and childlike an effect in all English statements of the human problem. For since meaning acquires positive reality only when it is expressed, this disregard of one's inner being leads only too frequently to real impoverishment. That this reflects the true state of affairs and not, as many Britishers assert, only a reluctance to reveal the inner richness of their life, is proved by the whole English literature of the novel. There is nothing particularly fine about the much-derided British habit of applying to the deepest problems, to the most inward values, the simple standards of "good form" and "bad form": or in the almost universal inclination to place the exclusive emphasis on the social significance of some life-question. We need only ponder on the fact that the one country in the world where blackmail can be so decisive a social problem is England. . . .

There remains for consideration the other characteristic which also has its roots in the same essentially social nature of the English: the sport spirit. This represents the deepest spiritual value which can be read into the human struggle for existence, just as it represents the highest sublimation of which it is capable. In the world of sport the protagonist tacitly confirms the rights of the antagonist. It is the rule of the game that one must rejoice in another's victory no less than in one's own. There must be no envy. Under such circumstances all life takes on the aspect of nobility. It is on the sport spirit that the prevalence of the ideal of the gentleman is based. It is a democratic ideal, in that every one can, should, and wants to be a gentleman. But in this, too, is revealed the animal character of the English. A gentleman is *bred*, like some noble animal; his instincts are trained. Thoughtfulness and insight are beside the mark. But we are compelled to admit that in this connection the animal character of the English psychological adjustment is an unmixed advantage. Young people can be trained only as animals are trained; and the animal, on its level, is more perfect than the human being. Why is it that the Boy Scout movement has meant so much more, in the affirmative sense, than all the other youth movements put together? Because Baden-Powell made it a basic principle that young people are like savages, and can therefore be mastered only by rules of conduct, independent of all abstract considerations. Whosoever belongs to this or that Totem must not steal, lie, etc. It is precisely in this super-sophisticated age, with its disbelief in all religious and moral standards, that this aboriginal way of dealing with human beings means salvation.

WE have now reached the point where we can properly understand in what sense the English world can serve as exemplar. We have only to envisage all the foregoing in the light of a widely known myth: the myth of the fall from grace. Man lost his innocence, and with it Paradise, when he ate of the fruit of the Tree of Knowledge. Thus the Englishman is by nature more wholesomely adjusted and more harmoniously trained than any other European. In him there is a fundamental right balance of the "I" and the "You." The common and the individual are mutually restricted, according to their significance, with separate spheres of operation. To whatever extent an Englishman may live for himself, there never occurs an inner isolation from the society to which he belongs and from the moral principles which hold it together. It is just this that gives his egoism—like the egoism of living for one's children in the case of every mother, and of nearly every father—a certain freedom and naturalness. And this leads to two consequences: on the one hand the Englishman appears to the outspoken Continental to be the embodiment, par excellence, of the ruthless egoist—the very thing with which the English reproach the self-centred German, whose egoism is only a path leading upward and outward from himself; and on the other hand that same English egoism seldom inspires resentment. Within himself the Englishman lays the exclusive emphasis on character, that is to say, on the harmonious co-ordination of the faculties; and in this he values the body not less than the mind, and puts the moral element above the intellectual. Thus he makes an "all-round man" of himself. Actually the English gentleman at his best is the one type that stands comparison with the Greek καλος καγαδος. If we add to this the two constants in his character, the human side of him and his high psychological gifts, we are able to explain why, after all, he carries conviction. He convinces simply by *being*. Thus the English never had to do any Anglicizing in order to make the world which came under their influence English. On the contrary: *because* they never set themselves that problem, the Anglicizing took place as a matter of course. On the whole, British supremacy offers the best proof of the truth of Coué's teachings and the best evidence against any system of culture based on the training of the will.

The foregoing observations hold true on the level of the average man. But what happens when this psychological conformation must serve to express a profound personality? In that case something altogether extraordinary ensues. It is a fundamental law with the Englishman that the personal element, that tender, delicate, easily wounded thing, must never be assailed or denied, but must be regarded as something sacred, in others as well as in oneself; it is something which cannot be violated by accepted norms; and finally, the conscious emphasis being always laid on the unconscious, English reticence and personal diffidence do not indicate a state of pathological repression: as a result of all of this, it is typical of the Englishman that the unique element in his make-up is in closer contact with his creative side than is the case with any other European.

It is for this reason that he gets the maximum number of ideas from a given situation; it is for this reason, too, that he displays so high a degree of personal initiative. It explains his profound understanding of reality, independently of all knowledge and experience. The Englishman is less given than any one else to obstinate preconceptions. In this respect, too, he is the most unembarrassed of men. Furthermore: a Spaniard, Salvador de Madariaga, recently remarked that England somehow represents that harmony between the ethical heavens and the objective earth which has the same significance for human progress as the instinctive co-ordination of eye and foot has for walking. This results from the fact that every psychological adjustment which is correct on its own plane can serve to express with absolute perfection the utmost human profundity. He who sees the earth in perfect perspective sees it potentially with the eye of God. The basic note of healthy human common sense is deepest wisdom. Thus it happens that England, which is the land of earthly positivism, of the highest appreciation of wealth, and of a kind of common sense which sees an enemy in any intellectual problem, is at the same time the land of the most sublimated European spirituality. English intellectuals seldom bear comparison with the intellectuals produced by other peoples. But nowhere can fine and profound souls be found in equal numbers. Thus it happens that England is the one modern country which instinctively understands happiness as a spiritual quality. If we observe the behaviour of the typical English youth we are compelled to think of the animal world, and to evaluate it as such. "To have a good time" seems to be the Alpha and Omega of their life-philosophy. Yet sometimes, within the limits of this innocent existence, we encounter a soul endowed with natural depth, and then its happiness is like the happiness of the blest. Then it means being anchored in that serenity which out of its strength can accept in joy all the world's pain. Then it means being lifted forever beyond the plane of the tragic. In itself the English view of life, to the extent that it is conscious, is devoid of the tragic element. Whenever possible, conflicts are ignored, problems are thrust to one side, and compromise is the rule of conduct. Thus the average Englishman stands on a lower level than any one who is aware of the tragic aspect of existence. Yet on the other hand the foundations of English character make it possible for the profound soul to lift itself suddenly out of this childlike acceptance of life into a divine joy; beast and angel stretch out hands to each other above the head of man.

Another function of the same faculty is the ability to "rise to emergencies," to "face things," which is signalized in every novel, without exception, as the fundamental virtue: it signifies nothing but the faculty to conquer every temptation with an absolute heroism born of the spirit within. There comes to mind the scene on the *Titanic*, when the women and children had been placed in the life-boats and the men, singing "Nearer, my God, to Thee," went down with the boat. From the same source, too, springs the profound religiosity of the Anglo-Saxon. But thence also springs, *per contra*, his peculiar sombreness when his life is not animal and has failed to take root in ultimate peace. Thus a profound representative of this stock recently wrote to me as follows: "It seems to me that the Anglo-Saxon, if left to himself, tends to gravitate more inevitably toward skepticism and denial than the German, and to take refuge in a bitter cynicism and general distrust of the reality of the spirit. This has of course been overlaid by religion; but in spite of his preoccupation with religion it has rarely gone very deep with the Anglo-Saxon, and as soon as he shakes it off he almost inevitably takes refuge in negation. It has always seemed to me that the true Anglo-Saxon attitude was admirably expressed by the Saxon chief who, after listening to the preaching of Paulinus, addressed the king to the effect that the life of man was like the sparrow that flew through

the hall, tarried for a moment in the light and warmth, and
then flew out again into the darkness, no one knowing whence
it came or whither it went."

W HAT is the outlook for the future of the English world
in the general European picture? It is quite clear that a
favourable prognosis is impossible. The conditions which make
possible the present situation, and which are essential to its
perfection, are steadily melting away. The more general social-
political conditions which threaten the old English life have
recently been so well summarized by Guglielmo Ferrero that I
could not do better than quote his arguments: "The peaceful
character of the English masses derives from the eighteenth
century; it was a result of the discipline and tranquillity in
which the great masses of Europe lived from the close of the
religious wars until the beginning of the French Revolution.
This pre-Revolutionary order persisted in England even after
it had begun to decay on the Continent. For in the nineteenth
century, too, the wars of England continued to be exactly
what they had been in the preceding centuries: that is to say,
matters which concerned the state, and not the people; as
against this, the wars which were waged on the European
mainland involved state and people in a common passion. Pro-
tected from all dangers by its insularity, the English people
could live tranquilly through the entire nineteenth century—
even in time of war. There was no such thing as universal conscription; the small armies needed by the state were recruited
from among volunteers—and these were almost exclusively
Irish. It was the state alone which carried on the war, the
people itself remaining sheltered not only from war service,
but from every anxiety. Thanks to this tranquillity, the great
English masses, concentrated though they were in a few cities,
within the sphere of influence of gigantic and ever-growing
factories, were nevertheless able to retain that high opinion of

rank, aristocracy, monarchy, and the possessing classes which had been proper to the entire eighteenth century. And this high opinion persisted in spite of a continually increasing labour activity and the rise of the modern school system. As against this state of affairs, all the Continental wars since the French Revolution have been the common concern of both the state and the people. The state declared war and gathered in the spoils if the issue was victorious; but the people—the workers, the peasants, the middle classes—were compelled to yield up life and limb, frequently without knowing what the war was about. And hardly was the struggle over when new anxieties began, for these peoples lived in imminent fear of new wars, which might break out at a moment's notice. Every people had its 'hereditary enemy,' whose behaviour had to be watched with unremitting vigilance. Wars and fear of war spread among the masses a spirit of unrest, of revolution, and of chronic opposition to the state: and only the English people was delivered from all evil—until the year 1914.

"The secret key which alone can open up the mysteries of English, as contrasted with European, history since the eighteenth century consists of a single phrase: Universal military service. The World War forced compulsory military service on England, too; for the first time in its history the English people as a whole was compelled to conduct a war. The consequences soon became obvious; they may be seen in the spirit of criticism and of opposition animating the English masses; in the leaning, new for this people, toward revolutionary doctrines which have hitherto left them cold; and finally in the attitude of indulgence toward acts of violence which less than ten years ago would have been regarded with horror. These are all signs which we Continental peoples recognize at sight. These are the characteristic reactions of the masses to a war in which they have been compelled to take part. These reactions were, and today still are, more violent in England and in Italy than in France or Germany, precisely because the Italian and the English peoples were less accustomed to war before the year 1914. The three years during which the system of universal military conscription had to be instituted in England did more than a century of history to transform that country into a Continental state. One of the principal differences between the great Continental powers and the Island Empire has disappeared." But together with this difference there has also disappeared the special privilege of England, the exclusiveness of the national nursery which was alone responsible for the insularity of the English type. And the material foundations of that supremacy which depended on England's monopoly of industry have likewise disappeared. Furthermore, the prestige of the white man has declined completely. All the dark races have begun to find the arrogance of the English intolerable. Yet all this would be of no consequence if the Englishman could only stand up to the struggle of a keen rivalry with all comers—just as the German does. *But it is exactly this that he cannot do.* He stands and falls by his *rôle* of ruler —he must play while others work for him. For he is essentially lazy. His attitude toward work is very much like that of the Greek. The beauty of English life stands out against the background of the other nations much the same as the beauty of the finest Russian aristocratic life stood out against the background of the dull Russian masses. This certainly does not mean to say that the English people is done for. Once again it will know how to adapt itself in good time to the occasion. Indeed, it has already done so; the island Englishman described in the foregoing pages, having heroically accepted his destiny in order that the Empire Englishman might come into his own, has probably committed suicide by now—an act of the highest moral significance; but an act of suicide nevertheless. The English colonial lacks most of the great attributes of the Englishman. He is a chauffeur among other chauffeurs. Thus it is that the American has hardly anything in common with the Englishman. Those Englishmen who still attach any importance to the survival of English culture are consistently becoming "little Englanders."

But is there any possibility of a moral and spiritual return within the borders of the Elizabethan age? Will it lead to anything more than a spiritual monasticism? It is precisely England which stands upon the threshold of the Mass Age. In a few decades the complexion of England will in all likelihood be much more radical than that of any other European country: we need only remember that the Dominions of New Zealand and Australia, based as they are on principles which lie on the further side of socialism, are also part of the world-empire: before long they will outstrip England in wealth, and will certainly furnish leaders to the Empire. England's victory has been ruinous; to be compelled, at this date, to provide military protection for colonies is hardly better than a Versailles Treaty. . . . Personally I am afraid: from the historic point of view the English world which I have described here has gone the way of all flesh. But as a private possession it can survive for centuries. And this it should do. With all its faults it belongs among the finest products of the European world. And if it ultimately disappears from the picture as a temporal power, it will survive as a gen in the body of mankind, just as the Hellenic world of old has done. For in accordance with the law of non-recurrence which governs all life, the *same* perfection as the English will never occur again.

FRANCE

FRANCE

Before the outbreak of the World War there was not a single country where men of broader spirit and emotions did not from time to time quote the old adage: Every man has two native countries, France and his own. And truly: it is impossible for any one who knows how to get out of himself—how to take a holiday from his "I"—not to feel at home in France, provided that he knows and understands the country and does not let fortuitous impressions interfere with fundamentals. And this hardly depends on one's personal attitude toward the French, whom few people understand and very few people like—especially since the world became de-Gallicized, so that the French type no longer has a universal but rather a specific—if not a downright provincial—appeal. It is very difficult really to get to know the Frenchman, if only for the reason that he uses his politeness as a shield to his tremendous reserve. The first reason for that home-feeling which every man of inward openness experiences in France, whether he be personally of the lonely or of the social type, is the following: this land embodies the one universally intelligible and universally enjoyable harmony between man and his surrounding world which is to be found in Europe. The Englishman, too, fits properly into his world; in the abstract sense he even surpasses the Frenchman in this, for if the latter is at home in France, the former is at home everywhere. But his life-form is incomprehensible, however attractive it may appear. The French is the universally intelligible life-form. It is universally intelligible because the focal centre which determines its forms of expression is not in the unconscious but in the conscious; and within the conscious, again, it lies in the intellect—and this intellect has created a perfect language for itself. Whatever becomes essentially conscious becomes, on principle, conscious in every one; just as the sun, once it rises at all, must shine on everybody. Further, intellect is essentially transferable: once it

41

expresses itself completely, it must be understood by everybody. For once it expresses itself completely it is *objectively*
clear; a point of view which is objectively clear represents a
necessary relation between the problem in abstract terms and
the general conditions requisite to human knowledge.

The transferable element in the mind is by no means exhausted by clarity of understanding: it applies to all correspondence between the meaning apprehended and the expression; and French expression is always and everywhere illu-
minatingly clear. It has the same advantages which enabled the
ancient Greek form, as a matter of course, to follow in the footsteps of Alexander and to conquer the whole Orient. It is logic
made flesh in the fullest sense of the words. The language
is so witty that even a stupid Frenchman—and even a foreigner of moderate intelligence who has caught the spirit of
it—makes an impression of cleverness out of all keeping with
the reality. The French taste is in itself so good that the *on* of
Paris—that impersonal, anonymous "they"—has a surer judgment than any save the most unusual individual. Thus all
Occidental ideology, whenever it can be expressed at all in
French, finds in the body of that language its most intelligible
expression: the lucidity of the language, in its widest sense; the
refining of the spirit which animates it, till it achieves an impersonal, inevitable grace: this creates a direct relation between
the specifically Occidental spirit and human nature at large in
a way unrivalled by any other European life-form. This is why
it is only in the French style that European culture makes an
immediate and successful appeal everywhere in the world.
This is why, until very recently, and with perfect justice, the
French language was everywhere accepted as the best general
medium of intercourse. This, too, is why most of the beautiful
life-forms of Europe which have been generally accepted are
of French origin. This also applies to social forms. As we have
seen, England gives complete satisfaction to the two polar extremes of the "I" and "You" *for herself:* the French life-form

does it for every one. The solitariness of the individual is not as absolutely respected as in England; social life is not as completely based on the group. On the other hand, a compromise on the plane of rational beauty is accepted as a norm —a norm which, while it makes social life agreeable, also enables the individual to set upon it the stamp of his personality.

The same set of circumstances determine, *mutatis mutandis*, all French relationship between the individual and his environment. The natural features of France are altogether those of a garden country. She is the mother of the Frenchman, for which reason the latter is always, in relation to the eternal world, a gardener first and foremost. This feeling of the gardener arises in him primarily from a desire to express all ideas in as universally intelligible and universally pleasing a form as he is capable of. Just as every animal constructs its own environment, so every man who is at all conscious of his surroundings feels the urge to humanize them; from this springs the original gardener character of women. And the Frenchman is wholly and supremely a gardener. The preeminence in cookery, the adornment and beautification of women, the sociable arts, fastidiousness of language, refinement of the love-life, *esprit*, the law of moderation in everything, and a proper regard for the vanity of others—all these are nothing more than the various arts of the gardener. To this, precisely, belongs that high morality implied in the French *le moral*, that lofty balance of character, governed by the ethos, which belongs to the Frenchman both individually and in the group. According to the teachings of the Chinese, morality means only nature trained and educated. Actually morality never means anything more than the harmony presented between intelligence, soul, body, and world; it has no metaphysical significance. But it is on the other hand the premise for all empiric harmony. And in the creation of this harmony the Frenchman is the most gifted of Europeans.

Thus, essentially, France is in all respects nature trained and educated; which means—a garden. On every plane— from the culinary to the moral—the state of France is essentially one of measure and harmony. In Paris, the highest expression of France, the solitary and the convivial, the cheerful and the serious, can all feel equally at home. Here all effects and conditions seem to have been happily devised with an eye to each other; French cheerfulness produces the effect of an overtone to a corresponding seriousness; irony is the balance to deep emotion; light-heartedness plays the treble to the deep bass of earth-rooted, primal strength—and even the shadow of the street-walker moves against the light of virtue. Such primal harmony cannot but have a liberating effect on every one who is at all able to feel it; it is bound to produce this effect, by the same law which makes a plucked violin-string set up sympathetic vibrations in another string of the same frequency. In the realm of the soul, Paris is Europe's foremost teacher of rhythmic gymnastics. In this lie the roots of its stimulative powers; it loosens the cramp which grips us within; the strength of the muscles grows in harmonious interplay; individuals otherwise unproductive suddenly get ideas, for once a motion is set up, a counter-motion or change must follow of itself. But the place which France has in the hearts of many foreigners—the place not of a favorite mistress, but of a true wife—must be explained by the following reasons in addition to those already stated: in the last analysis French life, for all its vibrating motion, is a state of stable equilibrium; the French love of change has as its ultimate object the preservation of tradition. Man is a creature of change; only he who takes this into account understands the unique rhythm of his nature. On the other hand, however, his life-melody is a ritornelle. Hence the truth of the saying: the more frequent the changes a people permits itself in minor matters (and this is also true of the individual), the more certainly can it be relied on to remain steadfast in essentials.

Frequently this truth is best illustrated by those individuals whose heaviness or lack of imagination leads them to believe that they can dispense with all changes: it is their lives which furnish the best illustrations of supreme instability: it is they who pass through the decisive revolutions. The same truth explains why the French, passing through so many revolutions, have changed so much less in the course of centuries than the British and the Germans; just because this feeling for fine distinctions makes them appear more changeable than all others, they are the most conservative people on our continent.

But all life is based primarily on adaptation to environment, and all enduring happiness on the balance between wish and fulfilment; in itself the innovation which springs from the spirit of human initiative has as little significance as an atmospheric change contrasted with the earth's rotation: thus the specific French way of life must make a happy environment for any one, and most of all for those who are the bearers of the spirit diametrically opposed to the French spirit—the bearers of the dynamic Faust spirit. This is the spirit of the unredeemed individual whose primitive nature, whatever the spirit may dictate, cries day and night for liberation in the sense of earthly happiness. Precisely in this respect, therefore, does the French atmosphere accommodate itself to all natural longings. It brings the need for change into true objective harmony with the need for constancy: thereby it disposes of the hankering after protest and revolution. It is a mistake, for the rest, to consider the Frenchman quick and mobile. He is this only as mind; and it is just this synthesis of volatile mind and steadfast nature which constitutes his greatest charm. Taken all in all, he is, in fact, too routinized. The reluctance of the France of today to understand the changed world, her rigid formalism, the stiffness of her administrative machinery, may all be traced to this. But even these defects fail to disturb the beneficent quality of the real French atmosphere. After all, by far the greatest part of that which fills the life of man has remained unchanged since the time of Adam. And when this self-constancy is thus affirmed, in beauty, without insistence, the individual feels an instinctive security. And this brings us to that factor on which France's chief attractive power is based. The static character of the French—their character of the gardener—implies a decisive affirmation of life. The French attitude toward the positive side of life is one of complete naturalness. They affirm it with all their five senses. They have a sensual understanding of the delight of love, but this is only one expression, among others, of a general affirmation of life, and can be understood only from that point of view. The word "sensual" as generally understood is more applicable to the Norwegian and the Englishman than to the Frenchman, for with the former the satisfaction of the erotic impulse is not something which he accepts as a matter of course: the result is that in the Frenchman this impulse seems to be over-emphasized, just as sex involuntarily plays a greater *rôle* in an irregular liaison than in marriage. The Northern races accept unembarrassed whatever is alive in them. Here, then, we have the primary reason why every one who is not a pedant, or a Philistine, or otherwise malformed, feels at home in France: a man's *impulses* will not countenance a denial of life. And it is the impulses which determine the immediate mood and tenor of one's life.

The France we have here examined endures and continues through all change. This is France the eternal. When I again reached France in 1926 after an absence of thirteen years, what made by far the deepest impression on me was the utter change-lessness of this eternal past, uninfluenced by the altered times —barely touched, indeed, by the world's transformation. For this reason I could think of nothing stupider than the idle chatter about France being "done for." A land with such authentic roots, a land with such unique attractive power, is never done for. If its inhabitants were to die out, or degenerate, it would soon be repopulated from the outside; and before long the immigrants would be transformed into the same essential persons whom we call the French today. In the case of individuals this would apply for the reason that it is chiefly elective affinities who become naturalized in France. And in the case of the mass it would apply for the reason that this garden-land irresistibly transforms the most diverse individuals into the French gardener type.

Y ET, if it is true that nearly every intelligent and unprejudiced person involuntarily feels himself at home in France, even nowadays—and this in spite of such reasons as he may have for hating the Frenchman—it is also true that the Frenchman himself feels anything but at home in this postwar period. And this, too, could hardly be otherwise. Never since the wandering of the nations has Europe been in such a state of flux as it is today. Tradition has lost all historic meaning, precedents no longer apply, the old established harmony is no more, all equilibrium has been upset. Under these conditions it is inevitable that the French mentality, which in stable times is eminently adapted to the world at large, should today be eminently unadapted. It is quite clear that the French cannot see matters in this light. And this is not only because of France's long pre-eminence among the great powers. However clear the intelligence of the Frenchman may be, his self-consciousness is emotional rather than intellectual: as such it is easily and violently aroused, and the emotions are their own ultimate justification. There is no purpose in discussing anything with a Frenchman unless there is a preliminary acceptance of his fundamental conviction. He is incapable of neutrality, and that not only in political questions; he does not understand extrinsic objectivity, in the German way, unless that objectivity rests on acknowledged subjective premises. This is why, in spite of all his sturdy common sense, he clings to prejudices which can be logically disproved: *les sentiments ne se raisonnent pas,* and for him the emotions are the final court of appeal. He is less capable than any one else of understanding what is strange to him: to this extent he is the most isolated of Europeans. This explains the extraordinarily narrow range of subjects in which he shows himself to be clever. He has the most finely differentiated consciousness in Europe; he is extraordinarily gifted as a logician. But the unconscious bases of his mind are in a state of equally extraordinary immobility. Even today the Frenchman's idea of Goethe or of Shakespeare is, with very few exceptions, childishly silly. His views on things not French may as a rule be taken seriously only when the attitude of the foreigner toward France is a challenge to the French point of view. No Serbian or Lithuanian or Esthonian newspaper would ever dare to offer its readers such childishly stupid opinions on foreign matters as daily appear in the biggest French newspapers. The Frenchman is actually the prisoner of his nature. Thus his repugnance to travel is based on the right instinct: outside the borders of his own country he produces an effect of provincial narrowness of mind. At home, contrariwise, the same narrowness has something touching in it. Just as the Englishman naïvely takes it for granted that he must conquer the world materially, so the Frenchman naïvely takes it for granted that the whole world desires nothing better than to be what he makes of it. And because of this very naïveté nobody takes offence at his opinion as long as he stays at home and only lets his spirit radiate outward. He is altogether incapable of understanding why any one should want to be different from him; and if an individual just cannot resemble him, he regards this as something temporary, and offers his assistance generously and in all disinterestedness. On no account can he understand that the world will not forever ungrudgingly accept him as he is together with his views. As the symbolic advocate of stable equilibrium, viewing the entire earth as a French garden, he is bound to see in the dynamic person—should the latter try to impose his will on him—nothing better than a criminal. He sees validity in *existing* equilibrium, *existing* morality, *existing* law, *existing* limits in every sense. Every shift and change is a dangerous threat to the very substance of his being. And the threat is all the more dangerous because the oldest cultural orders can hardly tolerate any change whatsoever: it is thus that the soil of Tuscany can bear only the ancient wooden plough. Because of all the foregoing psychological reasons, the Frenchman— ever since he became what he is today—has in every war felt himself to be the attacked party, has always seen in his opponent the enemy of civilization, has never failed to take up a position of absolute right. The present turn of world events was bound to lead only to one thing—a terrific intensification of this psychological state. On the basis of these observations the so-called French "hysteria of fear" becomes perfectly intelligible; the fact is that France has never before been so seriously threatened. For the first demand of France—as of every garden—is for external security; and external security no longer exists. It demands world stability—and that has been destroyed. Those who see in the French *rentier* class, in the French tacit acceptance of money marriages, etc., nothing more than the unpleasant facts, have completely failed to understand the Frenchman: these things are only some of the forms of expression of a fundamental attitude which calls for balance and permanence.

The French hysteria of fear arises from the additional fact that the Frenchman personifies the psychological type of the emotional introvert. In this capacity he lives simultaneously in two hermetically separated worlds, one of which represents the Freudian principle of pleasure, and the other of which represents the principle of reality. Beatrice Hinkle, whose book *The Re-Creating of the Individual* (Harcourt, Brace and Company) contains some of the best observations on the psychology of the European peoples which I have ever read, has this to say on the subject:

"In the French nation we see the most complete expression

of the duality of the emotional introvert. The achievement of
living in two worlds, side by side, the one dominated by the
pleasure principle and the other by the reality principle, each
entirely separated from the other by an impassable wall so that
there is practically no encroachment of one upon the other, can
nowhere be seen so clearly as in the psychology of the French
nation. In French realism, with its hard uncompromising, often
ruthless, facing of the facts of life, without pity or mercy, we
have an example of what forced acceptance of the reality
principle means to the emotional introvert type, and one which
reveals better than all explanations or description, the great
differences between this type and the subjective extravert.
There is no childish self-deception here, no smoothing of the
bare facts that man is egocentric, cruel, a destroyer of his kind
for his own individual power, ultimately holding nothing
sacred or above him; for this is the unredeemed ego reduced
to its primitive state. The absolute devotion to system, rule,
tradition; the measuring of everything by the criterion of its
utility; the intellectual honesty, the lack of all sentimentality
and even sentiment when reality is to be met; the narrow,
limited, and rigid attitude to reality in which no vision, dream,
or phantasy on the side of beauty and goodness is ever allowed
to soften the hard outline of the actual fact, either as it is, or
as it is feared it may become, all reveal the distinctions between
the reality of the emotional introvert and that of the subjective
extravert. The pain involved in its mastery, and the overwhelming *rôle* of fear as the motive power, are clearly shown
in her history, and are at the present time very obvious."

The French character has, indeed, its hard side. It is the
omnipresent compensation for France the gentle, the land of
beauty, of clarity, and of pleasure. In its most repellent quality
it is embodied, with primal graphic power, in Poincaré. The
characteristic peculiarity of the French, their ability to live
simultaneously in two hermetically separated worlds, is bound
to manifest itself in the production of forms which are diamet-

of the "peace period" proved that this circumstance necessarily relegates France to the background? Her victory just sufficed to enable her to keep her head above water. The fact is that catastrophes, as such, never call for abrupt and decisive changes in the life of a nation. In the long run, and despite all accidental occurrences, the advantage belongs to him whose aptitudes bespeak the spirit of the times. For this reason no German of any account has felt himself crushed by the defeat (and this is why, on the other side of the Rhine, they have to keep on insisting that Germany lost the war). This is why, in spite of German stupidities and German blunders, time is on the side of Germany, while, in spite of all the ingenuity of the French, it is just as inevitably against France. It may well be that, thanks to her external exhibition of power and her brilliant political, diplomatic equipment, France will long occupy a foremost place in the world of appearances. But the utter lack of correspondence which already exists between the external and the internal—that is, the ultimate reality—is revealed by every glimpse into the depths of the French soul. . . . Disillusionment, bitterness, an uncomprehending amazement reigns there. Did we not win the war? . . . Did we not put up a marvellous defence? . . . Is not justice on our side? . . . Do we not represent the old culture? . . . This does not happen to be false, but actually true—that is, from the French point of view. And when nations are fighting for their lives one cannot invoke impartial justice. But the French point of view no longer carries the historic decision. And it is on this that everything depends.

But in reality the greatness of France never did depend on her external exhibition of power, and much less on material expansion. If she ever burst her frontiers, it was only for a brief period of excitement: no matter whether it was the sacking of Rome carried out by the Constable of Bourbon, or Louis XIV.'s devastation of Pfalzburg and Heidelberg, or Napoleon's occupation of Europe—or Poincaré's occupation of the Ruhr. Nor was it ever a colonizing nation. Instead of Africa becoming French, it is much more likely that France and Africa will merge into a new hybrid—something which has already happened at least once in the past, during the neolithic age. Paideumatically expressed, in the language of Frobenius, the French are a people of the caves and not of the open spaces. Most of the time the King of France was actually more powerful than the German Kaiser; yet it was always self-understood that the former should yield to the latter the principle of space. It is in the nature of things that gardeners should feel themselves at home only in their own gardens. Any one who knows the French at all also knows that outside of France they actually lack the capacity to survive. And ancient tradition adds force to natural aptitude. France has not lived through a single period of instability ever since the early Roman days. Nothing essential was destroyed in France by the migration of the nations. The Franks, on entering the country, only became, as it were, the boarders of the Gallo-Romans. And in France the feudal order rose naturally out of the Roman private law: when the Roman state machinery crumbled to pieces, the surviving economic system became the foundation of the new political system (Fustel de Coulanges). There accordingly survives in the soul of the Frenchman an enormous segment of antiquity. Their primal concept of morality—*le moral*—is pre-Christian. One effect which follows with particular clarity is that the Frenchman shows the truest friendship and utmost generosity to any one whom he recognizes as his own—be it countryman, naturalized foreigner, or friendly guest (ξενος), while toward the stranger (barbarian) he can adopt an inhuman attitude which no other European can parallel. And this is true not only in a political connection: during my Paris period I once lay for months in a hospital, desperately ill. Before my French friends began to care for me, and thus put me through a process of moral naturalization, I experienced a lack of humanity which I would not have thought possible in Europe. For the Frenchman *le moral* means, fundamentally, nothing more than measure and harmony, for the individual as well as for the community—which is, properly, *tenue*, in the sense of the Roman aristocrat. On the other hand it is part of this attitude that the Frenchman is the only one nowadays who instinctively postulates a harmony between idea and life, the only one among the moderns who still knows what the ethos of friendship is. Furthermore: the living tradition of the French provinces is mediaeval. It was with complete justice that a young poet recently characterized his land as *un pays de petite noblesse*. Accordingly the modern element in France signifies not only something built upon primeval walls, but the rebuilding of a very ancient structure.

Yes; the real France is a *mixtum compositum* of the province of antiquity and the Middle Ages. To this extent the master who best understood her was beyond a doubt Henry IV., who, more than any one else, took into account this special nutshell character of France's structure, and under no circumstances aspired to world-conquest. France has just as little aptitude for this as Germany. All her imperialistic sallies have ended badly, because they never bespoke the deepest will of France. And the imperialistic gesture she is making today produces a directly comical effect, because those who rule and direct the country today are all of them outspoken provincials; the effect of the French Revolution and more particularly of the middle-class era which followed it was to give the spirit of the ancient province the advantage over the mediaeval tradition of space. It happened once that an honest peasant of the Rhineland, who wanted to ask a question of a Moroccan, addressed the latter with: *"Hé, victorieux!"* He had heard the word so often that he took it for the racial designation of black Frenchmen. This comic element even breaks through into the realm of the spirit, where the state of affairs is otherwise quite different. If Frenchmen interpret their *magistrature*, wherever it still exists, to mean that other nations took her as a guide in their thoughts and their behaviour, then in this attitude, too, their provincial character comes to light. For this human type is by its primal nature adapted to a small circle. In the same way their national vanity is nothing more than provincialism. Psychologically the Frenchman's pride in Paris as the only city in which it is possible to live—he holds this to apply to every one in the world—reminds one of no one more than of Sinclair Lewis's Babbitt, and his pride in Zenith. In the case of the woman, vanity is without doubt an unmixed advantage, for it is vanity which makes her pleasing to every one. To be beautiful means nothing else than to be for others. Thus vanity is the very foundation of pleasant private relations. To this extent French vanity is in itself a national virtue. But this high virtue becomes a vice the moment it oversteps the bounds of the intimate circle. This is why authentic world-nations are never vain: they never shine by reflected light; they radiate it.

No; the greatness of France was never dependent on her external exhibition of power. Thus, from the French point of view, it is a direct tragedy that since the year 1918 this country should be forced to play a *rôle* which does not suit it at all. The greatness of France emerges only when the intimate natural and radiating spiritual disposition of the race can enter into an harmonious synthesis. And that synthesis is just that thing which we call *culture*. Of all that is French, it is French culture alone which conquered the world for the world's good. To some extent it still rules. With this we come to the true definition of France: *the French are par excellence the culture nation of Europe.* They are this because their matriarchal disposition, which is the foundation of all deep-rooted and realistic culture, provides the framework for their particular will to form, a will which is fed by a particular sensibility.

CULTURE is a form of life as the immediate expression of spirit. Consequently only that people is called upon to be the creator of a culture which possesses both spirit and a gift

for form: a people delighting in the production of forms, to
that extent a people which faces outward, a people with a sense
of reality. In itself the deepest inwardness is without cultural
significance; in this instance everything depends upon transla-
tion into form, for the plane of culture is the plane of expression, and that precisely from the point of view of the spirit;
the only meaning which that plane has, is that it captures and
holds the spirit in the mesh of earthly life, that it lifts the
processes of the spirit above the accidents of interruption. No
one would refuse to admit that in the eighteenth century France
embodied the highest expression of the old European culture.
But it still does that today. And today, when the old culture
is in the throes of dissolution, this circumstance is even more
important than before. On the whole, this culture is certainly
without new creative force. That is in the nature of things.
The state in which our culture finds itself is exactly the same
as that in which the culture of Greece found itself; precisely
because the latter attained perfection in the fifth and fourth
centuries B.C., it ceased from that date on to bring forth anything essentially new. But in its stationary latter days, the
Greek culture produced something more than exquisite individual creations: it is precisely this subsequent period, down to
the latest Greek times, which became so important to the new
era. For it was only through this rigid, unchangeable norm
which it embodied that the swiftly unfolding flesh of the new-
emerging world was able to work itself on to the skeleton of
tradition.

This norm was always guarded by a group of the *élite*, and
not by individuals, for tradition is never an affair of individuals,
but of a collectivity. This destroys, from our particular point of
view, the objection which is so frequently raised against the
France of today; namely, that she has ceased to bring forth
great personalities. In the first place, great personalities in the
Russian and German sense are brought forth only by young
peoples. In places where the general cultural basis is very high,

even the most gifted individual finds it enormously difficult
to develop a unique greatness, for the most extraordinary
talents, too, know how to fit themselves into the existing
order, thus failing to obtain those conditions which are necessary to a hypertrophic development; in such places, greatness,
in the German sense, is achieved only by the barbarian or
eccentric individual; in this sense Balzac was the last great
man in modern France. But then France never was a land of
commanding individuals. In the first place the French spirit is,
as we have seen, essentially limited. And then again it has
always been too social to lay particular emphasis on the great
man, in whatever sense he might be great; it has always been
prevented from doing this by the ever-present fear of the
ridiculous. And the supernormal is, indeed, from the objective point of view, ridiculous, for it runs up against the law
of proportion. Thus the significance of France has always
lain in the high level of its *élite* spirits as a community, and
not in their individual representatives, however extraordinary these might appear. That level is today as high as ever
before. And it is just this that enables France to emerge more
clearly than ever before in the *rôle* of the culture-people of
Europe: in no other country shall we still find a representative
and authoritative group of the *élite*.

We shall best perceive the extent to which this is the actual
case if we consider the significance of Paris. This city is phenomenal. Something similar may have existed in the time of the
Greeks, but certainly not since then; even this goes too far:
even in the time of the Greeks nothing similar existed, for
the significance of Paris is based precisely on the fact that it
is a world-city. Let us first examine its position within France
itself. In the course of time this land has developed to such
a degree in the direction of a singular social organism that it
really has one, and only one, head, while the remainder of the
country seems to be there for the sole purpose of nourishment.
It is true that the French province—it is only in France, *et pour*

cause, that this expression of antiquity still has any meaning—
has a life very much its own, so much so, in fact, that the
regionalist idea is again coming to the fore. But it is the vitality
of the stomach, the liver, the limbs. If the province is aware
of its independent life, even to the extent of the case of
Bretagne, where the French language is actually not understood in certain places, still it never occurs to any one to dispute the hegemony of Paris; on the contrary, the rooted
authenticity and power of that provincial world is the pledge
of the security of Paris. Paris is both brain and solar plexus.
Wherever a talent arises, it strains naturally toward the capital.
And still, again, "meaning" demands that its ruling class
shall incessantly slough and renew the material which com-
poses it. For Paris stands and falls by its qualitative *rôle:* the
moment it ceases to play the aristocrat, its *rôle* is ended. But
to the extent to which it does this it naturally submits to timeless
norms. If one wishes to talk at all in Paris, one must master the
laws of conversation, of public utterance, and such laws exist;
the painter must have learned something definite and must
use his knowledge; certain eccentricities are once for all prohibited. But these timeless norms in no wise prejudice the concrete forms in which they come to utterance: this is proved
precisely by the fact that Paris is also the world-center of
fashion. The changes of fashion, too, follow strict laws; and
the surest and swiftest perception of the working of these laws
is in Paris. But before everything else, every mode must have
its own beauty. To this extent, then, the old adage that there
is no arguing about tastes fails to apply: granted a certain
situation, there *is* such a thing as absolute good and absolute
bad. Furthermore, France possesses the ability to work out in
such a singular manner the principles of judgment on timeless values, because the Frenchman takes such delight in
change; for thus he is always able to avoid the danger of forever locking the absolute norm within some unbreakable framework of form and content. Moreover, his sense of clarity

stands him in equally good stead: an idea is perfectly expressed only to the extent that it has been made clear; it is perfectly true only when it can be clearly seized. The very same applies to grace and tact. Because the feeling of quality has been so highly developed among Parisians, and because Paris feels itself so secure as the arbiter of taste, it is able to accept anything. In my twenties it accorded me very much the same position as I have today as a result of my work, but at that time it applied only to the specific form of future possibilities. The norms of fulfilment are all the more severe. Thus Paris readily takes up everything that is new, and yet never becomes its slave. There is not the slightest contradiction between this and what has already been said in regard to French narrowness and French inability to understand what is foreign. The norms of good and bad apply to every level. He who has any consciousness of quality retains it even in the presence of matters which he barely understands. Besides, judgeship, like kingship, hardly calls for originality or personal understanding for the original. Looked at as a whole, mankind has followed the same norms ever since Adam's time. The human race is altogether poor in invention. The very fact that statistics can serve to further knowledge and practice proves that even the limited intelligence can, by seeing life normally and accumulating sufficient experience, achieve the same results. The very same Englishmen who have to their credit such tremendous imperialistic achievements hardly ever think of anything which is not under their noses; they have not the slightest insight into the peoples they so wisely administer. And if their seemingly paradoxical practice of judging a man's ability to develop leadership in any activity by his behaviour on the athletic field does not reduce itself to absurdity, it only goes to prove how slender the connection is between intellectual originality—or even mere intelligence—and human leadership. Thus his psychological inability to understand whatever is foreign does not at all prevent the Frenchman from making judgments in the general run of human affairs which are very frequently, if not always, correct. Common sense and logical keenness prove their worth everywhere. A clear thought is clear everywhere; the exact formula is everywhere superior to the inexact. The mere expression *magistrature* with which France indicates her claim to cultural leadership opens the way to a right understanding: the teacher is often much stupider than the pupil, yet the former is in the right and advances the latter by his *rôle* of censor. Paris exercises the *rôle* of censor because of her aesthetic adjustment, her extraordinarily rich experience, her unerring good taste, her logical reliability, the remote perspective from which she looks at all that is foreign, and, last but not least, because of her traditional *courtoisie* and that *bonne grâce*, the like of which is not to be found anywhere else in the world. Is it any wonder that most of the world-reputations which are based on quality are made in Paris? Let Paris understand ever so little: he who has stood the test of Paris has stood the test of all humanity.

I T is from these data that we must evaluate the significance of the French mind in its relation to the new world in the making. It is true: there are in France today no great spirits, not even spirits of moderate greatness, pointing the way into the future; true that France's psychological inability to understand the new and the foreign seems to relegate her generally to the background. Because time moves only in one direction, and tradition—wherever tradition is the conscious rule of life—moves with it, it cannot but be that France must see her task as one of final clarification and differentiation. This explains why Marcel Proust, who unquestionably indicates an absolute close, occupies so high a representative place in her fine literature. Thus, while the rest of the world increasingly stresses the irrational powers of the unconscious, France lays the stress, more than ever before, on intelligibility. From this point of view we are at last able to offer a final evaluation of the significance of the French limitation of mind. The Frenchman believes in "definition" as natural peoples believe in the fetish. But we can clearly define, in the French sense, only that which we already know, or that which follows of necessity from accepted premises. In order to understand something which is new in essence, we must simply yield ourselves up to it until the new, necessary organs of cognition evolve. Submission of this sort is beyond the psychological capacity of the Frenchman. But this renders him incapable of adding to his knowledge; he is incapable of inner transformation. Hence the unequalled stupidity of French criticism in regard to all those matters which can be understood only from the premise of the new world in the making, with its new state of consciousness. It is for this very reason that the French so often see depth in the shallowest things, and significance in the narrowest things, if only they lift whatever seems to them misty and undefined on to the plane of the "already known." For this very reason, France can play the leader only in a time of fulfilment, when it is a question of imparting final perfection to an accepted world. The blazing of new paths is not for this race. This concurs definitely with the primal conservatism of the French world. But for all that, France does not stand alone today. Indeed, she stands less alone today than ever before. She also knows well that she no longer has the power to set the tone where she does not actually lead. Thus it is certain that with her great intellectual honesty she will soon recognize as her real leaders those among her sons who understand the new age. Once it has come to this point —and in certain instances it has already done so—the high French consciousness of quality will before long come into its own again. Then the French *élite* will once more emerge as the Areopagus of Europe, rendering final judgment on all questions of quality.

This leads us back to a re-examination of the point that France is today the only country which embodies the old tradition in an unbroken and undegenerated form. She will certainly have to confirm and stress much that is un-French if she is to maintain her place in the new-emerging world. Still, her world-significance depends, for the future as for the past, on the traditional element which she bears. For this traditional element embodies, under a temporal garb, eternal values. Thus we are led to examine how France must adjust herself to the new world and how others are to look upon it—for all destiny depends upon the meaning which we read into events. Should traditional France make its decision in favour of the Poincaré attitude, it signs its own death-warrant as a factor of significance in the Europe of the future, for this would be in total contradiction to the sense of the new era; and if the other nations decide to see such an attitude, no matter what the facts actually are, they will gain nothing by it. Things would be totally otherwise if French traditionalism and French statism were to be regarded as an integral part of the new mankind in the making; that is, when France would no longer be in fundamental opposition to the new, and the young races would no longer see in her the enemy—*but when both would see in her the necessary brake to the wildly careening chariot of the white peoples.* When this moment arrives, the mortal struggle is over. For the struggle would then be resolved into a fruitful mutual polarization of forces, by virtue of which the new would find a constant centre of reference in the old, while the old, as against this, would be able to rejuvenate itself. Thus the two poles of Europe, the static and the dynamic, would be mutually reconstituted, each induced and conditioned by the other. This readjustment, to be sure, calls for a great deal of renunciation on the part of France. It implies a kind of discernment which is made enormously difficult for her by her victory and by the frustration of the fruits of victory, beginning with the psychological and ending with the moral aspects—the discernment of the fact that for as long as can be foreseen, she must renounce all leadership and act only as a brake. But why should not France, too, the most spoiled of all the European countries, make a renunciation for once? Let her take a lesson from Spain, which since the time of Philip II. has lost every war and yet has never lost her proud self-consciousness. . . . In any case, this is the only way in which she can blossom into new life. And she *will* blossom into new life. Sooner or later the marvellous French feeling for harmony and proportion will help her to overcome the present reactionary phase.

One more word concerning the singular character of the French spirit. The French are not a philosophic nation; they are not really political, nor are they generally artistic; but as against this they are *the* literary nation. Nowhere else in the modern world does literature play anything like the same *rôle* as among the French. It is only in France that writing as an art is some seven centuries old. The relatively few recognized writers live only for themselves; but every one has to read them; in the last analysis they are decisive. And among them every nuance finds treatment. I was astonished that André Gide, who after all is only a moderate talent, should play the *rôle* he does: his importance goes far beyond the specific need of the French youth to react to their father-complex *en donnant du cher maître*. It was insisted: he has invented a form of narrative and a formulation of problems hitherto unknown. In the same sense the disproportionately important position of another writer, whom I had always considered of little significance, is based on the fact that as a *causeur* he has discovered shades of expression hitherto unrevealed. No other people in the world recognizes originality in this cameo sense more quickly than the French. On the other hand this very fact enables us to understand why no other people lacks the sense of authentic originality to the same degree. Balzac, for instance, to whom all French writers since the eighteenth century stand in much the same relation as water-beetles to a continent, is hardly honoured at all in his own country. It

seems that he lacks style . . . as though any giant, be he a
Cervantes, a Dostoievsky, or a Goethe, ever did have form in
the same sense as a Théophile Gautier! Gods and cameo-
workers are not subject to the same laws. True originality is
not founded on a semblance of originality, whether in relation to content or to form; it rests on the vitalization of a
phenomenon—be that phenomenon new or unknown—from a
new depth of meaning.* Accordingly, no essentially important
man was ever original in the French sense. Contrariwise the
French spirit has brought forth the new less frequently than
any other. It is inventive enough, but only on the basis of unchangeable premises; its fine spirit is that of a finishing-school.
However, to return to the particular matter of this paragraph:
in France literature is an aim in itself. This circumstance is in
itself no blessing to France; the point of view represented by
Ramon Fernandez and José Ortega, namely, that the spirit
must remain in its own sphere, impotent, contemptuous of the
world, is outlived; it is the last expression of that dying life-
feeling which is primarily Christian ("My Kingdom is not of
this world"). The new era rigidly demands the readjustment
of the human depths to reality, as the School of Wisdom
teaches. It is therefore no compliment to France to say that
she projects all values on the nullifying plane of literature.
It has exactly the same effect on the French mind as the mania
for putting all spirit on the level of theory has on the German
mind: it prevents it from understanding the actualities of the
spirit, if these happen to be new. But the existence of a purely
literary nation is a piece of real good fortune for the others.
In the last analysis, form is the decisive factor everywhere on
earth. Form alone can give reality to spirit-content, for it conforms to earthly law. Jesus did not become Saviour simply because he was a divine spirit—the heavenly rulers as such are
particularly impotent here below—but because in him the Spirit

* Cf. my deduction of the true concept of originality in the chapter *Was Wir
Wollen* in *Schöpferische Erkenntnis*.

became Word, and the Word flesh. In the twilight of chaos through which we are now passing, the symbol of form which has been saved with France out of the old culture is of inestimable value. And it is as the embodiment and carrier of this symbol that France will find the quickest way to the new content. It may take a long time. But once she has reached this point, she will as surely find the happiest perfections of formula for the new problems of the new world as she did for those of the old.

I CANNOT, however, close this subject without having taken up another problem on the existence of which perhaps depend France's greatest possibilities for the future. The new world is threatened by a danger which very few seem to apprehend: were it otherwise, life would not be taken so lightly. This danger is, that love may disappear from the earth. In most countries women are gradually becoming Amazons. It was to be foreseen that it would come to this. The "masculine protest" of the feminine liberators actually gave us nothing new: it simply aimed at the restoration of that matriarchal state which was everywhere the primal rule—a state which is to that extent truer to nature in that man, as a sexual entity, is by nature much more dependent on the woman than the woman on him. For this reason masculine bondage always naturally sets in wherever the man cannot compel and the woman does not desire. For the same reason it is in the nature of the man to seize the means for the external enslavement of woman wherever ethical usage does not stand in his way. That every gain toward independence on the part of the woman is bound to lead to a disproportionate loss of independence on the part of the man was first proved by America. In that country the husband has come to be just as oppressed as the wife used to be in the old Orient, with corresponding psychological recessions which are becoming more and more evident. Today, with the triumph of the feminine movement, the matriarchal state has been practically restored, with a form corresponding to the time and place, in the manners (if not in the laws—from which God defend us men!) of all those circles throughout the West where independent young women have caught the spirit of the age. And this brings with it the progressive atrophy of all those characteristics which define the woman as a love-being. The word Amazon means, literally, "breastless." The ability to feel and to yield oneself up is dying out. If it is typical of the American woman that she produces an effect of coldness, hardness, and soullessness, the cause is to be sought in this. Every Amazon has always been cynical. As soon as the centre of her being is moved out of the sphere of feeling, the woman becomes more rational, more matter-of-fact, than the most rational man. Hence Judge Lindsey's headlong revelations of the view taken by young American girls of the very newest school with regard to the sex-act; namely, that it is a purely biologic function without any spiritual significance. No man thinks as cynically as this, for if this is the way of his love, he knows he is indulging his vices, and thus the demand for love, at the opposite pole of his spirit, still remains. The boyish bob, the changed figure, the wearing of glasses, the destruction of all that is provocative of love by exposure to wind and weather, the sport fury—all these are the external signs in the change of feminine structure. More important from the viewpoint of type-creation is the changed mentality. Except as a mother the woman, by her nature, has no instinct for morality, but only for rules of conduct. It was a practice in Babylon, on certain holidays, for the noblest damsels in the land to give themselves as a matter of course to strange men. Of course only on those occasions: otherwise they would have considered it an abomination. But it would have seemed to them just as "impossible" to be prudish on the holy days. This explains why no woman was ashamed of dressing décolleté in pre-war days, or of following the most recent cult of nakedness today. Shame "as such" is unknown to the woman: for her the decisive factor is the rule of conduct. And in Europe today love has become openly "unmodern"; it could become this because in its spiritual sense it is a product of art, created by means which have not always been effective. In proportion as the distance which the girl must observe for the idealization of man was diminished, in proportion as she became his comrade and competed with him in physical exercise, and in proportion as the new morality removed the compulsion to concentrate all sense and thought on the cultivation of the emotions, in the same proportion did the motif of liberation from the man, who had so long enslaved her, emerge into predominance. True enough, the American example was rooted in other causes; but that did not prevent it from adding its strength to the change. To this was added the compelling fact that as a natural being the woman is more independent of the man than *vice versa*. From now on, love simply is to exist no more. The most modern woman of the world treats with man as with an equal. Whatever may happen in individual cases, the fact remains that no period has ever been more unerotic than ours. The dances which from the viewpoint of the old generation are "indecent" are in reality nothing more than a very innocent method of giving relief to the ever-present sex-impulse. Where the latter happens to be too strong for this, it finds expression almost normally in perversion. Since love between man and woman is no longer "fashionable," erotic men have their men friends and erotic women their women friends.

Thus the living moral code of yesterday is no more. That which seems to resemble it is either the inertia of routine or else a convention taken over at a distance; it is thus that only South American girls remind me at times of the closely-guarded young ladies of my boyhood years. The new-emerging moral code is that of a decisive Amazonian world. In certain cases this inevitably runs riot and becomes grotesque. I once observed in St. Moritz a young American woman who had a real tiger-face; it appeared that her specialty was biting men dangerously; also, she danced again only two days after she had broken a leg. Her prestige was enormous. Another woman of the world prided herself on having broken a limb five times during the previous season. But with regard to the traditional cultured class of Europe it came to this pass: women whose whole history demanded that, whatever they did, they should express themselves in their bearing and their inner discipline, behaved, now that the old moral order was dead, like nature-beings, like primal man, whose type was not to be found beyond the seas. This applies even to Englishwomen of quality. But with them this fishwife kind of dancing has a special significance. Even before the war the Englishwoman of quality used to behave, within her narrow circle, like a Bacchante. This was a reaction to the reserve otherwise imposed and practised, in the same sense that flinging cushions about is a habit among members of royal families. Now, however, they carry on openly and apparently without any shame. Yet this does not prevent them from being, outside the hours of licensed abandonment, women who have retained their *tenue* to a greater degree than others.

But we may talk of *tenue* from now till doomsday: love lies on its death-bed. It is not only in Soviet Russia that all sentimentality is penalized; in Western Europe, too, emotion is dying out. We sometimes still find men in the fashionable sets practising this atavism. But when the women on their side adapt themselves by mimicry to this situation—it is quite certain that the boyish bob and the boyish figure may be referred to the fact that during the war men had disaccustomed themselves to the company of women, so that boyishness had become the surest appeal—the contrary effect is bound to be produced under certain circumstances. Young people of today would certainly not be impotent by nature in such large numbers if there had not taken place, in the furthest depths of their nature, beyond the reach of all will, of all morals, a transposition of poles. We see this shifting in the life-picture going on everywhere. With the exception of one country—France.

Today France is perhaps the last refuge of love. In this country it still plays exactly the same *rôle* as of old. Thus all those who are still capable of love will make France the land of their pilgrimage. The rule of love is actually still so absolute in that country, that one cannot find there the slightest understanding of the new state of affairs as outlined here. Once, in Paris, when I turned the conversation to this subject, a handsome officer of marine broke into loud laughter: "All that is Nordic weakness! When our ship anchored in Copenhagen and Oslo it was found necessary to forbid us Mediterraneans to set foot on the land. . . ." I replied: "I am glad to hear that. But are there Mediterraneans enough to rescue love?" In this regard things are at a bad pass with the celebrated Nordic. An authority in this field, L. F. Clauss, the idol of the German Völkische Partei, has this to say in his book *Rasse und Seele:* "For the Nordic, even the sex-act becomes a sort of task. Even here he has his objective outlook. The Mediterranean type is free from this: he loves and desires and weds as a master of the game" (p.87). And again: "The young Nordic can stand for hours at the street corner where he has learned the young woman of his love must pass, swearing that this time, absolutely, he will accost her and tell her his love. But then, as soon as he sees the unsuspecting maiden approaching, he hides himself in the throng: from that undisturbed vantage he can watch her pass. He relinquishes his object from a distance and takes refuge in his world of dreams, there to celebrate in undisturbed possession" (p.56). Is it not a matter for astonishment that women should still want to have anything at all to do with Nordics? Is it not pure self-preservation when they plan to build up a world without love? . . .

In any case one thing is certain: love, no less than other things, calls for talent. There are entire peoples which are unerotic. The same is true of tremendous numbers of individuals of both sexes in every nation. In general, Spaniards and Italians know only passion. The majority of Germans, if they are not simply crude, pour themselves out in a Wertherian sentimentality. Englishmen are frigid to an unusual degree; nowhere in the world are there as many *mariages blancs* as in the Island Empire. In Russian life, love plays the minutest *rôle*; in fact it has recently been "scientifically" established in that country that love is a capitalistic invention: it is not a natural urge, but an ideological mechanism, which must crumble to pieces along with the capitalistic order; until then, a "League Against Love" must be founded. In the entire Orient love is of so little account that the centring of one's life about it, in the manner of the modern European novel, is absolutely incomprehensible. Yet all this does not contradict the fact that women, everywhere on earth, are love-beings; fundamentally nothing could be more alien to them than that pose of at best "friendly condescension" into which they have been forced by masculine "idealism." It was Eve that tempted Adam and not *vice versa;* so has it always been and so will it always be; it is the slyest feminine cunning which makes the contrary appear to be the case. . . . But most men are too stupid to play the game accordingly. Hence the involuntary position of monopoly occupied by those few who in one way or another, from time to time, tend toward the Don Juan type. I knew a German poet who in his later years found his pleasure in playing the Pietro Aretino to girls of the best society: so little competition did he encounter that not only was he literally besieged in his home, but his fame preceded him to all the capitals of the world, so that he only had to stretch his hand out and take. Again, I know of a Russian whose sexual charm was so contagious that once, in Venice, he won a wager which sounds fantastic; he wagered that if he were introduced into any house, preferably for the first time, he would in a high percentage of cases—exactly how high I no longer remember, but it was very high—

need no more than half an hour to win the lady. It is certain that in the art of love, as in every other art, we have to do with a special kind of ability: a self-understood swinging together of body, soul, and mind. It is this which makes love, as women understand it and as every man desires it for himself. Thus the French cult of love is something more than a question of a life-philosophy: it is based on a natural talent, a gift of grace. It is the expression of a wonderful ability. Enmity toward the senses, where it is not a sign of moral ugliness, is evidence of nothing better than impotence. For the saint transposes and sublimates only an innately powerful love-instinct. Never yet did an unsensual person become a saint. In this respect at least may France forever remain what she has always been.

SPAIN

SPAIN

No foreigner who writes about Spain ever satisfies the natives of that country. This is because the circumstance already treated in detail, namely, that what a nation means to itself, to others, and before God, calls fundamentally for three different answers, which can never be reduced to a common denominator, is nowhere more drastically clear than in Spain. Every foreigner necessarily sees Spain otherwise than as the Spaniard does, but whereas the same is true elsewhere, it is true to a lesser degree. It is hardly likely, then, that the Spaniards will accept as valid what I have to say here. But I can only set forth what I have seen and what lives in me as the fruit of this observation.

First of all the general impression, as it formed within me immediately after my journey in Spain. "In and for itself," Spain belongs not to Europe but to Africa. To cross the Pyrenees from France is to step out of a garden country into what is actually the desert. Whatever is not desert there is steppe or oasis. Again and again I was reminded in Madrid of Karakorum, the Tusculum of Ghengis Khan: the royal city is surrounded by a landscape of Central Asiatic harshness, magnificence, and width. That strange sky, with its pyramid-like clouds, those dusty-brown steppes, with their spare, shattered trees, those raw, snowy sierras which enclose the whole, furnish a picture of lofty desolation of which only the desert landscape is capable. I deliberately use the extreme expression *desert* in setting down the first characteristic of Spain in order to direct the attention, from the very outset, to the essential element: in the literal sense that description applies most certainly to Castile. But Castile *is* Spain. The spirit of Castile is the determining factor. And what characterizes the Castilian landscape is the cosmic, the stellar, in distinction to the sublunar; it is the predominance of the planetary as opposed to the living world, the very existence of which, looked at from the astronomic point of view, is nothing more than an incident.

The predominance of that viewpoint is what characterizes everything that is African. It characterizes all African landscapes, all African culture. And since primeval times Spain has belonged to the African sphere of culture. Her culture is a special expression of that primordial and primeval spirit which already animated the pre-Egyptian cultural peoples and has expressed itself in the Arabic and Berber cultures with no less authenticity than in that of Spain. It is really primeval: whoever wishes to learn the culinary art as practised in the Stone Age need only go among the shepherds of the Spanish sierras. Just because it *is* primeval, the Basque people can always keep on renewing the representative *rôle* which it plays for Spain: this applies today to Miguel de Unamuno as it once applied to Ignatius de Loyola. On the other hand, the country is also of immemorial culture; among authentic Spaniards there are no plebeians at heart. But essentially this spirit is properly African and not European, and we shall best understand it if we see it in relation to the Bedouin. The latter, having sustained himself for thousands of years in the desert, having mastered it, has on his side recreated himself in its image. He is harsh and sombre, elemental, mighty of will. At his extreme he is fanatical, like the desert storm. When has the Spaniard achieved historic importance except in this *rôle*? For the Spaniard of historic importance has always been either Castilian or else one of whatever blood, whether Basque (Ignatius, Unamuno), Andalusian (Primo di Rivera), Catalonian (Columbus), or German (Philip II.), who was born again into the living spirit of Castile. In the particular gloominess of the last-named, whose Escorial is, next to Tamburlaine's pyramid of skulls, the most convincing memorial ever erected to death in its cosmic sense, I find the most convincing proof of the elemental power of the Castilian landscape: it withered and dried up a soul which originally was probably too tender.

Furthermore: the harsh and sombre desert-dweller must on the other hand be in some way fantastic. Every desert-dweller is by nature quixotic. That is to say, his life signifies the self-assertion of the insignificant, self-willed in its insignificance and to that extent ridiculous, in the face of immeasurable cosmic forces. But this self-assertion looks ridiculous only to the outsider; in the eyes of Spaniards, the figure of Don Quixote is totally lacking in the comic element. For them, on the contrary, he emerges as the highest symbol of man, and this to a far greater degree than does Goethe for the Germans. For what have all the representative deeds of the Spaniards been, if not Don Quixote epics? From the Cid to the Conquistadores—Cortez burning his ships, Pizarro setting out with his tiny band to the conquest of Peru—and from the spiritual Conquistador enterprise of St. Ignatius to the single-handed fight of Miguel de Unamuno, whom few of his countrymen recognize as representative, against present conditions in Spain? Thus every Spaniard, too, stands solitary and alone, like Don Quixote: this is how every one must feel in the desert. He is isolated, even though, like every Mediterranean type, he always sees himself primarily from the viewpoint of others and consequently always remains, in contrast to the introverted German, equal to all social demands. The Spaniard knows that he must live out his own life, that in the last analysis no one can help him. Hence his cult of manliness, of manly worth, and, in its extreme form, of the passion for empire over men (over men, not women, not things!). Hence his particular concept of honour: the *honour* of the Spaniard is based on pure subjective passion, the *pathos* of the lone individual. As a man dependent on himself alone, the Spaniard neither offers nor seeks pity. He wants to be altogether himself, standing on his own feet. Thus it is hard for him to grasp the concept of justice in its Western sense; self-help alone appeals to him as being both sensible and dignified. The impartial judge who in cold blood sentences to death a man to whom he stands in no relation, must in the eyes of the Spaniard rank lower than the murderer. There always rises before me that drawing of Goya's, in which two duellists face each other at arm's length, buried to the knees in sand, so that neither of them can run, as there always recurs to my mind the report that even today there take place in Aragon duels in which the opponents are tied together, locked at their left elbows, while they flourish the knife in the right hand. . . . To the desert-dweller, personal courage is everything. To such a mentality, abstract justice can become comprehensible only where it emerges as the expression of the Inquisition idea. In this case it is precisely the personal passions of the will to live and the will to power which come to the fore. Nothing was ever more popular in Spain than the Inquisition; every movement for justice inevitably ends up, in Spain, as an Inquisition.

The desert-dweller is both harsh and fantastic. But above all he is hungry for life, for the dead desert in all truth cries out for life. But this feeling for life is realistic through and through. He dreams of no ethereal soul, he knows himself to be flesh and blood. I will never forget how Unamuno, in proving to me the continuation of the father in his children, described how his son once sat for hours in a café, scratching out on the marble top the words: *Soy de carne, soy de carne* (I am of flesh)—just like himself. Fleshliness, not spirit-being, is the primal feeling of the Spaniard. Hence the peculiar practicalness, in fact the earthiness, of the Spanish fantasy. The original of Schiller's Knight Delorge threw the glove which he snatched from the lion's den in the lady's face, because she exposed well-born people to unnecessary dangers. And further: the desert-dweller knows the tragedy of life at first hand. Thus the best Spanish pictures of Christ always show the agony of the Saviour. Affirming life as he does, the Spaniard also affirms death; as he loves life, he also loves blood, its most immediate symbol. Hence the indestructibility of the bull-fight. Manly courage and blood-lust live them-

selves out in him—but not cruelty. There is no cruelty at all in
the Spaniard: only petty people are cruel. To call the joy of
blood, or even blood-lust itself, cruelty, is nothing better than
moral and physical cowardice; for he who accepts life must
also accept death, and with death, in a world of freedom, also
the act of putting to death. As long as his passions do not come
into play, the Spaniard is, indeed, extremely humane. There
are no humaner prisons than those of Spain. Precisely because
this people gives full relief to its blood-lusts in the Corrida, it
is more humane than those peoples who refuse to admit their
own delight in blood—it is in just the same way that surgeons
and nurses are as a type exceptionally cheerful and friendly.
In the same sense Spain is thoroughly and completely unmili-
taristic: where courage and blood-lust are exalted only in reference to the individual, and unconditionally so, they need no
reinforcement in mechanical organization. Thus, if the question were intelligently raised, it is probable that the Spaniards
could more easily be won over to the idea of national dis-
armament than the Germans. And where the will to life is so
supreme it runs to extremes. In the blank spaces of the illimit-
able desert there arises a frenzied hunger for personal immortality, for a flesh-and-blood immortality. This is the root
of the unshakable Islamic certainty of immortality, in a Paradise of oasislike beauty; it is likewise the root of Unamuno's
doctrine, the source and origin of which is the revolt against
death; from the same fount flowed the idea of the vault of the
Escorial, wherein are ranged, one above the other, the sar-
cophagi of kings still unborn. We may observe in passing: the
Spaniard is essentially Catholic only to the extent that he recognizes the reality of the spirit only in its fleshly embodiment.
He is Catholic today in the dogmatic sense, for Catholic dogma
has moulded him into what he is. Yet in one way he does deny
his Christianity—he will forever remain Catholic in contrast
to the non-Catholic.

Thus it is: the Spaniard knows only of spirit become flesh.

This is the very reason for his ascetic streak. Where the spirit is experienced primarily as fleshly form, no flesh can ever be felt or ever can work spirit-free. Thus it is not only true of the Spanish woman that her senses awaken as a rule only when her love is of the soul; Spanish men, too, in spite of their extraordinary ribaldry, actually live closer to the feminine idea of chastity than any one else. Hence the marvellous spiritual texture of every Spanish body, even in the utter absence of mind and experience. Hence, too, in extreme cases, that impulse toward stripping the reality from things—an impulse which, on the basis of a realistic nature and in a manner hitherto unnoted, brings the Spaniard close to the Arab. In the presence of the tragic feeling for life, that unity of flesh and spirit, which in reality never becomes perfect, must again and again lead to an extreme division in the consciousness. Thus every Spaniard is simultaneously both Don Quixote and Sancho Panza. Extreme realization and extreme de-realization are the two poles between which his life and experience move in constant renewal. So that every dream at once runs to fleshly reality, and every reality, again, embodies super-earthly spirit. Judged by the German, Sancho Panza is less the clown than the ironist.

WHAT I have written till now is the direct expression of that which arose in me, visionlike, as the result of my direct impression. It should be valid for the essence of Spanish being. Reading it, modern Spaniards will assert that I have been writing about old Spain, not about modern Spain. But that is exactly what every non-Spaniard most profoundly feels in Spain—that the old continues with singular force in the momentarily new. For substance, as a timeless effective force, opens to the beholder a simultaneous revelation of the whole stream of time, and the past is always longer than the present. There would be no point in raising detailed objections, such as that Spain is still mediaeval, having passed through neither the Renaisssance nor the Reformation: to that same extent Spain is also still living in antiquity, and also in prehistoric times—she might, indeed, be living futuristically. . . . The truth is that the psychic atmosphere of Spain, like that of no other country in our continent, derives its character from the primal substance. It is *this* which first works itself out in the sensitive visitor.

But the extent to which Spain today appears different from what she once was is assuredly also of importance. A brief shift of mood in the basic theme from the tragic to the correlative comic will most quickly reveal the state of affairs. The foreigner, with his prejudices, naturally thinks of a Spanish Dictator in the light of a Philip II., or of his field-marshal Alba, or else of a Torquemada. I did indeed know, before my visit to Spain, that Primo di Rivera does not belong to this type; and I therefore asked, when a meeting between us was arranged, that this should take place in the presence of beautiful women and over the champagne. Yet, when Primo did arrive, I was astonished: not only did a *señorito andaluz* stand before me instead of a harsh Castilian—what he actually resembled was the plump, lady-loving gendarme of French vaudeville, who, casting his eyes upon the buxom maid, sings, *"Sapristi, quelle belle personne. . . ."*

I understood at once why it is fundamentally impossible to overthrow Primo: kings and presidents are overthrown, policemen never. And when I saw further not only what delightful mother-wit, but what sturdy common sense and what warmth of heart animated him, I understood something else: I understood why it was just this man, who is damned by all the intellectuals of Spain, whose attitude toward all men of spirit and all things of the spirit has been fantastically stupid, who is perfectly primitive and, in the last analysis, perfectly unimportant—I understood why it was just this man, who resembled the Russian general who was appointed to the rectorship of a university and who, finding only nine Muses in the Museum, immediately issued the command, "Have the tenth put up at once!"—why it was just this man who has perhaps done more for Spain than most of her rulers for the last hundred years: this judgment stands firm even for the time after the dictatorship has come to an end; on the basis of the dictatorship a new Spain, an improvement on the previous parliamentary country, will become possible—for Primo di Rivera embodies the complementary picture to the eternal Don Quixote. And who is that? The no less eternal Sancho Panza. In a chauffeur age, the latter, as the authentic ruler, is absolutely in the right place. Thus Primo di Rivera, too, belongs to eternal Spain. And so does her king, of all kings the most modern. The Spaniards, too, are hardly monarchistic any more in the traditional sense; within the younger generation there is no European of any account who is. It is true there are many who consider the monarchical as opposed to the republican the better form of state; as far as Germany is concerned, I am of these myself. It is also true that there are even legitimists among such. But this is only for the sake of historic continuity, and not because the offspring of certain families are by their nature higher beings. As a matter of fact, the members of the present or of the recently reigning families are least of all born kings. In the first place the centuries of constitutionalism have turned born rulers into born mediums; which is the reason for the particular leaning of princes toward occultism. And then generations of living in the show-window has transformed them into the representative type—and the representative *rôle* signifies something essential only in an old world, and not in a world in the making. But above all the fact is that the traditional court life has lost all relationship with modern reality, so that the very thing which imparted world significance to the court of Louis XIV. has lost all meaning today. Even today, assuredly, there are excellent—and even important—men in the princely houses. But today the type itself produces the same effect of artificial breeding as do those Japanese cocks which supply the yard-long feathers we sometimes see in the theatrical revues: as is known, these are born and bred up in very high but very narrow cages; the shape of the cage is such that every movement must be in a vertical line, submitting the tail-roots to a special kind of massage so that the feather-bearers must carry an increasing weight. It is for this very reason that princes today are inwardly the most uncertain of persons. Apart from new countries, like the Balkans, where the entire question is one of linking up with European tradition, the youngest traditional type of prince can live itself out beneficially only in those countries—England, for instance —where its *rôle* is purely symbolic. How dangerous this type can become, because of its absolute lack of feeling for reality, when it takes on more than a symbolic *rôle*, is demonstrated by the case of William II.—Alphonso XIII. is a king in what I might call the pre-traditional sense, as the founders of the dynasties were. He acts the king from case to case, and that is why he retains his validity. He is the only one among the living monarchs who has never been anything but a king; he is therefore devoid of the typically royal uncertainty. The naïve self-consciousness implied in this gains additional benefits from two circumstances: first, there is the structure of the Spanish soul which has remained mediaeval in some respects; second, there is the absolute absence of toadyism in the entire people—as a king he can never feel anything more than a free man among free men; all this enables Alphonso XIII. to be, precisely, a pioneer among kings. He does indeed master all tradition: whatever he does and says reflects before all the spirit of a *first* king. Thus the new direction taken by the world works for and not against his kingship. By and large, his kingship lives by virtue of attempted assassinations. Personal courage is all that the people demands, all that it honours. In particular, however, it lives also by virtue of futurity: long before the war he was the first Spanish chauffeur. And now comes the principal thing from the point of view of Spain: he possesses, to the highest degree, that self-irony which has always supplied the counter-weight to Spanish *grandezza*. About a century ago the world-empire of Spain fell to pieces. During recent years one South American state after another has been ordering its statues of independence from the fashionable sculptor of Madrid. Over and over again, the king was asked to dedicate them. He undertook this office *de la meilleure grâce du monde: c'est une manière comme une autre de reconstituer l'Empire où le soleil ne se couche pas*. In a new way the Spanish-speaking world is actually drawing together into a mighty unity.

As I write this, in 1926, Spain is being administered, in conformity with the spirit of the chauffeur world, by Sancho Panza; the first grandee, who is at the same time the first chauffeur, of the land, half-ironically concurs. But Don Quixote, in the semblance of Unamuno, sits at the Franco-Spanish frontier, his gaze turned toward the homeland which is both mother and daughter to him, and waits in vain for only one chance to seize the reins of power. That is what he is really waiting for. What is there in this modern world essentially different from the old? The word of Cervantes stands for ever.

THUS I see no reason at all even to retouch that vision of eternal Spain which I first unfolded. What I have established through a few examples could be confirmed by all the others. It is self-understood that Spanish humanity, like every other, is subject to the law of what the Greeks called Kairos. But the essential is precisely this, that the eternal element of the substance remains of decisive importance in the face of all the changes of time. This is already taken care of by the women, those mightiest and most steadfast female figures I have ever seen, who have always taken man as an adventurous, irresponsible child and have always let him carry on until he went altogether too far: thus, I am told, Count Romanones was once deposed from the Ministry by his own wife when he became too radical and the mother-instinct deemed it necessary to impose some drastic punishment. No woman in the world that I know of actually embodies the power aspect of the eternal-feminine to the same high degree as precisely the Spanish. But in the life of the man, too, it is the eternal substance which dominates. This is the reason why every non-Spaniard, or at least every non-Spaniard of sensibility who comes to the country, experiences the old Spain even today.

And of what significance can this eternal Spain be to the new Europe? Let us first of all turn back to the realization that a nation is threefold in the significance which it has to itself, to others, and before God. Nothing within the framework of our observation has been affected by the fact that a large part of the upper strata of Spain can be little distinguished from other Europeans, and that a leading spirit in Spain, like José Ortega y Gasset, is not simply a good European, but of the best. In the synthesis called "Europe" it is precisely the particular which acquires value in its own way. Within that synthesis, Spain, as such, will acquire significance precisely to the extent that it is different from other countries, uttering with special clarity and convincing power a living note of its own, which shall sound in all life. *It is, then, precisely to this extent that Spain can become of extraordinary significance in the new world in the making.*

Let us turn our eyes to that other land at the opposite European pole, Russia: wherein consists the European importance of its great literature, which, as a picture of purely Russian conditions, does not, after all, mean anything to the non-Russian? It consists in this: that the Russian lacks the inner fixations which have created thought and will in the European soul since the Middle Ages—Russia has passed neither through the Middle Ages nor through the Renaissance. Thus Russia is not frozen, but fluid, and to that extent near to nature, and, potentially, to God (elsewhere I have defined the life-mode of the Russian as the direct striving of the animal toward God,

over-leaping mankind). Since that which is fixed cannot create
—it is only the undifferentiated, the protoplasmic, on whatever
level it may be, which brings forth the new—it follows that
the European soul, if it is to renew itself in the creative sense,
could hardly find a better polar opposite than the symbol of
Russia. And furthermore, every Russian embodies in himself
a higher tension than any other representative European
hitherto. Now since the western type of the future—the ecumenic—can be realized only by means of a heightened tension
in the human being, it is not to be wondered at that even the
chaotic Russian could for a time become the ideal of the all
too fixed and limited European, and of the German in particular.—But Russia's symbolic *rôle* for Europe, in the sense indicated, is ended, because fulfilled. Looked at historically, the
old fixations have melted out, for only those strata which do
not count for the future are still fastened in them. Now another polar extreme is needed. It is such a pole that Spain, at
least to some extent, offers. In another sense than Russia, Spain,
too, has not shared the destiny of Europe. From the Middle
Ages until Napoleon, it actually experienced not a single moment of instability. The spirit of the Reformation passed over
its head. Since the time of Philip II. it has to an increasing degree led a life of its own, withdrawn and shrunk upon itself.
It had no share whatsoever in the French Revolution as a revolution; nor did it participate in the World War. But above all
it has not shared in the process of intellectualization, that of
Reformation and Renaissance, which has been an essential historic experience for all non-Spaniards. Till now this has been
Spain's disadvantage. But just now the contrapuntal counter-
movement to the eighteenth century and its fruits has set in.
And with it, Spain—conforming to the laws of the "symbolism
of history" *—*suddenly becomes the timely symbol*. This may
perhaps not be visible to her from her own viewpoint, but it

* Cf. the chapter of this name in my *Schöpferische Erkenntnis*.

certainly is from that of the others. For Spain takes into account only the *immediate* and *actual*, and not what that signifies in connection with another being; thus the intellectualism from which we thought to derive the first benefits serves to advance the Asiatic peoples.

What is it that we have before us, from the European point of view, in the case of Spain? It is nothing more nor less than *incarnated basic tones*. In Spain the primeval basic tones of earthly life sound forth in perfect naïveté, conditioning life to a degree no longer known anywhere else on earth. Miguel de Unamuno, the living Spaniard of most importance to Europe, and probably the most important Spaniard that has ever lived since Goya, unswervingly proclaims out of the wholeness of primal man the very few but the very deep things which he has grasped and knows: the significance of faith, of blood, of the tragic, of *tenue*, of Don Quixote as the highest symbol of man: precisely what we need today is to understand convincingly these thoroughly simple, thoroughly profound tones; for in the world of our representation, with all values become relative, it is just these tones which it is hardest to apprehend. The direct consciousness of the modern has almost lost contact with them. What the European, in this hour, needs more than all else, is to win through again to an immediate relationship to these basic problems of life, for these are the intestinal problems of earth-fast and heaven-storming man. It is not only as soul, in distinction to spirit, that man is inescapably fastened to earth: it is so with him as body, too. If it has been the special merit of Germany's chthonic thinkers to have raised the earth-conditioned psyche to consciousness as such, so that we are able to experience anew one side of the "Mother"-problem, it has been Spain's contribution to reawaken the experience of the body and that spiritual quality which stands immediately next to it, in the desire of life and horror of death, in elemental passion with its unconditional Yea and Nay. For these intes-

tinal problems, as I have called them, will forever remain the
intestinal problems of man, however high his head may be
lifted; for the man who has cut himself loose from his mother
there is no salvation. Thus, in the synthesis of the new Europe,
the Spaniard emerges as the representative of the primal cosmic
element, as the representative of that which was before all
history and will always be. On this quality of representative
of the pre- and super-historic, in the earthly sense, depends
all, yes, all, that Spain signifies to the non-Spaniard; upon it
depends everything that it can possibly mean as a monad within
the close-locked system of Europe. But now we can begin to
specify. We have already said that Spain represents the primal
cosmic element in a fundamentally different sense than Russia.
In what way? The Russian primal nature is obviously not
human in character; it is both sub- and super-human at once.
Whenever intellectual Russia has felt itself diametrically opposed to Europe, it has been in reference to Europe's specific
human characteristics; that is, to its ethos and its logos. But
looked at biologically, what is man, as man, if not the logical
and ethical animal? The logos side of the Spaniard has received
a relatively light development; however highly it may be
trained in certain cases, it still means little nationally. But there
is no people with a more primordial and deeper-rooted ethos.
The Spanish tone is wholly that of bearing, *tenue*. It is true
that one might also say that the quality of Spain is wholly that
of passion, for there is not a more passionate people. One might
even say that it is that of relaxation, as the Spaniard himself
also calls his bearing *dejado*, indolent; but all these things are
comprehended in the freedom of those who have *tenue*. What
is typical is the fact that the Spanish pathos, the pathos of that
which on the one hand clings to earth and on the other hand
quixotically storms the heavens, emerges on the plane of human
existence as a perfected ethos, as that which is within form and
imparts form. The Spaniard never runs away with himself,
either earthward or heavenward; his manhood, which is his task

and his pride, he never abandons.* And from this it follows as a matter of course that every Spaniard who has not broken with his race is a master, to the extent that mastery naturally implies a sense of worth and the acceptance of the device, *Noblesse oblige*. Man, as man, *is* in fact the lord of nature. Only lordship befits him. In the modern chatter about service as the highest form of activity, of giving oneself up to the forces of earth or to experience or even to our fellow beings as an ideal, of the necessity of denying the world-conquering spirit, is expressed only the abjectness of the under dog. In Spain every one knows that man only starts with *tenue*. In that country no popular leader would ever hit upon the idea of cultivating a "proletarian sense of pride," for there even the beggar has the self-assurance of a chieftain of the Stone Age. It is this which, for the crude and uneducated, is the equivalent of the self-assurance of the *grand seigneur;* it makes him, there and then, the equal of the latter; while the man who is self-consciously a proletarian or who, proudly conscious that he is child of the new world, claps every superior familiarly on the back, actually displays his lack of self-respect.

For me no doubt exists that ethically, Spain stands at the apex of European mankind today. In other countries all those bonds which condition nobility are falling to pieces. In Spain, thanks precisely to such bonds, a condition of *modernity* is being created. In that country there is being created the only humanly worthy democracy, for such a democracy can arise only among those whose rights are equal—not on the level of a "lower class" but on that of an "upper class." I shall never forget the impression made on me by a young peasant woman—one who had, in five years, brought six children into the world—when, after an automobile accident, I found shelter, together with two Spanish dukes, in her poor hut; she conversed with these dukes not simply as if she had equality of rights with them, but she

* The chapter *Das Ethische Problem* in my *Wiedergeburt* shows the extent to which the question of bearing or *tenue* is bound up with being human.

was their equal, for she was no less conscious of the dignity of her position than the Duke of Alba was of his. Nor is there anything different in the intercourse between King and people. The populace shows respect for itself by observing the rules of etiquette, but the King, on his side, knows well that it would go badly with him if he did not treat the poorest Spaniard as a man of equal rights. Spanish *castizo*, the strong emphasis on purity of blood, has long since freed itself of its excrescences by according respect and permitting pride only to what is higher, without awakening a sense of inferiority in the lower. As regards the attitude of the great toward each other, the actual impression made on me by their athletic contests was that of a tourney held in days when the King had to maintain his rule from one single combat to the next. In that country the members of the aristocracy address themselves very seriously to the task not of pleasing the King, like courtly toadies, by letting him win, but to that of defeating him. The authentic Spaniard is really devoid of all snobbishness, of all middle-class vices, and certainly of the menial sense of inferiority which is the first characteristic not so much of the waiter as of the flunkey. The Spaniard is ethics become flesh. Lack of *tenue* seems to him to be humanly unworthy—as it indeed is.

Well, my own feeling is that this element of highest ethos, both as an actual ingredient and as a creative symbol, is the very thing this unbridled Europe of ours most keenly needs. No kind of culture is possible among people whose character has not been built up on human foundations; that is, on foundations laid down by the ethos. Only when it has absorbed this element will Europe be able to weather the crises of this transitional period with good results. And this is true, above all, for one more reason, which is again the clearest symbolization of Spain: *tenue*, inner discipline, implies immunity from the dangers of these changing times. From the time of Philip II. until a few years ago, Spain seemed to be, outwardly, on the down grade. Yet it is in no way decadent and never was. On the contrary: in other countries of a more logical character—the logos is the principle of initiative, the principle of transferability and therefore of change—the very physiognomy of the national type has so changed from century to century that the modern in the dress of his ancestors seems a masquerader; whereas the Spanish grandee of today is the perfect image of the portraits of Velasquez and El Greco; that is, he knows how to do nothing, how to stand in one place. He knows how to wait. He is timeless, like his brother of the desert, the Bedouin. He is, in his essential substance, as unshakable as the latter. Does he not, in this bare possibility, supply the exact counterpoise to the fluidity of the rest of the world? If the European of the future is to attain perfection, is it not absolutely essential, under all circumstances, that he become, as an ethical being, a Spaniard?

I N these large, exaggerated lines—exaggerated because one-sided in their emphasis—I have indicated what Spain means and can yet mean to Europe. And at the same time I have paid attention here only to the positive, for Spain's failings and drawbacks are without any symbolical significance. They are simply facts, unfortunate or indifferent; in no instance that came to my attention could they be held up as warnings. It is to be taken for granted that the masses of the poorer Spaniards are far behind those of other peoples; it is not for nothing that they are almost identical in blood with many Africans. When Abd-el-Krim was a student in Madrid, wearing Spanish dress, he was hardly to be distinguished from the Spaniards. It is also to be taken for granted that in the case both of Spanish indolence and of Spanish indifference, which manifests itself in a lack of interest in intellectual, political, and religious matters—among the men, it is this last which is most striking—we have to do not with superiority, but with arrested development. Thus even today the Spaniard has much the same outlook in the matter of money as the Cid and the Conquistadores—that the only dignified way of obtaining that very necessary commodity is either to commit robbery or to find a treasure; to this day, treasure-hunting has remained a national idiosyncrasy in Spain. In many ways there has been little change as compared with the early Middle Ages; in other ways, again, there is much that still harks back to the time of the counter-Reformation and much that echoes even the prehistoric state. But this plays no part at all in the general picture of Spain. Thus no foreigner of standing who has written about Spain has ever had anything of interest to say with regard to her negative side. The reason for this, once again, lies in the primeval, elemental character of the Spanish: elements simply are—one does not criticize them. For the Spaniards themselves, the problem naturally bears another aspect. To make this thoroughly clear by concrete example: it is possible that to the Spain of today the eternal Spaniard Unamuno represents an inhibition, while the European Ortega offers the nearest road to salvation. Of course even Spain must first of all modernize herself, must learn, in her own way, to adapt herself to the emerging ecumenic state. In Spain, too, it is the chauffeur in the mass who is coming to the fore—from the *torero* to the chauffeur is a very short cut; precisely in that land where mind has hitherto meant so little is intellectualization especially needed, and the overcoming of superannuated mental prejudices. And yet I believe I may affirm this: just from the Spanish point of view, the emphasis, even for the future, should continue to be laid on the timeless, the eternal, Spanish element. A Spanish friend of mine once said to me: "Lack of snobbishness is not an advantage but a disadvantage, for the reason that the snob most rapidly becomes like the thing which is above him." I objected: "This, if it applies at all, applies solely to those who are intellectually and mechanistically disposed, for a scheme of progress can affect the development only of such people." The Spaniard is, indeed, distinctly dynamic, and yet anti-mechanistic; he has all the passions of conviction, but not those of criticism. For that reason he can lose only if he tries to adjust himself as if he were an Englishman or a Frenchman. The advantages of Spain lie in the ethical field, that is, in the field of character. He is essentially *not* progressive. He is the eternal African in the best sense of the words. That is what he *should* remain; for that is what he is bound to remain under all circumstances, as long as he retains his substance. When Ortega, speaking of the future, assigns to the intelligence a lesser *rôle* than it has had in the past, he is wrong as regards Europe, but right as regards Spain. In that country it is impossible for the intellectual function, for intellectuals, ever to play a decisive *rôle*. It is a remarkable effect which just this man, José Ortega y Gasset, produces against the background of his homeland: he is one of the finest and most universal of Europeans; he will some day be acknowledged as one of the leaders of this age. But the statement of European critics that he is a leader in his country is incorrect; for a spirit of his kind, this is an utter impossibility. It is not insight that rules the life of the Spaniard. But is it not perhaps better that this should be consciously so? How much true insight is there at work among us? Are not instinct and blood, to the extent that they can still be determining factors, the better leaders? . . . It is quite certain that the essential substance of Spain can embody itself in the form of modern conditions. It will do this beyond a doubt. But this process, if it runs its course undisturbed, will take place as a differentiation and a shaping of what is eternally the same, and *not* as a changing of form. It has always been the same Spaniard: the Spaniard who, in primeval times, created the glorious rock monuments; who, as Roman Emperor, more than once ruled the world; who conquered the New World; who painted the great portraits; who fought for the faith; and who once more today, through the lips of Miguel de Unamuno, proclaims with magnificent bias the gospel of tragedy and of agony. And when we bear in mind that very few peoples have passed through so many racial changes as that of the Iberian peninsula, we are compelled to ask ourselves: Is not change everywhere, in the last analysis, something external? Is not all substance, in the last analysis, eternally the same? It is above all as a model of essential substance that Spain means something to a Europe which takes such delight in change. In any case it is only as substance become reality that Spain has a European future of a new kind. Not for nothing did the new rise of Spain—for she is incontrovertibly on the rise again—begin with the close of the age of progress. Thus may she, as essence, for ever remain what she has always been.

GERMANY

GERMANY

I T was not difficult to determine why the Englishman is fundamentally misunderstood. But why the German? His nature is not animal, but all too human; and with him, too, as with the Frenchman, it is the intelligence, the transferable *par excellence*, which has the upper hand. Any examination of Germany which is to be both sound and generally intelligible, must set out from this question. But *the* German, in any exact sense, does not exist. When the German world first became a disturbing problem to me, no one was more helpful to me than the white-haired Russian Ambassador to London, Count Benckendorff, who, when the subject of Germany was broached one evening, broke in with: *Ne dites pas* les *allemands: il n'y a que* des *allemands*. Every German is actually a window-less monad; this is probably the reason why the creator of monadology was a German. And this necessarily results in such manifoldness that, however numerous may be the common features based on similarity of type, one cannot speak of "the" German in the same sense as one speaks of the Englishman or the Frenchman. In this, his case resembles that of "the" Hindoo. In spite of all this, the mass-German emerges today as an historic phenomenon which only America can parallel; to this extent "the" German as such does exist from the viewpoint of others. He is seen as something very definite, and as this given quantity, he is misunderstood by everybody. So it is after all permissible to speak of misunderstandings as they apply to "the" German, and of the general German characteristics which these misunderstandings evoke. As far as I can see, there are some five or six of these which claim our attention before anything else. I will deal with them in sequence, but not in strict order, since they overlap.

The first reason for the incomprehensibility of the German is his preoccupation with the object. He is in all likelihood the one object-creature that God has created. It was only among

Germans, out of all the beings we know, that there could arise, without provoking a counter-movement, the Fichtean definition that to be German means to do a thing for its own sake. It is taken for granted that no work achieves anything unless it is carried out with love and is, to that extent, an end in itself; but from that definition to the one which makes the object mean more than the person is a very far cry; and for Germany, and Germany alone, does it hold good. Let a work be ever so personal in its co-ordinates, let the sense of it lie ever so clearly in the quality of life which it embodies—the German sees in the matter only what is intrinsic. In the early days of Bolshevism I once went to hear a lecture by a reliable German authority on Russia who had just returned from the soviet state and who was to render a report on it; he delivered an objective address on the idea of surplus value; that is to say, on the one thing which lacks all meaning in an evaluation of Bolshevism. Thus the German revolution was in its very nature contrary to sense and to that extent devoid of practical danger—to those of my relatives who were threatened I made these representations from the very beginning, and I even guaranteed that nothing would happen to them—the reason being that the revolutionaries were accessible to objective considerations. It is obvious that an upheaval never pays; it is obvious that the first result of an agrarian revolution is to decrease returns from the soil; and it is obvious that the innocent must suffer. In his actions the authentic revolutionary is impelled by a primal passion which expresses itself in a blind "and yet. . . ." The German will have none of this. For him the decisive factor lies at all times in the "objective." The ninth of November, 1918, which I happened to spend in Berlin—this, the most stereotyped of all events, was the fourth revolution that I went through—made itself memorable for me through two experiences. On the morning of that day I met a Balt, a former Russian marine officer, in a state of moral collapse: "Have you read the proclamation of the Kiel sailors?" When I answered in the affirmative, he went on: "I was the one that drew it up; I did it at a certain moment in Helsingfors, hoping by a skilful deflection of events to prevent a massacre of the officers. And now these jackasses have copied it out and repeat it by rote." Later in the day I was walking with a professor on Unter den Linden. He sniffed the air and declared: "It is, I believe, high time to proclaim the republic. Are you coming with us to the Chancellor's palace?" I did, though the business was no concern of mine. The scholar wanted to speak to one of the deputies of the people. They seemed to be in a hurry; he would have to leave his request verbally with one of the adjutants, who would pass it on later. Whereupon the professor stated that the republic ought to be proclaimed at once. Before long the adjutant came panting back and, clicking his heels together, asked: "Is it the opinion of the Herr Geheimrat that a republic would suffice, or must it be a democratic republic?" That is what I call German absorption in the object itself. It is a quality which defines almost all of that German life which is directed outward. It lies at the root of the purely German idea of the expert; it is purely German in spite of the fact that experts may be found everywhere, because it is only in Germany that the man has his functional centre in his specialty, and not *vice versa*. In this respect I learned a great deal during the inflation period from a young waiter, who found fault with the owner of his café, a dealer in Turkish carpets, because he, as owner, wanted to see for himself that things went right: "The specialist can only laugh at that," he wound up, with the tone and expression so often to be observed among Geheimrats. Later on I happened one time to be sitting at the corner of a table at a Berlin luncheon party, with Lunacharsky and a great German naturalist. The latter wanted to know how his Excellency—Lunacharsky being Minister of Education, he was of course to be regarded as in all respects on the same plane as his German colleagues—was carrying through the building up of the inhabitants of Turkestan into civilized beings. "We, of course, are continuing the tradition

of Wilhelm von Humboldt." Lunacharsky and I could hardly
keep our faces straight. It was and it remained quite impossible
for this good Professor Teufelsdrökh to grasp how instruction
could possibly be conveyed otherwise than from a purely objective point of view. This primacy of the Thing in the German
soul also lies at the psychological root of most German idealism; the German does not dare to stand up for something
which he cannot justify objectively. This explains the unfortunate expression of Bethmann-Hollweg at the beginning of
the war. Thus I recently read in a prospectus of the Krone Cir-
cus: "The object of my creation is not entertainment; its purpose is to teach, to spread knowledge, and to enrich one's life-
philosophy." There is no feeling whatsoever for the value of
enjoyment in itself, for its spiritual quality, which is so characteristic of the Englishman; and in this wise festivities are
made to depend on a life-philosophy, and the festival itself is
institutionalized in the spirit of some object. Thus even the
foxiest German business man claims to be serving an ideal at a
sacrifice. Germany's inner attitude toward the war was of a like
spirit. The one thing which was least comprehensible to Anglo-
Saxons, the chief buttress of their later belief that the Germans
are a nation of fiends, was precisely this constant striving to
justify all action on metaphysical grounds. They understood
well enough that the Germans were striving for power, fighting for life; what they could not understand was that something which they regarded as quite naturally justifiable should
have to be supported, in addition, on metaphysical grounds; in
their opinion that could mean only one thing—a bad conscience.
And in the same way the defective German sense for national
pride is based on the predominance of the thing. Honour can
never be motivated objectively. Either the feeling for it is
there, a primary element, or else it is absent. All definite sense
of honour has always meant, in German life, the honour either
of castes or of individuals who broke away from the norm and
who attempted to impose their specific nature on others. This

is best illustrated by the German compulsory duel in contrast with the recognized freedom of choice in such matters among Roman or Latin peoples. With regard to this point, as well as with regard to another—namely, how all plastic expression, all that is based on beauty, that is, all form and all stateliness in Germany has been Latin-born in spirit—the reader should turn to Otto von Taube's *Betrachtungen eines Römlings* in *Navigare necesse est* (Insel-Verlag, Germany), one of the profoundest treatises that I know of on the essential being of Germany.

But the German life-element lies, once for all, in that which, externally, emerges most typically in the cult of the object. And since it lies in this alone, it produces an effect of the incomprehensible and unnatural. It was an Englishman who made the quip: "If there were two gates, on the first of which was inscribed *To Heaven*, and on the other *To Lectures about Heaven*, all Germans would make for the second." This man saw deep. Thus a very well-known philosophical publisher once told me enthusiastically that nearly all the books of one of the most important living German philosophers whom he was publishing were lying unsold in the cellar: "And that's how it ought to be." This good man was capable of discouraging the sale of the books, at a personal sacrifice, in order to sustain his belief that great works could not possibly achieve success during the lifetime of their author. With this we reach the real root of German absorption in the thing, and are also in a position to understand how that same motive can find equal expression both in the mastery of reality and in the fictitious. In the eighteenth century there was in France a place called Versailles, where a powerful monarch lived. In Germany there were a good five hundred images of it, where, outwardly, things went on in an identical way. Yet in Versailles history was made, and in the miniature courts of Germany history was played at. But just this game befitted the German. It is in exactly this way that the military demonstrations which the Allied Commissions so thoroughly misunderstand should be taken. As parades they are ends in themselves. And how was it in the Middle Ages? If one reads the history of the early German Empire, one encounters almost exclusively minutes of sessions; the Emperors went from city to city, like regular committeemen, for this purpose. Today it is no longer the Emperors who sit in session, but the artists, the savings-bank officials; and even the School of Wisdom has its sessions. That which lies at the psychological root of the parades and sessions also lies at the root of German "protests"—from historic Protestantism down to what we encounter, day in, day out, in the form of "resolutions." The protest is an end in itself; it is not supposed to produce anything. This explains why German protests, as experience has shown, carry so little conviction; every one feels that they were never intended to be successful. For this reason the German refuses to keep his protest to himself even when he knows perfectly well that he can attain his end more certainly by keeping quiet. The utter harmlessness of the German protest was recently demonstrated in the case of Theodore Lessing; the entire German student-world, and with it the majority of the German people itself, rose as one man against him. And the only result was this, that Lessing obtained a sinecure, a research fellowship without teaching duties; he thus realized the dearest wish of the great majority of scientists. Of all this, the German proverb speaks: *Viel Feind', viel Ehr'* —Many enemies, much honour.

But the same psychological circumstance explains, again, German exploits in the realm of things and facts. Given a prevailing idea which conforms to reality, and the objective meaning of which consists in the fact that it can be transposed into reality, the German people can achieve what no other people can. Only Germans could have been blessed with the marvel of the Rentenmark; indeed, every one was perfectly ready to sacrifice all that he had for the sake of the *idea* of the gold basis. It is the same, fundamentally, with every great German enterprise; its possibilities depend, time after time, on German self-sacrifice for the sake of the idea. Furthermore, only Germans could so redispose themselves as to turn the Versailles Treaty into a direct advantage for a new German rise. This faculty for changes of position is only a particular expression of what commonly emerges as German conservatism; its psychological roots are the same as those of German dogmatism and obstinacy of opinion. The German is not conservative in the English sense; he does not live in the line of historic continuity as a matter of instinct. As against this, however, he believes in timeless values and in persistence through time; but even the possibility of sudden, complete rebirth, too, is an allegory of timelessness. From the same motives the German believes, as no one else does, in hard-won rights, while on the other hand he is prepared unconcernedly to compromise with every injustice. German objectivity, therefore, is the psychological root of specifically German idealism as well as of German spinelessness. And all these characteristics have their origin ultimately in the fact that with the German the representation takes precedence over the actuality. This may at times be an ideal, or the will of the state, or money-making, or existing law, or a personal grudge. I know of representative Germans who were happy that in the Versailles Treaty they had found a steadfast instrument, and the mere idea that they might lose this inward sense of certainty through a revision of the Treaty terrified them. It has always been the same. In the Cathedral of Assisi there is a window glowing with a picture—by Giotto, if I am not mistaken—in which Barbarossa lies on his back while the Pope sets a foot on his belly. The Italians in the picture look on in a sort of embarrassed amusement. I should like to wager that the Germans had insisted on this ceremony; they regarded it, in some way, as an expression of *de facto* law. German loyalty, too, derives its peculiar character from this predominance of the thing over the person. From the generally accepted point of view the Germans are, of course, the most faithless of peoples; this thesis of Leopold Ziegler's, the most German of present-day German thinkers, must be accepted as proved. No one collapses, or "changes his position," as frequently as the German does; for with him the principle of living continuity, the purely personal, is not the ultimate and immediate authority; the German ideal of loyalty (*Treue*) is to that extent an ideology of contrast. But there is another kind of loyalty, unknown to any one else. In a certain war between the Poles and the Lithuanians some German soldiers of fortune were engaged on the side of the latter, and fought so well that the Poles sent them an offer to change sides. Back came the answer: "Delighted—but you will have to wait until tonight, when our contract expires." But by the evening they were all dead.

WE have now come to the characteristic German feature which I have dealt with more than once (cf. first the chapters on Germany's task in the changed world and the phenomenal world and the power of spirit in *Philosophie als Kunst,* and, again, that on Germany's true political mission in *Politik, Wirtschaft, Weisheit*); and that is the unreality of the German spirit. It is typical of the German spirit that it lives for itself in a sphere of its own; its knowledge is not something that lives, but something that has been constructed and projected. And the result is that fundamentally German knowledge is out of touch both with personal and with external reality. To one who is freely and naturally centred in himself —as all the European peoples, with the exception of the Germans, more or less are—the German must appear actually unnatural, for the impersonal motivation of his life which thus emerges produces ultimately an inhuman effect; the personal element in a man declines in direct proportion as his consciousness becomes centred in detached, externalized ideas; and for those who have to deal with him it really becomes impossible to know what they can expect and what they can rely on. To which this should be added: whenever a perception, at the very moment of its incidence, is formulated and set forth, i.e. devitalized by utterance, it at once eludes the complete organism; then, by the psychological law of compensation, the personality, as it continues to develop, becomes primitive instead of more differentiated. German sentimentality, German lyricism, even German soulfulness, owe their special and typical character not to the education of the emotional side of the German, but much rather to its lack of education.

And the same unhappy effect is produced in his contacts with the external world, by the absence, in the German, of a relationship between thinking and being. What he likes is to dictate ideals and programs independently of the will of the participants. He demonstrates this in every official order; I have never yet read one which has not thoroughly annoyed me. This is implied by the dominance of stark formulation of ideas, whose logical content and logical sequence are regarded as of more importance than the living persons to whom they are applied. The primary impression of the Russian is that the German is soulless; how should it be otherwise? There *is* something monstrous in the mere idea that the will just does not count as long as "the thing in and for itself" is good.

This characteristic adjustment of the majority of Germans quite naturally results in the absurdity that whenever castes which deviate from the type do not play the determining *rôle*, Germany is practically ruled by scholars. This would be the right place, then, to say something on the nature of German caste. The Germans are physiologically a caste people, in the same way as the Hindoos. And that for the same reasons. As a nation, the Hindoos, too, are introverts; with them, too, it is reflection that dominates. Under these conditions the only way to allow for actual differences is by an arrangement which takes into account a pre-existing framework of life—one which offers a normal field of development to variations; and a limited number of such frameworks suffices for the purpose, for every man belongs to some type, and there is only a limited number of types. With a few rare exceptions, neither the German nor the Hindoo can become the same unfettered individualist as the Briton or the Italian; he must find some sort of self-justification in the world of explicit ideas. Just as we had and have the Kshatriyas and the Rajahs in India, so we have in Germany types to whom the general characterization does not apply and who are distinguished by the typical freedom of the Nordic ruler-type. It was in the nature of things that these should, in their day, constitute the ruling class. German aristocracy is under no circumstances the product of the normal state of mind of a master people; it is rather the product of the fact that in the midst of the Germans, the born ruler is in the nature of things in much the same position as the pike in a fishpond. Yet it has always been evident that the basic disposition outlined above belongs to the Germans at large. As for the German aristocrat, no sooner did the peculiarity of his type fade out than he reverted to the original scholar-type. And for a long time past the nobility has felt that it constitutes a class in exactly the same sense as mail-carriers, business men, and doctors do—a point of view which defeats the very concept of aristocracy. Thus it is: as a type, the German is a scholar. This surely was true even of the Cimbres and Teutons, and it is an eternal pity that there was among the camp-followers of Marius no sociologist with a satirical bent to give us a description of the scholar in his original state of complete ignorance. What is it that makes the scholar as a type? The scholar is the man who by his nature, calling, and profession lives fundamentally in the world of externalized and explicit ideas. It goes without saying that he justifies his existence; he is even very necessary. It is his business to work out the tangible and the objective, and to follow up results to their final consequences; it is his business to supply specialized information for the young. But by his very nature he is, *par excellence,* not the profound but the shallow person; he is such primarily as a philosopher. Depth of thought is an attribute of those who have their roots in the depths of reality; a man is capable of deep perception to the extent that his consciousness directly mirrors these depths. And for the scholar as a type this is by its very nature impossible, because his consciousness does happen to live in the world of externalized and explicit ideas, and he is correspondingly out of contact with the depths of his reality. If scholars pass for deep, it is because of the fact that the dear public does not know how to distinguish between depth and toploftiness. In Germany it is only the exceptional few who really understand the distinction. It has happened over and over again with me that at the Darmstadt sessions there have been acclaimed as the crowning glory of the season learned speakers who, as men of knowledge, were not fit to tie the shoe-laces of lesser celebrities. They happened to be the most intelligible to the majority. And the fact is that for the average German audience, no abstract theoretical lecture has ever been too difficult. Yes, the scholar is the essentially shallow person. And for the most part he is even the essentially stupid. This statement is no paradox. In all intellectual work quality alone is the decisive factor. If every shoemaker is to be respected because he is useful, every poet and painter who falls short of greatness is superfluous. Thus it is only the great scholar who is a higher type of man. If a man has only the inclination of the scholar, but is not gifted as such, then he stands below other types, for, as every comic journal amply witnesses, outside of his specialty the scholar is peculiarly incompetent.

How, then, can an entire people of scholars do anything but bring forth an overwhelming majority of insignificant scholars? It cannot be otherwise, for the average of even the most gifted people is low. Thus, in the case of at least 70 per cent. of Germany's learned literature, there is barely one original thought for every thousand pages. If this statement should annoy any German, he has only to realize that, considering the vast quantity production, even this percentage proves that there must be living in Germany a greater number of important scholars than anywhere else in the world. It goes without saying that it is precisely the unimportant scholars who are the appointed teachers; their business it is to provide knowledge for the masses, and only he can succeed in this who resembles the masses. The value of high talent is considerably overestimated: in very ma~y fields of activity it is the talent below the average which reaps the most brilliant successes; for, after all, we all understand only him who somewhat resembles us. But, conceding all this, the fact nevertheless remains that an untalented man of scholarly inclinations is on the whole inferior to every other type. In Germany the most pitifully uninspired scholar ranks as a being of a higher kind, just because he is a scholar. In this we may perceive an absolute misunderstanding. It is illogical to ascribe high value to a man just because he is engaged in a disinterested pursuit of truth; everything depends on whether or not it is his vocation to find it. In this respect the American view is superior to the German. It is true that as a nation, America is organically indifferent to the value of the great and free spirit. But when it judges the average scholar by the standard of social service, by the extent to which his accomplishments can serve the common end, it does well. In every rightly adjusted social organism, the rôle of the scholar as such was properly a modest one, purely regulative. In Germany, whenever no higher caste dominates, they belong at the top, for it is only in the scholar that this scholar people instinctively recognizes its authentic representative. And this does *not* mean the same thing as in China, for there the scholar must be, by definition, the perfect noble. And thus most of the misfortunes of Germany's history are due to the domination of the scholar-world. It is probable that those who overthrew Arminius were by inclination professorial natures with a Ku Klux Klan turn of mind. Since the fall of

Bismarck it is everywhere the scholar who has dominated in Germany, even if the absolutely ignorant scholar. Since the war, things have become even worse. It is the nature of the scholar that he should be devoid of any understanding for psychological reality. It is the will of God that he should be tactless. He can grasp only that which has become, not the thing in process of becoming. He lacks every organ for a living life. This, then, is the ultimate reason why the greatly gifted German people, having achieved greatness under the guidance of great men, has never enjoyed that greatness long.

THE German scholar-spirit is all the more uncanny to other peoples because it finds its instrument in that lack of moderation which is traditionally German. I do not need to examine this characteristic in detail; it is the one characteristic which foreign critics have always unanimously observed, and which the German himself only imperfectly sees as a function of his feeling for space, his longing for infinity. The generalizing of the scholar in the field of abstraction finds a parallel expression, in the case of the people, in overwork and mass-production. If the so-called feeling for space and longing for infinity put themselves at the service of the scholar, they must issue, empirically, as mere immoderation; the result is something uglier than anything America has produced, for back of it there lies not naïve exuberance, but dry, soulless calculation. For the fact is that what we are concerned with here is not only longing for infinity and feeling for space as determinants of values, but also the chaos of a still unconquered dynamic nature and the assertive hunger of the introvert who does not feel safe in this world. The uncanny element in German immoderation becomes wholly incomprehensible when that element rages without aim. The deepest impulse of the German is opposed to purposefulness. He does that which an inner force compels him to do. But if in the case of an ideal, or of great spirits, this leads to the rarest kind of achievement and creation, it has, in the case of the people as a whole, and throughout all its history, characteristically led to what, in *Deutschlands wahrer politischer Mission,* I have defined as "senseless heroism." The original model of the German man of action has really been, at all times, the soldier of fortune. The senseless hero-life of the warrior is not without beauty; it is the affirmation of tragedy, and built itself up on it; and all tragedy is deep. No corresponding tragedy of the business man exists. Even though the latter again and again risks everything for nothing, even though he plays the aimless conqueror, it is not only without sense, but repulsive of sense. And since no man believes in the absolutely senseless as long as anything else is possible, the German, precisely when he is laying about him without the remotest purpose, gets himself suspected of the most fiendish machinations. The naïve fury of the German Hans is then misjudged as the bottomless cunning of Satan himself.

Yet the foregoing observations do not exhaust the sources of misunderstanding. By the German, primary importance is accorded not to life itself, but to experience (*nicht auf dem Leben sondern dem Er-leben* *), to the pathos and not to the ethos. With him every other phrase is, "That was a tremendous experience." A great experience can have the most diverse origins. Thus, under certain circumstances, a defeat may constitute a greater experience than a victory. The defeat of 1918 was such. It has certainly been more fruitful for Germany than their victory has been for the victorious peoples. It is for this very reason that, since that time, Germany has been uninterruptedly on the rise. How can this be understood by the French, for whom *la gloire* is the highest thing? Or by the English, whose psyche, it is true, is profoundly influenced by every event, but less in the sense of subjective experience than of organic transformation? Or by the Italian, who is subject

* To which is added, in the original: "A word significantly untranslatable into any other language."—*Translator's note.*

to no experience at all? And then Germany presents the incredible spectacle of a nation composed of monads, each for itself and without apertures, and yet with the collectivity functioning as one machine! Herewith we reach that tension in the German nature which is of decisive importance. To the extent that the German, as a type, is a scholar, he is an introvert, and therefore incapable of direct contact with external reality. No real scholar ever sees anything other than his own idea; this accounts for his absent-mindedness and his lack of tact. But on the other hand it is just this scholastic centering of the consciousness in externalized and explicit ideas which, if it once becomes "practical" (in the Kantian sense), can produce a high degree of mass-organization. For in this wise the life of millions simply subjects itself to an idea. The rule of the idea becomes absolute; individual personality is simply wiped out of the picture. Now we can understand the proverb of the Russian moujik who is ready to credit the German with everything he himself cannot understand: "The German has even invented the ape!" The German actually does not see "the other man." He is not, like the Mediterranean, a child of the market-place; he fails to see himself primarily from the viewpoint of others; in practice he knows of nothing at all except himself. And even himself he really does not "see"—whatever one sees, one must see from the outside; for which reason he is, more often than not, wrong about the character of his effective being; and for the same reason whatever he says and writes about himself is, from the viewpoint of others, usually phantasmagoric. It may be true within the sphere of experience, but it is what it is only for him who has passed through this experience. German all-understanding actually operates only in the sphere of the imagination, which, in compensation for the narrow sphere of real experience, runs riot in boundless space. This explains many things, above all the incessant German cry for the common interest—a cry which is never uttered by one with whom the common interest is natural. The meaning of possible common interest is wholly unperceived in Germany. The German insists on achieving a common interest precisely where each one is a unit apart and must therefore remain lonely. Correspondingly, German common interest nearly always means a trespassing on the sacredness of the individual. For this reason it is typical of German organizations that they are founded to serve a common end, whereas such organizations can be productive of good only if they spring up spontaneously out of a thing or a person.* Hence the unspeakable atrociousness of German *Vereine.* All of them have their *raison d'être* in the fact that the German in the first place does not look at others at all. It is a condition of his special psychological adjustment that he should be incapable of establishing a contact with his fellowman on the basis of feeling or emotion. This is why he attributes so much value to the revelation of the emotions of the heart. The man of deep tacit sensitiveness is instinctively reserved in his self-revelations. The German believes in the emotions of the heart only when they are exhibited, for he cannot perceive them otherwise. Nor do things stand differently with the scholars of other lands. But it is only in Germany that the majority is like this. And this same majority is organized; it is a tremendous world-force, and it sets the general tone! For the tone is not set by the silent in the land, the one type which the German, in unconscious self-knowledge, prizes above all others—he feels that, being what he is, he ought to keep as quiet as possible—the tone is set by him who makes himself seen and heard afar, that is, primarily, by the travelling salesman. And if, under all these circumstances, the others don't become anxious and afraid, fright must be outside the range of their spiritual possibilities. There are other reasons why the German is not understood. But those already cited will abundantly explain, in my opinion, this fate of the German.

* Cf. my studies *Von den Grenzen der Gemeinschaft* and *Vom falschen Gemeinschaftsideal* in Sections 3 and 14 of my *Weg zur Vollendung* (bulletin of the School of Wisdom).

L ET us now turn to the origin of the characteristics we have observed, and let us begin with a closer examination of the last mentioned. This characteristic lies at the bottom of the idea current in the country that there are two Germanys, Weimar and Potsdam. The fact is that there are two Germanys, but it does not happen to be a case of "either—or," but rather of polar co-ordinates. As a nation, the Germans are in the language of the newest school, objective introverts; i.e. a type of thinker who is turned inward toward himself. This does not mean that he is incapable of extraversion, i.e. of adjusting himself to the external world; but it does mean that such adjustment can take place only through his inferior functions. Of course this judgment does not imply that the German is less "able" than the other peoples; on the contrary, he is acknowledged to be the ablest being in the world. It does imply, however, that his active ability does not embody his highest significance. Our purpose here is to remove a fatal misunderstanding. The German too easily sees in two fundamentally different things one and the same thing. What constitutes the worth of the German artisan under given circumstances is *not* his ability; what comes to expression here is the spirituality of the mediaeval craftsman, who, for his soul's sake, found his life-work in the elaboration of some church ornament invisible to the world at large. In relation to this kind of "love of the thing," the correlative name "the silent in the land" becomes a title of honour; and this kind of "love of the thing" remains to this day the real soul of German quality in work. But this soul can be lost; and if it is lost, the quality which defines German work becomes inferior instead of superior: that is, it becomes his "ability," which is the quality whereby the worker identifies himself with the work as such. In this case the artisan's joy in his work becomes the expression not of the soul's absorption, but of lack of spirit; and then the step-by-step process, the attention bestowed on trifles, the patience which can be neither exhausted nor disillusioned, mean, in the German, nothing better than adaptation to the laws of the world with a minimum of soul and spirit; then his world-success derives from the fact that inertia and routine best bespeak the spirit of the world. It should not be forgotten that the spirit of the donkey is fundamentally better adapted to the laws of the world than is the spirit of the genius. Something of this was in the mind of Victor Hugo, too, when he wound up his poem on the world's creation with:

> *Et Dieu et le pourceau immonde*
> *Se regardèrent.*

If German ability has achieved such fantastic results, then, judged purely *a priori*, it can only lie in the fact that something low is involved. We should remember in this connection what has been said about the narrowness of the French and the athletic spirit of the English, qualities which have not stood in the way of either people in their aspiration to world-mastery; the talents which are needed in order to achieve the successes of ability are fundamentally *inferior*. Thus "ability" is the exact opposite of love of the thing in its best sense; it is a purely mechanical quality; in matters of the spirit it derives its inspiration from Satan, not from God. We need only call to mind how closely this kind of German ability approaches American efficiency, and we see the whole thing clearly. The creative, the intellectual, the spiritual, the metaphysical in man, tolerates neither routine nor overwork. If the Germans were simply a nation of arms and legs, then, and then only, would they have the right to be proud of that which the majority regard as their chief glory. But the essential and the best in the German does happen to belong to the realm of mind and spirit. Thus, if his joy in work ever has a spiritual, intellectual determinant, that can be only when it issues from the spirit of the silent in the land. Once he lays the emphasis at all on world-power, he is compelled to exaggerate a function which is by its very nature inferior.

This more than anything else explains the fate of the Germany of Wilhelm II. It needed a tremendous, almost superhuman harnessing of energy in order to remould a nation of poets and thinkers—such as the German people was to some extent acknowledged to be—and transform it into the worldpower of yesterday and today. This excessive strain, on its side, was bound to lead to a tremendous loss of personality and soul; in becoming essentially "able," the Germans had to suppress the best that was in them. In this we shall find the cause of that soullessness and mechanization which every one of any account has emphatically observed in the new Germany. Nor is this state of affairs to be overcome by the demand for quality work in mass-production; German soul and German spirit are such that they are even less capable of survival in the forms of Americanization than in those of an exaggerated Prussianization; it is thus that German-Americans are of all Americans the most materialistic. Furthermore, since any understanding of the world can be achieved only through soul and personality, it necessarily follows that the abovementioned inner loss must lead to an increasing inner isolation. In the period of Wilhelm II. it became a decisive historic reality, leading up, finally, to the war against the whole world and to the defeat.

But the fact that the German of the most recent period has misplaced his inner emphasis does not, we repeat, mean that his inferior functions will not live themselves out at all: he should simply know that it is something of inferior quality that is involved. The shortest cut to an understanding of that adjustment which, for the German, with all his faults, would be the right adjustment to the cosmos, leads through the example of Kant. This man, while attending the funeral of a beloved sister, suddenly became aware of the fact that he had not seen her for twenty-five years, although she had lived only a few hundred yards from him. This came about because of the fact that every day, at exactly the same hour, both used

to go for a walk, but in opposite directions. In Kant this was
no proof of inferiority; the extreme regularity of his outward life was much rather the necessary psychological compensation to the inner freedom of his spirit. The same thing
applies to the German love of system as a whole. And also to
German middle-class psychology (*Bürgerlichkeit*). This is not
fundamentally concerned, as in the case of the French, with the
rentier psychology; it has to do rather with the demand for
external security which characterizes the introvert, whose most
personal life is lived in the inner world. To this extent one can
have little to say even against German pedantry. *But then the
emphasis should be laid on the other side, on inner freedom.*

That which applies to the individual applies to the nation
as a whole. The macrocosm of the latter always mirrors the
individual soul; i.e. within the nation there is the same distribution of emphasis and value among the various types as
there is among the various functions within the *individual*.
In both cases all possibility of perfection depends on this, that
the emphasis should be laid on what is of highest value, and
that inferior values should play a subordinate *rôle*, which, as
such, ought decidedly to be regarded as useful and even worthy
of respect. Thus there is in Germany the middle-class, organized, systematic type, a type which even constitutes the
majority. But even at his best he represents the inferior section
of the nation, and not, as in the case of the English and the
Americans, among whom the introverts are inferior as a type,
its best section. It follows, then, that he should not be the
decisive factor. And it is perfectly useless to call up, in this
connection, considerations of equity based on numbers; a
man who is essentially a drill-sergeant really has no desire, in
his inmost depths, to be anything else.* Should he happen to
rise above the station for which Providence destined him, he
shows himself up by dragging down all life to the level of a

* Cf. the detailed *exposé* of the false ideal of justice, to which this sentence
applies, in the chapter *Indische und chinesische Weisheit* in my *Schöpferische
Erkenntnis.*

drill-sergeant's ideas. This is what has been taking place in an
ever-increasing degree, in the last few decades of German
history. And if more recently it is less the drill-sergeant than
the savings-bank official who feels himself destined to occupy
the post of Chancellor of the Empire, this can scarcely be
regarded as a gain.

But again, it does not follow from what has been said that
we should take the advice of Germany's enemies, renounce our
striving, and fall back into that romantic state which, on the
basis of the *Tales of Hoffmann,* they consider the only true
mirror of the German character. The man of ability must be
retained, but only as a draught-horse, without special significance; he must be the security for inward freedom. The
orderly type must be retained, too: external freedom, like that
of the political nations, has never been a real desire of the
Germans; ever since they have obtained it, they have put it to
the worst possible uses—they even seem to be doing everything in the world to cancel that freedom through the discovery
of new bonds; the German *needs* external discipline as the bal-
ancing weight to his inner freedom. A Dresden bookseller once
said to me: "Before, when we still had a King, I could close
up my shop and go home and look up at the lights in the castle
with a feeling of security; on holiday evenings *he* was still at
work, on things beyond my understanding. Today I feel insecure. I need a close-fitting coat to feel safe in my skin."
Because the same thing applies to the overwhelming majority
of Germans, democracy in the English sense is of little use
to them. Hardly had the preceding ruling castes disappeared
when dominion passed into the hands of minorities whose
power was based on money or personal connections, and these,
lacking a historic background, are all the more intemperate in
their exercise of power. And then, with the predominating
objectivity of the majority, the point of view of the gentleman
ceased to play a determining *rôle.* This, more than anything
else, accounts for the fact that in all her great periods the

German structure has, in one way or another, been aristocratic;
if a noble view of life is to play the determining *rôle*, the tone
must be given, for this caste-people, by a real caste which has,
as it were, taken an official oath to have a noble point of view;
nothing else will do with a people which has the German turn
of mind. We must probably take it for granted that the
security-type and the orderly type will always constitute the
masses in Germany: it was on this basis that, in my *Deutschlands wahrer politischer Mission,* I called the Germans the
middle-class people *par excellence.* But for that very reason,
no rule of the masses, or even of a majority, can ever be worth
anything to Germany if she wishes to "keep fit." In her case the
majority cannot give expression to the *volonté générale,* which
Rousseau had already learned to distinguish from the *volonté
de tous.*

Whatever has any worth in Germany lies on another plane
than German "ability." But, to repeat, this function, too, must
live itself out. The fact that the possibilities for this consummation were lacking before 1870 explains psychologically the
hypertrophy of mechanization which followed. There is a
particularly instructive example which illustrates the real relationship between that hypertrophy and the German inner spirit.
What does the German love of wandering about to the sound of
music signify? It means that that which is purely inward, even
in the realm of free art, calls for mechanical external compensation. For this kind of rambling is not, for its part, the
expression of a spiritual intellectual experience; it is essentially
a grand march.

We have thus defined, by implication, who should be the
ruler in Germany; *namely, the exceptional type, whose inner
freedom, by its very nature, externalizes itself in world-
power.* This is why Germany has always been the land of
princes and courts. This is why democracy, interpreted in whatever sense, has never led the Germans to high achievement.
It would be right to say that in one respect Germany finds its

closest affinity in America; it is far more capable than any other European country in the matter of mass-organization. But *this* Germany lies furthest of all from the best German spirit (just as the German-Americans on the other side are, as I have already said, typically the most unspiritual Americans). It is with real terror that I note the increasing idealization of the conditions obtaining in the United States on the part of Germany's "spiritual leaders." After the terrific *débâcle* everything must naturally be done in order to bring about the economic rehabilitation of Germany as quickly as possible. And for this the adoption of American methods, and co-operation with America on the basis of these methods, is the swiftest method. But woe to Germany if she sees in this anything different from the work of preparation which preceded the wars of liberation! Woe to Germany if she sees an ideal in Americanism! And unfortunately this is already true of far too many Germans. To the man who sees all value in objectivity, one ideal is as good as another, as long as it is only an ideal. And here the suppressed personal quality comes to utterance in such fashion that it uncritically transfers its affection to anything and everything. A certain art-critic whom I knew in my youth, a man of some importance, always had to see, in the painter about whom he happened to be writing at the moment, the greatest artist of the time. And thus I knew a certain bacteriologist who was profoundly offended by the human organism because the typhus bacilli could not survive the sickness which they themselves had occasioned. . . .

No; if a people so introverted as the German is to find its proper form, then the rulers must consist of types with a different kind of adjustment. In this regard it is India which, as a symbol, should show the way for Germany. The Brahmins rank as the highest caste. Yet it is not they who rule in this world. That labour is performed by princes specially bred for the purpose, and in order that the stamp of their particular order may stand out, it is even the custom to feed them, in the

face of all Indian tradition, on meat. Now I certainly do not
believe in a restoration of the rule of the princes in Germany; our development has carried us beyond that point.
Nevertheless its *equivalent* will have to emerge once more
if Germany is again to become "fit." The ruling class will have
to be recruited not from the ranks of the scholars, in the widest
sense of that word, but from the ranks of a special and different breed of men, quite alien to the masses of the people.
If, in the next few decades at most, no restoration in this
sense takes place, then Germany will inevitably evolve into a
caricature of America: into a caricature, because that which is
essentially colossal avoids becoming a caricature only when it
finds a colossal form.

I T is on the basis of the last observations and reflections that
we shall best approach an understanding of the special
character of the German inner spirit. It is a spirit of pathos, i.e.
of feminine character. In every feminine person the masculine element which is always present supplies the inferior
function. It is typical that precisely this function should be
overemphasized through the urge toward psychological compensation. Thus the German emphasis on the masculine is just
what betrays the feminine character. And the fact that the
primal masculine model is presented in the character of the
drill-sergeant again demonstrates the inferiority of the masculine function. It is assuredly not inferior in the case of every
German, but as a rule Germany produces men, in the best
sense, only as members of a special caste. No really masculine
people would ever have hit on the idea of representing that
man of supersensitive nerves, Bismarck, as the smith of the
German Empire, with sleeves rolled up. In this lies the psychological root of the overemphasis on the will to power which
characterized the era of Wilhelm II. The essentially masculine Englishman never emphasizes it; he seeks rather to soften
it, by restraining himself, by speaking gently, working through

feminine suggestiveness, etc. From the very same source flows the German contempt for woman. The Briton idolizes her, which does not, however, prevent older women of this essentially masculine nation from betraying much more masculine traits of character than do the majority of smooth-shaven German men of the same age. The German despises his own feminine element in the woman, and this, of course, reacts in turn on the feminine type. Furthermore, one respect in which the Frenchman is superior to the German is in his regard for woman's work, from the kitchen to the boudoir, as of equal worth with his own profession—which it naturally is. But here, too, the "masculine protest" of the German stands in the way of a clear understanding. The essentially feminine character of the German proves, for its part, that he is not by nature his own master, but that he needs the restraint of externalized ideas; this is in no way different from the need of the woman to receive her law from the man. The German delight in organization means the same thing; as Walter Rathenau so often justly remarked, the Germans are not an organizing, but an organizable people. The same significance attaches to the German ethics of duty. To regard the fulfilment of duty rather than personal responsibility, as the highest virtue, indicates a primal need for yielding oneself up. The instinctive question which the man puts to himself is not "May I?" but "Do I want to?" And in this lies the psychological root of the German hunger "to have both feet planted on solid fact"; this, too, is the root of the German lack of civic courage; it is only the exceptional woman who has this; it is typical of her that she has courage only for the things that are allowed by custom. Finally, the very physique of the majority of Germans is sufficient to prove the predominance of the feminine principle: the broadness of the hips, the formation of the skin, the putting on of flesh and the corpulency which characterizes the type, all belong to the female sex. But the decisive proof of the feminine pathos element in the fundamental German character lies in the emphasis on inner experience as distinguished from living. In this the specifically feminine element is transferred to that which characterizes the introvert as such. If the German is forever asking himself "May I?" this, too, can only be accounted for by the lack of self-assurance which the introvert feels in relation to the problems and tasks of the external world; the same thing, again, is at the bottom of his blustering attitude when he is at all certain that he "may"—especially when he knows that he is backed by great masses; simply as an introvert, the German cannot emerge as a free and naïve individualist, like the Italian. This explains the impression of a herd-people made by the Germans. The fact is that no other people in the world so uncritically permits itself to be commanded. In and for himself, however, the German is just as outspoken an individualist as the Englishman, the Frenchman, and the Italian, but in another respect and with a different adjustment; he is the individualist as the man who experiences, i.e. *for himself*—for himself only. Out of the consciousness of his individual singularity he cuts himself off from all others; it is only as the creature of the herd—and every one is that, as a member of a genus—that he comes in contact with them. As an individualist he is something of a crank, which individualism as such does not demand. The introverted individualist needs, as compensation, external order. To this extent the herd-element in German life is the substitute for the "rule" of monasticism.

From all the foregoing, the reader might gather that in the psychological adjustment of the German it is disadvantages which predominate. The contrary is the truth. *If the German is, to the extent indicated, an introverted individualist; if he is, as such, highly gifted; if he recognizes at the same time the limits set by nature on his type—then he is the leading European.* Why? Because the uniqueness of the individual is the last and deepest value in man, because all eternal values enter the field of life only through the unique, and therefore exert their profoundest creative forces through the man whose centre of consciousness lies therein. This explains why, ever since Germany attained the necessary stage of development, the overwhelming majority of all great Europeans have come from Germany. They are of German origin even when their greatness was exercised in fields which seem alien to the national talent: William of Orange, Frederick the Great, Stein and Bismarck, were Germans, too. The German psychological adjustment is the most favourable to the full development of *every* extraordinary talent. Only the German can so candidly and naturally think first of himself, and himself only, to the exclusion of others, that the unique element within him attains its greatest possible expansion. France is an example of the contrary. But something follows from all this for the people as an entirety, something which definitely puts a quietus on the democratic ideal as far as Germany is concerned—that is, if Germany is to be important for humanity, if Germany is to become great, the national emphasis *must* be laid only on the unique; and on the plane of historic life, it must be laid, therefore, on a few individuals. If, in France, Paris is the one head, then Germany, as a value, exists only by the grace of a few unique personalities. We are faced here by something which is of the essence of things, a structural fact which no effort of the will can alter: something as essentially basic as the fact that in France it is the group of the *élite* which decides, or as the fact that among Anglo-Saxons every individual is equally important from the social-political point of view—for which reason both of these nations do well to lay the chief emphasis on external freedom. In keeping with the law of polar extremes, neither France nor England produces individualities at all to be compared with those produced by Germany; even the finest representatives of the French *élite* have never measured up to the greatest German individualities. Contrariwise, however, the German masses are destined to be inferior to those of other peoples. On the basis of these facts we can rightly evaluate the primal phenomenon of German envy. This envy obviously indicates a metaphysical misunderstanding. If the German puts the emphasis, as he should, on the unique, he certainly cannot put it on *every* individual; but in every case the emphasis belongs to the uniqueness of the individual. And since that uniqueness is always alone in its kind, the question of comparison becomes illogical. But, as I shall show in more detail in connection with Hungary, that consciousness of uniqueness can become externally manifest only in the peculiar form of the *grand seigneur*. And the German is essentially a man of the middle classes, and moreover, as an introvert, feels himself insecure in the world. He is therefore unable to perceive that the implications of determinant uniqueness, namely, the rule and leadership of the few in the sense of value, do not deprive the lesser types of their particular worth. And we must admit that for the little man without metaphysical consciousness it is really very hard to acknowledge that the great man is the all-important thing. England is free from envy, to the extent that every person really counts. Germany may play the democratic game to her heart's content; the fact remains that, in his inmost being, every German knows that as far as Germany is concerned everything depends upon the few, and only the man of inner nobility can tolerate the idea. This explains certain peculiar phenomena which hardly any one understands. In the first place one of the principal roots of German monarchism lies in this, too: instinctively the German dreams of a leader who, by virtue of his very standing, is lifted above all comparison; that leader, again, be he ever so German, is by his very position free from envy. In this we also find the explanation of the remarkable fact that so many hard-headed business men play the patron to saints and spiritual leaders. They know that these others stand above them, but to the extent that they are the providers, they can tolerate the idea of their own inferiority. This explains, further, the tacit mutual recognition and mutual commendation of the professors; to the extent that equality exists within the caste, and mutual recognition is the proper thing, personal inequality becomes tolerable.

But no sooner does the majority, as such, come to the fore, even to the slightest degree, than envy inevitably comes into play, here more than anywhere else on earth. Then democracy uncovers its ugly face. Then all values are negatived. Then cheap equity triumphs over justice; * then quality production becomes impossible, and the last word rests with the ethos of *Gemüt,* "soulfulness," the enemy of all worth. The specific socialism of Germany, which seeks to remove competition and which would like more than anything else to turn the working class into a branch of the civil service, with promotion solely by seniority and the rank of *Geheimrat* as the climax of ambition †—this socialism is one of the bitterest enemies of culture that has ever appeared in history. Thus, if the Germans want to become and remain fit as a nation, they must, in spite of the fact that they are not an aristocratic people, seek an aristocratic form of organization. They did this in all great periods of the past. They will do it again in all great periods of the future. The external impulse in this direction is provided by the pathos of their need to yield themselves up; the German mass wants to be led. But the profoundest contributing cause lies in the instinctive knowledge that only under an aristocratic constitution can the German people acquire value, not only as the producer of great individuals, but as a people. That is why, whatever may be said against the majority of courts, all the cultural values of Germany come from the age of the princes.

WHAT external act is most representative of the German on his best side? The confession of faith. The man in whom the chief emphasis is laid, if it is laid rightly, on inner

---

* Cf. my study, *Gerechtigkeit und Billigkeit,* in Section 12 of the *Weg zur Vollendung.*

† I had a charming experience of this kind at the beginning of the German revolution. I inquired in a certain house for the janitress. I was informed the *Frau Rat* was not at home. *Frau Rat?* Yes, her husband had become a member of the Workers' and Soldiers' Council. All the deep significance of the revolution was contained, for this worthy family, in that fact.

experience (*Er-leben*), and thus on the subjective, can be true to himself only when his self-expression has no purpose. Hence the peculiar egotism of all great Germans, with Goethe at their head—a man whom no Britisher has ever understood; the faith of the German must be directed firstly toward himself, if his activity is to bear good fruit, for if his faith turns toward others, he at once loses contact with his personal being. All German greatness was actually a confession of faith, in one sense or another. And, for that matter, just as every genius has his apes, so the worst that Germany has produced has always been, and still is, a confession of faith. Luther's "Here I stand, I can no other" was a confession of faith, but so is the exhibitionism of German couples on their honeymoon. German lyricism is a confession of faith, but so is the German passion for outraging every principle of good sense and good taste by "telling freely the whole truth." German music is a confession of faith, but so is the German weakness for the peddling of private emotions. The introvert can play a useful *rôle* in the world's activities only by the act of confession, for it is only his inner life that has reality for him. If he is creative, his confession gives expression to what is most intimately his own. If he is not creative, then he lives by the repetition of the confessions of others. This explains why the Germans are forever quoting Goethe; it explains their interminable singing; they must sing the songs of others in order to feel themselves. At this point it becomes clear to what extent the Germans are really the nation of poets and thinkers; it is only thus that, as a people, they are themselves in the best sense. But it is also true that quantitatively, too, they are the nation of thinkers and poets. No nation in the world produces so many philosophers. Quite apart from the innumerable works that have been published, I hardly know one German who has not a strictly personal philosophy of life—be he a shoemaker or a captain of industry. As for the poets, their number is simply incredible. By a happy chance I came across the following summary by

Moritz Lederer: "It is necessary to have worked at some time in a theatrical office to appreciate the justice of the claim that we are a 'nation of poets.' Who can ever calculate which people has produced the greatest poets? But one thing I did know after a brief period of theatrical activity; there is assuredly no other nation in the world which has produced so many poets, and, in particular, so many dramatists, as the Germans. It is nothing exceptional for a single theatre to receive twenty or thirty dramas in one day. During my connection with a certain State Theatre in South Germany, an average of 450 plays was entered each month. It is accordingly safe to assume that the number of plays submitted in one year was 5,000. Of course not every one of the four hundred theatres in Germany receives such generous attention. Experience has shown that theatres of the second or third size receive more numerous offers than do the great theatres. But it would be close to the mark to estimate the number of manuscripts submitted yearly to German theatres at 2,000,000. To these must be added 300,000 dramas forwarded to publishers' offices and returned direct to the authors without ever having reached the theatre. In any case, it is safe to say that there is one manuscript play for every ten adult Germans. To get an idea of what these 2,300,000 manuscripts mean, one has to remember that the average copy weighs about 600 grams (a pound and a quarter); altogether they therefore weigh 1,380,000 kilos (about 1,400 tons); 275 railway trucks are needed in order to distribute the dramatic productions of a single year. An army of 25,000 mail-carriers is needed in order to deliver them. Five hundred readers or dramatists would have their hands full for a year reading the manuscripts. Laid end to end, these manuscripts or books would stretch out for 700 kilometres; a local train would need about twelve hours to cover the distance. But if we tear out the printed or written pages and lay *them* end to end, we can almost girdle the earth. We repeat: these are the production figures for a single year. If we begin to calculate the total dramatic production for an entire German generation (thirty years in round figures), the figures become positively fantastic. It is only then that we see with what justice we call ourselves 'the nation of poets.' " We must remember that Lederer has dealt only with the dramatists; he has omitted the considerably larger number of lyric poets. The quality undoubtedly remains unaffected by the quantity. Germany assuredly produces more bad philosophers than any other country. In the matter of percentage it certainly compares poorly with unphilosophic England. For if the latter has very few philosophers to show, at least the majority of them merit attention, while 90 per cent. of the German philosophers are absolutely worthless. The same holds true of poetry. But on the other hand, it is a result of the national inclination toward poetry and philosophy that Germany should produce the largest numbers of the very greatest poets and philosophers. It is right to say, then, that in Germany the emphasis should be laid on the spiritual creator. A well-known writer once asked me, during a Presidential election: "Counting the two of us out, whom would you vote for? Gerhart Hauptmann or Hermann Sudermann?" This was, of course, naïve. It was also somewhat naïve of Thomas Mann to acclaim Gerhart Hauptmann as King of Germany. But there is no doubt that in the German state the national emphasis should be laid on the poets and thinkers.

And in addition, I repeat, on the element of uniqueness. For Germany to take its stand with the majority, with the mass, is to accept a faith which represents an inescapable inferiority. The German people is once for all so constructed that it must seek its worth in the individual; not in classes, as is the case with aristocratic nations, like the Hungarian; not in the élite, as is the case with the French; and certainly not in the masses. Let Germany, for her part, think what she likes; judged from the viewpoint of Europe, from that of mankind,

and from that of eternity, things are thus and not otherwise.
This is the meaning of the words of Goethe:

Höchstes Glück der Erdenkinder
Ist nur die Persönlichkeit.

It is quite natural that the sense of uniqueness should only too
frequently blossom in the most curious forms. If Germans
without a sense of uniqueness are jealous of those whom they
feel to be more than themselves, the same is also true of little
people who do possess a sense of uniqueness; but in their case
the jealousy takes on the form of a grotesque self-esteem; this,
when projected onto the plane of external life, leads to that
overrating of the "silent in the land" which is the pest of
Germany. For the homunculus who canonizes any one of the
"silent in the land" naturally means himself. Among the
"silent in the land," only those can obviously claim to be important for the general public whom a God has gifted with the
ability to tell what they suffer. Instead of this, every one who
produces nothing outwardly, preferring to nurse his lofty
emotions and refusing to have anything to do with the world,
considers himself superior to the man who is able to stand up
to the world. Unfortunately emotions as such prove nothing;
emotions of the utmost loftiness can be produced by an attack
of indigestion no less than by a metaphysical experience. And
what is more, it is up to every lover to make the simple assertion: Never has any man loved as I love. The "silent in the
land" have become a public calamity since they gave up the
only business which really suits them—which is the business
of keeping quiet. Nowadays they shout at the top of their
lungs; it is they who are chiefly responsible for public opinion.
And as often as not, they actually suffer from pathological
delusions of grandeur. Every year I receive upward of three
dozen manuscripts or books without the slightest value, concerning every one of which the writer, or some friend of his,
assures me that I have before me one of the greatest works

of all time, and that the author is positively greater than Jesus Christ. Errors of this kind arise from the fact that in the case of the extreme introvert the whole libido, recoiling from the outer word, is redirected toward the ego, which thus expands into world-greatness. This, as Margaret Müller Senftenberg first made clear, is the real root of the delusion of grandeur of the schizophrene. Actually this is the root of most German self-applause. In the same way the German is generally given to overrating the little as compared with the great. There is something fantastic about the importance which the "little groups" assume in their own eyes. Once a thoughtful Geheimrat came to me and said: "There were three of us sitting together in Schlachtensee. We held the destiny of the world in our hands. Unfortunately we let it slip out." He was, in a general way, an able fellow, and, if I remember rightly, one of the highest officials in the State Treasury Department. The very same thing is true of the circles which congregate around really important figures. The majority of those who make up these circles are utterly devoid of a sense of proportion and of relative values. Because a man happens to be "creative" or "absolute," or because he is in any degree a pioneer, he must at once become the man upon whom everything depends, the greatest of all men. In the light of all humanity's growth even a Nietzsche is only one captain, among others, of the shock-troops of the new era; the peculiar world which is the sole province of the intellectuals is only one province of life; only the very few who, like Jesus, can radiate a world-impulse of unique force to all men represent what, in so many small circles in Germany—each small circle hermetically separated from all the others—is attributed again and again to so many individuals. . . . Yet one should not be misled by such excrescences. They are bound to occur wherever growth comes to the front. The entire importance of Germany actually depends on those who feel themselves primarily to be unique.

Much that is otherwise inexplicable is connected with the

above-mentioned circumstance. First comes that dislike of Germany which is typical of the important German. If we ignore the reticence and the evasions dictated by tact and good sense, we shall see that this dislike was absent only when the great German looked upon the people as if he were the father of his country. And how could it be otherwise? If the structure of a people is such that all importance must rest with the individual and the unique, the man of uniqueness and individuality must feel himself in contrast to the mass. It is for this very reason that the highest type of German has always felt himself impelled to leave the country. This is why Germany, of all peoples, could become the producer of those princes whose specialty it was to identify themselves with every country. Philip II. of Spain, Katherine of Russia, Edward VII. of England, Albert of Belgium, and Ferdinand of Roumania all came from Germany. Many of them were outspokenly hostile to Germany. And if they were not, they took it as their most obvious duty to attach very little importance to their national origin. The German of importance, judged by the standards of the Frenchman or the Englishman, cannot appear other than a-national. If the emphasis of significance is to be laid on uniqueness, then there is no such thing as a nation. That is why every member of a religious order must, by definition, break off all earthly connections. The same circumstance accounts for the fact that the German people has never created new nations, but has always, from the earliest times, been absorbed into others; this cannot be explained simply by its patriarchal character. In this connection Georg Groddeck (in his *Arche* of March, 1927) has found the appropriate expression: "The pot-house politician [Groddeck's name for himself] knows that this people does the work of life quite otherwise than the English and the French. Un-aging in her eternal fecundity, young as on Creation's day, she, as the Mother of the world, dedicates to the advancement of the sacred white race her inexhaustible children, creative, meekly patient, turbulent, un-

wearying. What cares this Mother for the bickerings of the
states? For millenniums past there have streamed out of her
nations and races, in all directions, north, south, east, west. It
does not break her heart if her children fall away from her,
if, as the English did yesterday, they turn against her; she
suffers, but, inwardly unbroken, she turns her eyes from this
day to the future. And scarcely have the wounds inflicted by
her children turned to scars when she sends forth new hosts
into the world—Anglo-Saxons and Franks, Alemanni and
Swabians. She does not need to play the empress, to conquer
the world, to force her name to the lips of men by deeds of
heroism and adventure; she does not need to become anything:
she is." The foregoing obviously does not mean to imply that
the German nation should surrender as such. She must assert
herself as much as she possibly can, for it is only as long as she
remains herself that she can remain the never-aging mother.
But she certainly must not seek her task where she sought it in
her latest period; she must seek it, instead, in the fact that she
is the blessed and eternal mother of ever-new sons of exceptional greatness.

THIS brings us to the definition of the German task in the
world. To repeat: Germany must naturally continue to
assert herself as a people and as a nation. Just as there are
general human rights, so there are general national rights; and
particularly in the age of the self-determination of peoples
would it be a crime for Germany to relinquish without a struggle one jot or tittle of her rights. But the world-significance of
Germany certainly does not lie in her ability, her capacity for
work, her organization, her system, or her social-welfare
machinery. It is ridiculous, at the present juncture, to take any
pride at all in what we understand by "ability": ability, system,
industrial and mechanical skill, competent educational institutions, and the like, will before long be as much a matter of
course as the fact that man has two legs. From this viewpoint,

it was a shocking exhibition of an inferiority-complex for the entire German people to hail with such pride Eckener's trans-Atlantic flight. The youngest people in the world can do the same; savages with their keen senses will before long be able to do much better. Nor does Germany's world-significance depend upon the place of power which she will occupy. Today Americanism is becoming, psychologically, the substitute for Prussian militarism; and if the same emphasis continues to be laid on it, it will lead to a more terrible catastrophe than did the latter; that is, not to external defeat, from which every strong people always recovers quickly, but to inner degeneration. The Prussian officer is, in himself, a man of the finest breed, but he is narrow as a type; his relationship toward the German who can rule to good effect is that of the individual Dominican toward the Curia. Only to this extent has he been found wanting. Personally I do not doubt that sooner or later the German people will bring forth a new, acknowledged ruling class, whose duration, under the new circumstances, will of course depend not on heredity but on co-optation; this ruling class will be able to govern Germany better than it has ever been governed before. If meanwhile the state loses in importance, as I expect, the same applies to all matters of foreign policy within the framework of Europe; thus with the predominance of the purely objective view of government which this development implies, it may very well come to pass that Germany will be the best-governed country in Europe. But it is not on this that the world-significance of Germany can be based. Other nations can govern well, too. Only that which a people *alone* can do, or can do better than any one else in the world, makes that people important for the time being. In this sense Germany's prospects of world-significance depend solely upon her intellectuality.

In the matter of intellectuality, Germany leads the other peoples of Europe in the same sense that France leads in culture and England in political tact. The Hindoo Ghandi astounded the modern world by showing that the Indian equivalent of the Christian doctrine of non-resistance to evil, the Ahimsa, could become a political force: the fact is that for the finest Hindoos, religion is the one thing of decisive importance; that is why only a religious figure can be a *Realpolitiker* there. In the same way it is the intellectual element which is the thing of decisive importance for all Germans of any account; this is true whether they admit it or not. This difference is so vital that I must take it up in greater detail. The Germans are by no means the cleverest or the most intellectually gifted people in Europe; on the contrary, it is much rather the traditional figure of Hans which represents the aboriginal German. Yet to no people in the world do intellectual values *mean* as much as they do to the Germans. The implications of this definition can best be clarified by a comparison with America. The American is very often exceedingly clever. But it is only in exceptional cases that the recognition or the realization of intellectual values, in any sense at all, can be for him an end in itself. When he manifests an interest in the highest intellectual values, he does so only to the extent that these can be applied to a definite business or social problem. Now in the realization of intellectual values, it is primarily not a question of great gifts, but of the things emphasized by the conscious mind; let the man with the greatest mind but emphasize the external, and he is no longer intellectual. In spite of this, the value of the individual achievement depends, of course, on the degree of talent. Nevertheless, in the case of a *people* the degree of intellectuality can be measured only by its original psychological adjustment; here the question of talent does not enter at all, for every people produces men of talent. The intellectuality of the national achievement depends solely upon whether or not the emphasis is placed on the intellectual and *his* achievement. The Germans do this more than any other modern people. Moreover, only this adjustment brings out the best there is in the German. The materialistic German, placed

side by side with an equally or even more materialistic Englishman or Frenchman, always produces an unpleasant effect. And,
per contra, the intellectually adjusted German affects everybody with a direct sense of conviction and attractiveness. Thus
it is also to the practical interest of Germany to adjust herself,
or, where necessary, readjust herself, correspondingly. At this
point we need only call to mind German music; let every
German city institute a music festival twice a year—they would
certainly be overrun, either at once or in a short time, by the
entire world. The most recent rehabilitation of Germany in the
world's public opinion, after an unparalleled overthrow, can
be accounted for only by German intellectuality and its prestige. No; the entire significance of Germany depends only on
what it can do *apart from its ability.* And everything else must
be subordinated to this point: *apart from its ability.**

Accepting, then, the premise of the particular characteristics
described in the foregoing, what is Germany's true task in the
world? It can consist only of the following: in the first place
Germany is, once and for all, the *laboratory* of the world. It is
predestined to the fulfilment of this *rôle* by the majority of
those very characteristics which, applied in other directions,
produce so injurious an effect. The idea and the imagination
mean more to the German than reality; the thing means more
than the man. It is, again, essential to him that he prosecute
these ideas without aim or purpose. And finally, it is experience
(Erleben) that is most important to him. All this makes of him
the ideal experimenter. Thus, in all her periods of historic
ferment, Germany was really a laboratory. It was a laboratory, to the extent permitted by the framework of the Middle
Ages, in the time of Eckhart. It was a laboratory on a grand
scale in the time of the Reformation. It is a laboratory on the
grandest scale today. If the intellectual movements of Germany were placed in one scale and those of the rest of the

---

* See, in this connection, the chapter "The Peter's Pence of Literature" in the
English edition of *The World in the Making* (Harcourt, Brace & Company).

world in the other, it is the German side which would sink. In one way or another, everybody in Germany experiments. Even business men do; otherwise they would not be running so many risks; they would not be so proud of making sacrifices. And it is surely the laboratory in his factory which is the greatest source of happiness to the German captain of industry. Inwardly he cares much more about the experiments as such than about their practical results. In defining Germany as a laboratory we begin to see it is not to her detriment if, in the field of social culture and comfort, the German people does not perhaps stand comparison with others. The last thing that can be said about a laboratory is that it is habitable. But the right thing must first be found before it can be put to use. Thus the nation which cares more about seeking than about having found is doing more work directly for humanity than any other.

In the second place, Germany is the *conscience* of mankind. It has long been known by this name. But the word was used in a one-sided, moralistic sense, and those who used it thus were misled by that element which necessity imposes upon every one in political life. How things stand in a right definition may best be perceived against the background of England. England never knows what she is doing. Germany never does anything before she thinks she knows what her action means, and once she has done something, her foremost need is to make clear to herself the significance of what has been done. This is followed by the need to confess what she has perceived. Germany is therefore properly the mirror of the world, a description first applied to her, if I am not mistaken, by Leibnitz. Furthermore, Germany is the one clean mirror that we have, for, at bottom, the clarity of the French has much too much of purely French prejudice. The Frenchman is never objective. The German is objective throughout. He can therefore acquire tremendous importance wherever matters of general validity are concerned. Henceforth at least one half of all political life will have to be mastered to good effect on the basis of a universalistic outlook. A new code of international law will have to arise.* Altogether the relations between nation and nation will have to be founded, as far as possible, on law and justice. That subjective nations are still incapable of this, in spite of all their efforts, is shown by what France and England have made out of the League of Nations. If this last is ever to become a blessing to the nations, it must be animated by the German spirit. And further, a new form will have to be given, in keeping with the German spirit, to the relations between the white and the coloured races, and the old policy of conquest and exploitation will have to come to an end. Lastly, because of her unpolitical nature, it will be Germany's vocation, above all, to institute and to subordinate the particular law system of politics, as best represented by the spirit of Italy, in its relation to the particular law of the human will to culture. It will have to come to this. In the long run a purely egotistic policy will achieve little. And just as in India only the religious leader can be a *Realpolitiker*, because in the consciousness of India religion represents the deepest reality, so is it natural for Germany to give the primacy to intellect and to the intellectual—and thus to culture—as against the political. Otherwise we will come very soon to a new European war, and then Europe is done for. I have often asked myself how it was possible for the horror of the years 1914-1918, which branded the modern machine war as an unconditional crime, not to have called into being a united European front against war. Today I know the answer: the overwhelming majority of persons have neither memory nor imagination; they live in the moment, actuated by primitive impulses, and among men these will, to all eternity, call for war. Now the German has more memory than the others, also more imagination, to the extent that he lives in the realm of ideas more than the others do. He is therefore the predestined protagonist of the idea of world-peace.

* I refer the reader to the specific proposals contained in the Baltic chapter of this book.

Yet the possible importance of Germany in the sense observed is not confined to occasional tasks; in the world in the making, in which all the emphasis will be laid on the transferable, that nation will have a privileged position to which the all-human, from the outset, means more than the national. For in this lies the root of German universalism. German universalism is the very last thing we should try to overcome; henceforth it is just this universalism which can give national importance to the German people. The exclusively national element will assuredly not lose in importance in the future; quite the contrary; we shall see in the chapter on Italy to what a degree also the national element will have the highest significance for the future. But the world in the making—I allude here not to the book of that name, but primarily to my *Vision der kommenden Weltordnung* in the *Weg zur Vollendung*, Section 10—will be a bi-polar structure of the highest tension; on the one side nationalism, with its origin in irrational roots, and on the other side internationalism, embodied in the powers of science, metaphysics, religion, law, economics, capital, will hold the balance against each other. No other people in the world is so clearly called to occupy the universalistic pole as is the German. Should it perceive in this *rôle* its authentic significance, then its impulse toward expansion, its very immoderateness, will lose its dangerous character in the consciousness of others. For the struggle toward infinity properly bespeaks the universal, and no measure is too great for the all-embracing. Then Germany will become the land that lives *for all*, which is what every great German has always done. There has never been a single German of European value who has not had this universalistic scope. The nationalistic German, in contrast to the nationalistic Frenchman, is of no account in the cultural and all-human sense; he is a local and private matter, Pomeranian or Bavarian, as the case may be; that is, when he is not simply club property. Within the framework of the universal even the inferior function of the German can work for good; if any objective problem can really be resolved into a mere question of practical objectivity, and thus dismissed as a life-problem, it will be for the appropriate type of German to do it. And as for what passes as "practical ability," it should function decently as a matter of course, just as we expect of the mail service, or, if the personal element is to be introduced, as we expect a policeman at street crossings to act as guide.

With this we come to what is the deepest and most sacred task of Germany; that task rests on the foundation of the deepest German pathos. Out of his inmost depths the German, as an introvert, can do only one of two things: either achieve inmost experience (*Erleben*), or else break forth, and that out of the ultimate depths, with volcanic force. And in the phenomenal world this means that out of those ultimate depths he can engender and bring to birth. The great storm-figures of European history after the period of antiquity are all German, from the political storm of the wanderings of the nations down to Luther and Nietzsche. But above all, the Germans were the great elaborators, who assimilated every intellectual impulse, then reproduced it and continued it in the form of a universal intellectual creation. For since the Germans are a feminine people, it is exceptional for them to take the *rôle* of begetter; while bringing to birth is the rule with them. But it is in this that we may perceive the complete all-human significance of the German world. The last German word, whenever uttered by her great mother-spirits, never claimed to be the ultimate utterance of its kind—as is the case with the French; its clarity was never in the literal sense the clarity of finality. In a world of continuous emergence and dissolution, the ambition to frame the last word never indicates anything but narrowness. As long as mankind lives, the absolutely last word will never be uttered; for ever and ever, the problem of mankind will present itself anew, and life will forever remain a thing of problems. And only the German sees it thus. The only one who sees it at all similarly is the Jew, and, as the creators of the Old Testament and therefore the founders of that ethos from which the entire world-force of the Occident derives, the Jews are one of the very greatest peoples, however it may fare with them in other connections. Thus the great advantage of the German resides precisely in his problematic and even his indefinite character, just as the greatest disadvantage of the French lies in the excessive exactitude of theirs. Naturally the above-indicated German aptitude implies that only its highest expressions possess significance for the good. Most of the German storm-figures are merely disturbers of the peace, most elaborators are merely ruminants incapable of form, who, under the mask of intellectual interest, indulge their bovine Philistine inclinations; and most problematic natures are problematic in the bad sense. Yet the very structure of the German people implies that only the greatest can matter. Everything else in it is, from the point of view of mankind, preparatory.

On the plane of these last-mentioned values the German people brings forth, from time to time, forms and figures which no other European people equal. Here, primarily, lies the root of German music, the greatest music of all times. Music is not being, in the sense of plastic form; it is rather a continuous process of birth and death in the framework of a unity of meaning; * the greatest music can therefore be created only by a people whose life is a continuous becoming, a people to whom it is essential to live by inward experience (*Erleben*) and to confess that experience. Here lies the original root of Germany's great philosophy; the philosopher is to the realm of understanding what the composer is to the realm of emotion. Here, too, lies the original root of the incomparable human greatness of those Germans who have achieved this consummation. The greatest example of this kind hitherto known is found in Goethe. Wherein lies the all-human significance of Goethe? It lies in his ultimate and extreme exemplification of

* Cf. the detailed observations on the nature of music in the chapter *Werden und Vergehen* of my *Wiedergeburt*.

how all that is inadequate became, in him, productive. The exemplification is ultimate and extreme because to be human means to be inadequate; it was thus that even Christ saw His miserable human existence in relation to the divine spark within Him. But since for the majority of non-Germans the human significance of the German world is questioned from the very outset, it would be well at this point to enter into a more detailed analysis of the case of Goethe. Goethe was typically German; most of what has been said in this chapter about the Germans is valid for him. Luther's depth of conviction echoes again in the *orphisches Urwort, "So must du sein,"* etc.; that curious, theoretical approach toward himself was, among other things, an expression of the unreality of the German spirit; through that approach, too, he strove toward spiritual experience. True, he sought to develop his nature dynamically, but what mattered most to him was to turn its substance into a living experience. For him, too, the experience as such, *das Erlebnis an sich,* was the centre and focus of life, even though he did speak about it less than the moderns do, and strove to seize it as something objective, something objectivated, above all as something conceptual; thus his ultimate, extreme appeal lay in his affirmation, in his "eternal Yea" to himself; like most Germans, he, too, lacked the finality of will which leads to fulfilment on the plane of ethos as distinguished from that of pathos. This emerges with particular clarity precisely in *Faust,* that strange poem in which we see successive states ranged side by side with each other, without any state deepening or intensifying the state which precedes—that drama which is so epic that it can end only with natural death, for there is no climactic effect whatsoever in the fact that Faust ends a life so rich in action and experience as a large-scale agriculturist. If we bring up for comparison the life of any great saint or man of action, the meaning of this circumstance at once becomes clear. The manly element of Goethe, too, was on the plane of the type of ability and system; it should always be borne in mind that Goethe was an able minister of a small state, and an excellent business man; he is, in fact the real founder of the system of protection for authors through copyright. As a type, therefore, Goethe was a German intellectual, such as the others were. And the mere richness of his German gift in the sense of extension did not by itself make him the great man he is now recognized to be. Goethe's greatness derives from the incomparable depth, authenticity, and intensity of his Germanism. Expressed in terms of our basic definitions, it derives from the fact that his life was one long experiment, a probing of the conscience, and that his whole existence signified one long process of "dying and becoming." But this is where the uniqueness of Goethe comes into play. By its very nature his life vibrated between the two German poles, passive experience and unreality of the spirit; he took the former as his base; in the latter he externalized it again and again, and from this latter he strove continuously to return again to the former; but from this plane of being he attained to another and a higher plane. Because, as a great German exception, he took with ultimate seriousness not the "thing," but himself, not the externalized perception, as the scholar does, but his personal life—because of this he attained in the latter decades of his earthly development to *a fusion of subjective experience with objective perception, to the synthesis of a life conditioned by understanding, a life which never did and never could reach its end because its very sense was that of eternal advance.* And not only did everything that was inadequate in Goethe's person and being become thereby productive in the highest sense; because of his incomparable gift of expression it became productive for everybody. Viewed historically, this meant the rise of a new consciousness of reality, a higher kind, because it was conditioned by a profounder understanding. For thereby the spirit was called out of that unreality into which it had been cast by Christianity, to new mastery of life. Thanks to the attainment of a higher con-

sciousness, the curse which attended the tasting of the fruit of
the Tree of Knowledge began thereby to be transformed into
a blessing. Thereby new possibilities of perfection rose upon the
horizon. From this, then, flows the tremendous suggestive
power of Goethe's personality. It derives primarily from the
specific movement which he symbolized, and thanks to the
epic course of his life, he did this with such clarity, down to
the details, that we are reminded of slow-motion photography,
the movement from the unreality of the spirit to perfected consciousness of reality. Today all men, whether they know it or
not, are seeking for the way which leads from alienation from
self back to consciousness of self. This alienation from self began at the very moment when consciousness awoke, and together
with consciousness, the faculty of entering into relationship with
the things of the world not directly and immediately, but on the
plane of ideation; this represents, among other things, the myth
of the fall from grace. But this self-alienation grew steadily
greater; today it has become so great that man as an imaginative
being has lost all relationship with his inner reality. More
than this: the one-sided development of the intelligence has
caused the entire soul-organism of western humanity to disintegrate; advanced as it is beyond all others before it in the
power of ideation, this soul has, as a being, relapsed into a
wilder chaos than has ever been known since the Flood. And it
is impossible to win back the old innocence. Only one thing can
help now, the deepening of our insight into things to such a degree that it will no longer work destructively but constructively.
New life can blossom forth only out of perfected knowledge.*

The first really great example of such conditioning of a life
by knowledge and understanding was provided by Goethe. And
this should make clear wherein the deepest possibilities of the
German world lie: briefly, they lie in the eternally renewed

---

* Cf. the development of this line of thought in the chapter, *Was uns Nottut,
Was ich Will,* in my *Schöpferische Erkenntnis.*

possibility of a rebirth out of the mind. In one form or another, every great German has been the realization of just this possibility. This applies to Luther, in the way of religious self-determination, to Nietzsche in the form of psychological self-realization, to Stefan George in the sense of spirit-born self-moulding. Of course it does not follow from the foregoing that the German people is the great of all peoples. This idea, unfortunately still current in Germany, has back of it nothing better than the delusion of grandeur typical of the introvert, a delusion which always borders on schizophrenia. Not mind and intellect, nor intellectual development, nor even culture itself is an end in itself. In the last analysis the end in itself is, for every man, his individual salvation, and this becomes clear to every man ultimately, if only on the threshold of death. A psychological adjustment which looks to this salvation as its goal is deeper in the absolute sense than the psychological adjustment of the German intellectuals. Thus the English concentration of life on the practical improvement of the world, the French culture of expression, and the Spanish culture of *tenue*, are by no means inferior to German intellectuality. The haughty high priests of German intellectuality always remind me of those three men who sat at a table in Schlachtensee and held the destiny of the world in their hands. It is high time that this absurd toploftiness came to an end. The deepest and most honest thinker is, as a thinker, not superior to any human being with any kind of adjustment. He is not even richer in substance; he is merely different. The Germans are simply a particular kind of people with a resultant particular kind of task. They are the people of determinant consciousness, determinant intellect. This is the very reason why they can be much worse than other peoples. As human beings it is typical of them that they are specially inadequate. But in spite of their great defects they are, as men who are eternally becoming, the born pioneers in times of renewal. And that is much. And they bring forth, from time to time, great striving figures, never perfected. And that is something tremendous. For to be human means to be forever striving and never perfected.

A WORD, in closing, about Austria. Whether the union will ever come about, in space and time, I cannot tell. But that this union has already essentially transpired is therefore all the more certain. It is equally certain that the international frontiers of Europe will mean less and less as time goes on. Austria is primordially German—that can never be altered. Whosoever thinks of Germany must also include Austria as an integral part.

The Austrians are nevertheless different from the Germans of the *Reich*. But when was there a German who was not different from every other German? At this point I refer the reader back to the opening of this chapter; the German stands and falls by his particularism. In any case he stands and falls by it in his good points; for since in him the emphasis, when rightly laid, must rest on the unique element in him, this must emerge into the outer world in the form of extreme multiplicity. National uniformity in the French or English sense is impossible for the Germans unless they are to abandon the best that is in them. And in this connection the possibilities and necessities of their particularism go so far that the Germans can include within themselves wholly un-German types— which means not only particular castes which have reverted from type, but peoples which are of direct non-German origin. In the realm of life there are no such things as monads in the absolute sense; inwardly and outwardly all things are interrelated; we have no such thing as "I" without a correlative and polar "You." Thus no cultural unity was ever hermetically isolated. In actual reality the man of antiquity lived in relation to the cultured barbarian world. In modern Europe the necessary You-and-I relationship is represented by two essentially non-European countries. First there is Russia. "In and for itself,"

Russia is in every respect becoming exclusively more Asiatic—
and this in spite of all intellectualization and technical transformation, functions which as little posit an inner relationship toward Europe as the ability to count posits a personal relationship to the multiplication table. But who could possibly understand the state of the soul in our part of the earth without re-
ferring to Dostoievsky? How will it be possible, before long,
to understand it without Lenin? And it should be observed
that neither of these spirits means the same to Russia as to us.
Dostoievsky stands in much the same relationship toward his
beloved country as Jesus does to the Jews; he is essentially
not Russia's Messiah. As against this, Lenin is becoming, in the
Orient, more and more the model of a saint, while for us,
looked at absolutely, he represents the Satanic, and looked at
historically, the awakener of the compensatory Fascist counter-
movement. The second non-European country which nevertheless unconditionally belongs to the new Europe is one we have
already examined—Spain. The case of Germany is analogous,
in the sense that Germany serves as the mirror of Europe just
as the best individual German intellect serves as the mirror
of the world; elements which are directly un-German are
fundamentally part of the whole—first, because the concepts
of Germany and the German mind are more necessarily connected than are the concepts of Germany and the German
nationality; the whole of Central and Eastern Europe is ruled
by the former; then second, because among the Germans the
entire concept of the national plays a less important *rôle* than
among other peoples. That is why the political formlessness
of the Holy Roman Empire of German nationality represented
the German essence much better than does the modern national state. The state is not an organically German idea; today
no less than in the times of Arminius the German feels himself
more a member of a clan or of a party than of a national entity.
Further differentiations follow as a result of the self-contained
isolation of the German character. Here fundamentally dif-

ferent individuals live next to each other, without trespassing on each other, like different flowers in a garden. The unintellectual Cologne type is much closer to the Belgian than he is to the German of the Goethe type; the pure Lower Saxon, the Hamburger, stands nearest to the Englishman. On the other hand the Russian justly sees in the Czech a German speaking a Slav language: actually his particular Protestantism is, if anything, German. The Czech has not a soul of his own; the setting up of an independent Czech state was much more a social than a national revolution. All the higher classes in Bohemia had long been Austrianized, and on the other hand an extraordinarily large number of important Austrians were of Czech origin. The Austrian, then, however much he may differ from the new German, belongs in the German Reich by nothing less than the right of the first-born, *for he represents Germany's oldest cultural type.*

Austria is the one representative German country—the "silent in the land," in all their types, may be found among the German races, too, but they mean nothing politically or historically—whose living psychological roots do not go back to the Thirty Years' War. Its inhabitants are the only Germans who are culturally of the same age as the other western peoples. It is the only country in which the tradition of the Holy Roman Empire endures, where even today German universalism thus finds a body for itself; thus it is not to be wondered at if the idea of that Empire has again gripped the imagination of the best Austrian youth. If, for the rest, Austria is different from the other German countries, it is only a particular expression of the fact that Germany is capable of taking up within herself every possible type, and yet of giving all of them a common denominator; the Austrian, too, in the last analysis acknowledges the German spirit. The Austrian is not the introvert type of thinker; he is not a man of system; primarily his gifts are psychological and emotional, and to that extent he resembles the Englishman. He is tactful and has form in every realm of life, possesses a sense of quality equal to that of the French, for which reason world-reputations are made, apart from Paris, in Vienna, too. With particular regard to this town: its relationship to Germany is such that its culture is personal and not objective; grace and charm balance ponderousness, ease of manner balances seriousness, *esprit* balances thoroughness, and the lyricism of the Mozartian spirit balances the soulfulness, the *Gemüt*, of the German. But the Austrian is on the other hand of weak character, and there is very little to be said for his practical ability. He is by no means devoid of intellectual gifts; a wide range of discoveries stand to his credit, but on the whole he has been too lazy to insure his rights as inventor. Above all, however, because of his position as the ruling class in the Danube monarchy—a class which had little to do, and carried no serious responsibility—the Austrian became a sort of exotic plant; this applies first of all to that highest expression of Austrianism, the Austrian aristocrat. The life of the Austrian nobleman had long been a decorative affair. Little wonder, then, that when the structure of the Danube monarchy collapsed, he crumbled into dust, like the stuccowork when the ceiling of a palace caves in. In the sons of many living Austrian aristocrats we can in all probability salute the founders of dynasties of faultless head waiters. For the waiter is really the final sublimation of the cavalier; wherever they did not die out, the culturally overbred races of all time have always finished up as waiters.

But if the fine flower of the old Austrian world is historically done for, this by no means applies to Austria as an essence and totality. Its lands are still healthy to the core. As the economic centre of the Near East, Vienna has more of a future than ever. But above all it is the Austrian spirit which still lives: that old and highly differentiated cultural spirit which has always been ready to permeate any kind of stock, which assimilated racial groups of the most varied languages, and was able, because of this, to perform for centuries the political miracle of keeping them externally together by the gentlest means. This spirit is the antithesis of the Prussian. Its mode of life lies in *laisser-faire* and not in action; in softness, not in hardness. To this extent the world of Austria, looked at politically, is the second focus in the German field of force, the first being Prussia; it was not a coincidence that first Austria should have led, and then Prussia, after the Mediaeval state had once been left behind and differentiations on a small scale had been replaced by those on a great. But for the future it would be just as wrong to think of "Germany" as being entirely covered by the Prussian-Austrian tension, as it would be to think only of the Weimar-Potsdam tension: *only Weimar, Potsdam and Vienna taken together delimit with some exactness* the full richness of the German substance as it presents itself today. Once again does the world-law of "dying and becoming" work itself out. The old Prussia is dead; so is the old Austria. The theoreticians held that after the *débâcle*, Weimar alone should have taken the lead. In actuality, however, there arises out of the death of the old a new and richer unity than ever before existed; that which in separate articulation is no longer capable of life now becomes an integral part of a greater whole, hitherto. Potsdam is the focus, on the one hand, of Little Germany, and on the other, of modern German world-force; to this extent Potsdam is also the symbol of an Americanized Germany. Weimar is the focus of the pure and universal in the German mind. And Vienna is both the symbol and the focus of German culture. Culture exists only as form, as external expression, as life. To that extent only the extraverted type of German was at all able to create culture. That culture, though bearing the particular and special stamp of Vienna, is no less universal than the spirit of Weimar. From Vienna, German music set out to conquer the world. As a cultural type, the Austrian everywhere exercises a force of attraction. Vienna lies in the East; from her the young nations, become independent today, received their first culture. But at the same time

Austria is Germany's window to the West in the same sense that St. Petersburg was Russia's. Psychologically it still belongs to the old cultural commonweal of Christendom. It is not different in essence from France and England. Little wonder, then, that the reconquest of Europe by the German spirit in the cultural political sense, should, since Versailles, have issued from Austria. No matter how weak Austria may be, the living idea within her is today the same as once created the Holy Roman Empire of German nationality. Inwardly Austria is not only *still* but *already* European. Of course Austria will never again be ruler. The Holy Roman Empire will never arise again; history never repeats itself. But in the greater Germany of the future, bounded by the Vienna-Potsdam-Weimar triangle, Austria, as the representative of German culture, will play a greater *rôle* than during the last centuries of the Danube monarchy. For in the interrelated and correlated Europe of to-morrow, the spiritual root of that which once blossomed forth in the form of the Holy Roman Empire of German nationality—the supernational European idea—will once again become the determinant factor of history, in a greater, more expansive form, conforming to the spirit of the time.

ITALY

ITALY

H E who wishes to draw a faithful picture of Italy must find for it, more than for any other land and people, the true ground-plan, and distribute the fundamental values upon it in the right proportion. For nowhere else in Europe is the natural and the primordial of such decisive power.

This applies first in the sense indicated by Alfieri when he said that nowhere else does that plant, Man, flourish as well as in Italian soil. There the growth is really plant-like, as if independent of history. Italy is one of the oldest cultural countries; it harbours the most ancient historic races of Europe. And yet the phenomenon of decadence is, by and large, unknown there. More than this: the bearers of the most time-honoured names, the individual personifications of the oldest traditions, emerge in every generation (with rare exceptions which give one the impression of freaks of nature) with renewed natural force; regarded as social types, they are, correspondingly, like *homines novi*. The first comparisons that occur to one in this connection are India and China; every Chinaman is healthy just as nature herself is healthy, and the most ancient Brahmin families of India are, in spite of their age, so vital, that the very idea of degeneration seems to lie outside the realm of possibility. But the comparison holds good up to this point and no further. For in contrast to India and China it is characteristic of Italy that the people seems to renew itself periodically as plants do from spring to spring, and therefore not as cultural monads. Its basic character is unequivocally primitive. More than one Italian of the best classes would at once be written down by a foreigner as a savage, were not his nature essentially humane in the sense of the primal concept of humanism—the very humanism, that is, which evolved in Italy. By the time of Dante the Italian *gentilezza* was already the expression of cultivated primitiveness.

The second fundamental trait of Italy is directly connected

with the first. I allude to the natural constraint of the primal forms of her life, by reason of which they seem to bear a super-historic, even an eternal, character. If we give ourselves up first to the spirit of an old Etruscan grave, and then to that of an ancient Roman patrician house, and then finally to that of a modern Italian *casa* of tradition, we shall find them all the same. Everywhere an unparalleled seclusion of the house, held together by molecular cohesion. Even he who enters as a guest feels like one who is living with an oyster. For its born inmates there simply is no escape, except in the form of liberal emigration. I have used the phrase "molecular cohesion"; that intimacy of relationship depends upon the fact of Italian matriarchalism. Italy is today the European country of the most outspoken rule of the mother and the mother-in-law. Here alone, among European countries, do the young women look forward, as they do in China, to the time when they in turn will be able to rule as sexagenarians. Thus it is in Italy that the fact most strongly emerges that the woman is the conservative part of humanity. In all places where man the inventor has not intruded, the woman conducts the kitchen which her mother conducted, just as naturally as she brings forth human beings and not animals; so certain of style is she, that I have often amused myself by reconstructing genealogical trees with the data of the *cuisine*. And since woman herself takes no interest in food, mankind, in a purely matriarchal way of life, would have clung until this day to Mother Eve's original menu. This is almost the case in Italy. I believe I am not mistaken in deducing from the excavations of Cervetri, the mother-city of Rome, that the Etruscans ate the identical *pasta asciutta*, and prepared it exactly as the modern Italians do. Further, woman desires wherever possible to have all her offspring by her, and she can hardly see enough of her other blood-relations. In accordance with this, the molecular cohesion of Italian houses of tradition encloses entire clans; the only limitation is set by the question of actual space and the number of members in the family. Whosoever marries into an Italian house marries, as it were, all of its members; isolation of individual families, as among the Germanic races, is unknown here. And yet if no one feels himself burdened thereby, if every couple feels it is living for itself, and rightly so, this is explained by the fact that the Italians, like all Mediterranean peoples, do not need external solitude. They are all of them, like the ancient Greeks, "born in the market-place," with the result that a hundred Italians living together in the same house and having continuously to do with one another are actually less in each other's way than a German and his neighbour who seldom see one another. This frictionless social life—I call it frictionless in spite of noticeably frequent bickering and scolding, for these mean nothing in Italy—which in Germany is a problem and a high ideal, is a natural form with the Italians.

This basic structure implies, as it cannot help doing, an unequalled stability. Wherever traditions exist at all, they are as firm-knit as molecular conglomerations. Thus the Italian people seems, more than any other in Europe, to be held together by prehistoric habits. It is much more firmly rooted than the Spanish, for if the latter is culturally older it consists, as a desert folk, of single elements and not of communities. Taxes are paid in Italy more readily than anywhere else, for since the time of the Romans the paying of taxes has been the normal expression of subjection to rule. The clients of ancient Rome subsist until this day in the circles which gather round the high Italian aristocracy. And thus it is, *mutatis mutandis*, with all tradition. Until this day, in spite of all constitutions, the commune and the *signoria* remain the real organs of Italian life and being, and I doubt very much whether Fascism will succeed in breaking them down.

This brings us to the third fundamental Italian trait. The structure of a preponderantly molecular relationship naturally implies limitations of space; a molecule expanding beyond its natural limits explodes. This explains why the regionalistic form of life has always been and still is proper to Italy. The demographic disruption of Italy was of course at one time connected with the multiplicity of the stocks which inhabited it. As a race the Ligurians were distinctly different from the Etruscans; so were the Venetians from the Florentines. There is no doubt that the old Roman type originally had a substratum of Nordic blood, like the Lombards of today. South Italy is preponderantly Greek, and Sicily is partly Moorish and partly Spanish in blood. Nor must we forget to take into account the fact that Italy lies across three climatic zones, the temperate, the warm, and the sub-tropical. Yet these are not the decisive considerations; because of the unity of language which has already been maintained for thousands of years, all the inhabitants of Italy would long ago have achieved unification, as the inhabitants of France did, had it not been for the natural ties which made regional unity the decisive centre of their lives; and by those natural ties is meant the bond between the Italian and his landscape, together with the molecular character of his social relationships. Regional unity is still the decisive factor today in all the non-external respects which are the first to attract attention in a modern mechanized world. Until this day the Italian, looked at with regard to his life's source, is primarily not an Italian, but a Florentine, a Romagnole, a Sicilian, etc.

It is this very structure which imparts to Italian universalism its special character. The new Italian unity which was intended by the Risorgimento is only being perfected by Fascism. But in what manner? Not by the fact that it embraces all Italians in one uniformity, but rather by the fact that it creates a new unity which is, once again, a molecular relationship,—a molecular relationship in which it is essential that its field of force extend to great distances. It was exactly thus that ancient Rome ruled. Essentially it was one city among others. At no time did it ever really Romanize Italy—had it done so, the Roman type of the republican age would have endured longer. It was only as a city that Rome conquered and ruled first Italy and then the world; to become *civis Romanus* meant much the same as achieving membership today in the Fascist party, except that it was a more exclusive distinction and more difficult to attain. To that extent ancient Rome was almost closer in resemblance to the *camorra* and the *maffia* than to what is understood as a modern nation. Even in the imperial days of Italy, therefore, it was the regional unit which was decisive, because it alone was really alive.

The regional unit always had as its centre a *city*. In this, again, we find an element of the Italian world which is unique for Europe; its culture has always been regionalist and yet urban at the same time. Even its aristocracy was of the city. And for this reason the most universal form which has been created by the Italian spirit is rooted in a city; I mean Catholicism. From the Italian point of view Catholicism is either Roman or else it does not exist. From the Italian point of view the States of the Church neither were nor are a paradox. From this it becomes clear to what extent the Roman Church and the Roman Empire are of one spirit. The Curia as such has always been, and today still is, purely Italian; it is a molecular unit, just like an Etruscan grave. But as such it rules the world. Thus the ancient Romans, too, never really maintained, outside the city, anything other than legates and *nuncios*. Their machinery was assuredly Roman. But as long as that world-empire subsisted, one could as little become a Roman, if one were not one already, as one can become a virgin. Italy never became Roman, it remained Italian; and this was all the truer of the more distant provinces. It was for this very reason that the meaning of Latinity could later on be so peculiarly misunderstood. What we call Latinity today is not of Roman but of Greek cultural origin. It can be only this, for the very simple reason that a Roman culture never existed; the very concept of it is almost as contrary to sense as the new concept of a Fascist culture. In Rome the *res publica* was one city structure, one molecular relationship, among others. If molecular relationship once becomes the basic form, then direct radiation into space becomes impossible. Only the forms of rulership as such were transferable; this applied to Roman law, the Roman system of administration; the same thing applied later to the framework of the Church. But the content of this framework was and is everywhere different. We shall see further on the complete difference between what the Italians, the Curia itself, and the extra-Italian would respectively mean by Catholicism. It is only the formal origin of language which, for the rest, justifies the concept of Latinity. The spirit of the Latin was never taken over by non-Romans. In Spain it was the Iberian spirit which found embodiment in its form, in Gaul the Gallic spirit, in Roumania the Dacian-Byzantine spirit, and in Italy the primal Italian spirit. What have the exuberance and the *esprit* of the later Romance nations in common with the reserve, the conciseness, and the gravity of the Roman? Only the Spaniards may perhaps have a certain resemblance to the Romans. But they had that from the earliest times; that is why such a large proportion of Spaniards became Caesars. And it is precisely the Spaniards who typically repudiate the modern concept of Latinity: they take their renaissance of today to be exclusively Iberian.

There still remain for examination the fourth and fifth fundamental Italian traits, and we shall take them both at once. To the extent that the primal forms of this life are a plant-like naturalness and a molecular relationship, it is clear that Italy as such is predestined to be not a subject of history, but its object. It is extremely difficult to liberate the fixed energy of a molecule. But on the other hand every molecule has its ruling centre, and new molecules can form only around new single centres. It is quite impossible to group such structures together from without. This leads up to an understanding of the specific individualism of Italy. In every society a type actually "sets"—to use Hegelian phraseology—its counter-type; Jesus was a diametrically contrasted product of Judaism;

the docile Russian mass "sets" the tyrant of the type of Ivan the Terrible, Peter the Great, Lenin; the mediocrity of the German masses evokes the unique type of intellectual giant. Among human beings a structure of molecular coherence is *ipso facto* a *personal* relationship. This applies to every family, to every authentic spiritual commonweal. And where molecular coherence is the basic form of all group-life, it must result throughout in an extreme emphasis on the personal element; whatever occurs, occurs for some one's sake. Hence that beautiful Italian *gentilezza* which belongs equally to all classes of the people, the gracious attitude toward the sick, that especial courtesy of the heart which characterizes even the majority of Italian scoundrels and robbers. This matter-of-course acknowledgment of the personal element as a value makes it possible, first of all, for every individual to feel himself a monad. But it also enables the outstanding individual to become effective in a unique manner. In the realm of intellect, Italy has never really had schools and disciples in the German sense; *far da se* has always been a ruling principle in Italy. But in Italy the man of significance has always found a personal following such as would never come together in national structures of objective orientation. The greatest example in centuries is furnished to-day by Mussolini. As far as his position goes, it is he, the man, who matters, and not Fascism; it is toward him that all the enthusiasm is directed; nothing could be wider of the mark than to apply to this case the German category of objectivity. If the German cannot think of living himself out and of maintaining personal relationships in disinterested terms, it merely shows his particular form of narrowness. In Italy the decisive *rôle* has always been played by individuals who have thus lived out their own lives, and have thus maintained a personal following. The greatest era of such individuals was the Renaissance. It could achieve such greatness, first, because it was precisely at that period that the Italian blood-fusions produced their highest tensions; second, because the spirit of the age was particularly auspicious to the individual who was then achieving self-emancipation for the first time; and lastly, because the re-establishment of contact with antiquity and all its delight in earth liberated the primordial Italian energies which had long been suppressed. We have thus obtained the last co-ordinate needed to determine what it is that makes historical motion possible in Italy. In itself the mass is harder to set going here than anywhere else; if things depended solely on the mass, they would forever remain as they are; this mass is pre-destined to be ruled. The typically Italian world of conspirators and bravos demonstrates, for its part, the truth of this observation: an essentially secretive anarchism is never the germ-cell of a political future; it is only the safety-valve of a state of oppression which has on the whole been accepted. But in Italy the outstanding individual can, more easily than elsewhere, create out of himself and around himself a new molecular relationship. And if only the minority which has thus arisen—however small it be—consist of mobile and energetic elements, it will soon achieve a disproportionate degree of power. As far as history can be read, such minorities were first represented in the ancient Romans. "In themselves" they were of course something different from the other Italians, whether we account for this by their descent from a brigand people or by the original infusion of Nordic blood. Yet the prestige which they achieved—superiority of arms could alone at no time be responsible for it—was based on the fundamental structure of the people. And in proportion as this special type of men died out or was used up, the typical breed of the population came to the fore. And this implied that everything depended on the individual Caesar or *condottiere*. Mussolini therefore by no means represents something unheard of—let alone something unnatural; if he is at all a producer of historic values, he much rather represents what is normal for Italy. Whenever there were no "Mussolinis," the life of Italy was unhistorical, like the life of peasants. Democracy in the French or English sense has never existed in Italy. If there was no outstanding figure, the power fell into the hands of the secret societies, who after their fashion, again, represented the principle of minority rule. In the decades immediately preceding the Fascisti, the *de facto* ruler was Giolitti; if he stepped down and seemed to make place for another, it was only that he was retiring for the sake of his health or was waiting for the storm to blow over. In Italy the democratic façade was never anything more than a façade; if it ever became anything more, anarchy inevitably followed. And from this point of view we may gain a deeper insight into the true nature of Roman Catholicism. It calls for a "superman," but a man, nevertheless, who commands a following. He then rules by virtue of his personal authority. Parliamentarism and democracy really are, as the Fascisti claim, un-Italian. The Fascist cult of order and discipline has nothing in common with the spirit of the Prussian cult; a régime imposed from without is untenable in Italy; it can endure there only when it is carried along by the personal enthusiasm of individuals. It is the personal passion for the *res publica* which makes of the Fascist the replica of the ancient Roman. In the same way all authority in Italy is exerted only through the inner centre of the personality. Thus, again, the concept of authority in the Roman Church cannot be divorced from personal faith in the Church. It is just because personal consent alone constitutes authority for the Roman Catholic (and not the essence of authority itself) that one must be born a Catholic. That is why, in spite of all statements to the contrary, the Church has always maintained an instinctive attitude of mistrust toward its converts.

L ET us now turn to more particular matters. In order to put things in their proper light, I shall have to use, from time to time, now Spain, now Russia, as the background of my observations. The Italian differs from the Spaniard almost more than he does from the German. The flesh of the Spaniard is, throughout, spirit become flesh, and is therefore expression. The Italian face, as Rudolph Kassner has properly remarked, is in general expressionless. In all his acts the Spaniard is the man of reality—even when he tilts against windmills. The Italian, the moment he steps out of his intimate circle, within which he seems to be the soberest of men, is by nature an actor. His language of superlatives is essentially rhetorical; so are his gestures. But this does not mean that for him the theatre exists for the purpose of presenting the reality, as it does in the case of the Frenchman, or in order to create, as in the case of the Russian, but rather that for him the theatre is an end in itself. Which, again, does not mean that with him the emphasis lies on experience, *Erleben,* as with the German, but on doing, on acting. For a cultural people this is an altogether remarkable constellation, and, as far as I know, unique. The Italian theatre simply provides an abreaction for primitive instincts; it enables things to achieve unreality in the world of ideas. That is why the wildest mass-demonstrations of the Italians mean so little. But on the other hand the instincts *must* find an abreaction in this form, for, with the explosive primitive vitality of this people, suppressed passions would lead directly to assault and murder.

The key to the problem of the Italian comedy element lies in the fact that the Italian becomes an actor only when he steps out of his circle of intimate relationships. *For it is only with these that he stands in immediate contact.* About other things he merely rants. Those are the things that other people can do for him. But they must, again, give him the opportunity to live out his instincts, to applaud or to hiss as the case may be. Hence the theatrical element in Mussolini's speeches; hence, too, the theatrical element in the earliest Roman speeches. In and for himself, Mussolini is, with all his passionateness, probably the most sober of latter-day statesmen. And Italian statecraft has from earliest times been extremely sober. The fact is that in Italy politics were carried on by those exceptional men to whom they were a natural element, men who in the realm of politics found vent for the same characteristics which the average Italian expresses in eating his *pasta asciutta*.

But this by no means closes the subject. Because of the national disposition described above, it is only in Italy, of all countries, that a hero of the theatre can at times make real history; this is the meaning of the case of D'Annunzio. No Italian that I know who deserves to be taken seriously—and I know many such—ever considered this man more than an artist in language. He is exceptionally poor in substance, and what substance he has is bad. Nevertheless, in the war and later as a *condottiere*, he played in his own eyes and in the eyes of others a *rôle* which eventually created historic reality. Thus the people again and again took him seriously. An example— *relata refero:* it came to the knowledge of his legionaries that a number of ladies had set out for Gardone, where D'Annunzio was. Horrified by the idea that these evil persons might make an attempt on the virtue of their "saint" they simply *abducted* him. Shortly afterward, D'Annunzio had a fall in which he nearly broke his neck, and the story goes that this was only a means to forestall further efforts for his salvation. But even so shrewd and circumspect a person as Chicherin once took him seriously. The following anecdote is authentic—I have it on unimpeachable authority. It appears that Chicherin accepted an invitation to Gardone. After the superb dinner a servant brought in a naked sword, and then locked the doors. Chicherin stared in amazement at his host, while the latter declared: *Eh bien, mon cher ami, pour certaines raisons je n'ai pas voulu vous orienter d'avance—mais, j'ai resolu de vous trancher la tête.* Chicherin turned pale, and thought to himself: "I'm done for. This crazy loon is capable of anything. Compared with the Fiume crusade, this would be a perfectly harmless little adventure. Because if he does kill me, it wouldn't cause even a ripple. The Chancelleries will have no difficulty in finding grounds on which to justify this extremely opportune incident." Meanwhile D'Annunzio tried to read his guest's thoughts, and kept testing the edge of the blade with his finger. Finally, pretending to be annoyed, he said: *Quel ennui, je ne suis pas en forme ce soir. Je crains qu'il faudra remettre cela à une autre fois.*

But on the other hand, no one could make a greater mistake than to see in the Italian nothing but the comedian. In matters which are of serious personal concern to him he is the soberest person in Europe; in this respect he is closely related to the Russian. From earliest times on, the motto of the Italians has been *panem et circenses,* which means this: whenever the Italian is not acting, the matter concerns him as seriously as his daily bread. He wants either the practical—or else the theatre. This brings us to what is always strikingly prominent in the average Italian: his absolute lack of understanding for any viewpoint which is not practical and positive, from the sentimentality of the romantic to idealism. His conscious mind is alien to the middle ground between the theatre and action. That, it happens, is the realm of the real intellectual interests. The result is in no other country do these play a more insignificant *rôle*. Not only is the conversation of the average Italian— I include also their *grand monde*—the most insipid in Europe; even the intelligent and important Italian is, as a type, devoid of cleverness and wit. He has not English humour, nor French *esprit,* nor German *Tiefsinn;* even his irony falls flat. In this respect D'Annunzio once again emerges as the Italian prototype; his dazzling language is shockingly devoid of meaning, his rhetoric is empty. Just as in England the tiny circles devoted to intellectual matters shine all the brighter by contrast, so there is no idealism purer than that of which Benedetto Croce is the ultimate symbol. Thus the authentic Italian humanists—there were never many of them, for the average find their exemplar in Pietro Aretino—were particularly exquisite. But these circles have at all times constituted a world apart. In the national life they played a *rôle* only to the extent that they were encouraged by princes who wanted to show off with them.

The fact is that all pathos of the spirit, in the French or the German sense, is alien to the national character. But this does not cancel the fact that in exceptional cases the Italian can be extraordinarily spiritual *in action.* As a spiritual being his realm is, in fact, ethos, not pathos. The purest ethos, with almost no conscious pathos, characterizes Italian man of action from the ancient Romans to Napoleon. And the same fundamental disposition also characterizes the Italian artist. The Italian ethos derives its singular character from the fact that it asserts itself through a nature which is primitive, and, as such, affirmative; that is to say, it is not based on tensions in their nature, as is the case with the Spaniard, the Jew, and the Puritan. Hence the naturalism which runs through all Italian art, even in its periods of spirituality. Hence, too, its supreme shoddiness when it is not inspired by genius. Hence also that element in Italian politics which produces on the observer an effect of the most fantastic cynicism. No other people could have produced a Macchiavelli, no other people would tolerate that its latest hero—Mussolini—should refer himself to him with exaggerated emphasis. As a statesman, too, the Italian is a naturalist. He finds the necessities of political life just as natural as the mother finds the needs of her little children. In this connection there are no problems beyond the range of practical expediency. The comparison with the mother came naturally to my pen; all Italian intellectual spirit-life is of this kind, natural, tied fast to nature, directed toward her. This conditions the singular shallowness, the astounding *terre-à-terre* character of the average Italian when he takes up spiritual matters. In the great individual the same qualities issue in a marvellous earth-bound realism of the spirit. In this lies all the meaning of the perfection of antiquity. In this, above all, shall we find the key to the mystery of the Renaissance.

The real Italy, as we see, has as good as nothing to do with what a traveller out of the North experiences there. The discrepancy begins with Nature herself. The country impresses the visitor as being rich; but with the exception of a few regions, it is meagre and poor. The same discrepancy emerges in the realm of art, from *bel canto* to Raphael. The man of action is absolutely not the man of inner experience. The Italian sings like a bird in order to live himself out, he paints because he has to, he writes poetry or commits murder because he cannot help it. If ideals have made him their instrument, he sacrifices himself as a hero. If he has in mind anything at all besides the act in itself, it is the practical advantage to be gained from it; in this respect Titian should certainly be taken as prototypic. What the actions of the Italian may mean for others is no concern of his. This inborn realism assures to Italian politics, potentially at least, the utmost conceivable continuity, for politics is the art of possibilities. But in the realm of the spirit or the mind, only genius can amount to anything considerable in the Italian body. This explains the incredible heights attained by Italy at her highest, as it explains the extraordinary inferiority of her average intellectual production. What applies to Germany in the realm of politics applies to Italy in the realm of the mind. The number of important Italians has presented a broader front only when the national psyche has received, from one source or another, an accelerating impulse, and when, at the same time, a considerable number of unusual individualities were born. Otherwise the picture as a whole always found its type in the States of the Church, such as they were shortly before their end: a tiny, politically very shrewd, ruling minority, illumined now and then by a man of intellectual gifts, usually imported. Underneath, without an intermediary class, lived an ahistorical peasantry.

Let us now turn to the latest Italy, Fascist Italy, and thence to the considerations which impart to Italy an all-human significance in the new world in the making. Let us take note first of some popular misunderstandings. Both the Fascisti themselves and their friends throughout the world believe that with Fascism there has come to power a system of government which is, in the theoretical sense, of an absolutely higher type. It is of course nothing of the kind. There is no such thing as a better or a worse form of government; there is only a form which is badly adapted or one which is better adapted to conditions as they are, and good or bad applies only to the degree to which it gives form to these conditions and makes them productive of great achievements. And the particular line of progress which may at any time be plotted has only one meaning; namely, that the minds and souls of men have achieved a higher development and that external conditions have taken this circumstance into account. Now, no impartial observer could possibly assert that the Fascisti are, in this sense, superior to their predecessors; they are incontestably more primitive, nearer the savage. All the merit of Fascism as a political form lies in this relative fact: a people anarchic by instinct, lacking for centuries a strong national statehood, demoralized politically by an era of liberalism uncongenial to its nature—such a people needed and was benefited by the very thing which Germany forfeited when her strength gave out: Prussian statism. This remains valid even though, as we have seen, the psychological origins of the two culminating stateforms were fundamentally different. For Germany, too, this statism was at one time a pure advantage; except for it, Germany would still be what it was before the time of Napoleon. But when the living impulse had become lifeless routine its effects were evil; which is the very reason why Germany is benefited today by democracy, for it is only through democracy that the set, frozen forms can again become fluid. But Fascism, too, will be a blessing to Italy only as long as it retains its living impulse. As soon as the Fascist bureaucracy, which is already being built up, enters on the phase of rigidity, something else will again be needed. For to repeat: it is not the principle that matters, but the living forces it releases. And there is only *one* absolute political evil: routine as such.

But if the pro-Fascist doctrinaires read the situation falsely, the same is not less true of their doctrinaire opponents. There is not the slightest doubt that Fascist practice runs counter not only to the letter but also to the spirit of the liberal ideal, nor is there the slightest doubt that the liberal ideal represents human values. *But not always are these values to be realized on the basis of the liberal ideal.* Since the one enemy of all life is routine, even a petrified ideal state is an unmixed evil. The following considerations speak further against it: The liberal ideal, with its absolute demand for justice and equity, bases all life, as it were, on acquired rights. But it does not take into account the fact that life is a process both of birth and death; it juggles death out of the picture. That is why it inevitably breeds an unheroic outlook. It follows from these considerations that, as far as there is good in it, the liberal ideal only bespeaks *an ultimate condition.* But for that very reason it must break down with every new beginning. All justice and equity to the contrary, it has to be relegated to the limbo of the outlived things if a new life is to blossom forth. Death is a perfect negation of both justice and equity, for, from the liberal point of view, the longer a man lives the more thoroughly has he established his right to go on living. There is, then, little to be said against the Fascist method of violence, *assuming* that, thanks to Fascism, Italian life will actually be renewed. When did a renewal ever come otherwise? When radical reforms were the need of the day, every great king ran to Bolshevism. In such times there is no other way of doing things.

The question is not, therefore, whether Fascism has introduced a system of government which is best in the absolute sense—there is no such thing—or whether it is to be condemned for having dug the grave of liberalism; the question is whether, as a phenomenon of the times, it serves Italy and,

radiating from Italy, the rest of the world. And this it unquestionably does. It does this if only for one reason—but that
reason one of ultimate, decisive force—in that it has made
the principle of the heroic its Alpha and Omega. And this
principle is the highest by which nations can live at all. But
even this circumstance has nothing to do with the Fascist idea
in and for itself; at one time it was the liberal idea which
brought the heroic principle into play. If today it is no longer
able to do so, this is due to the fact that, psychologically, it has
completed its circle. This brings us to the credit side of Fascism.
To achieve forward progress today there is needed not merely
emphasis on the heroic, but its *extreme* accentuation. Why?
Because the liberal era was one of domination by abstract,
externalized concepts—the program, ideas of equalization,
impersonal objects; the living man was pushed out of the
picture as never before. In order to break through that crust
of petrified objectivity, he had to assert himself with primitive,
primordial force. This explains primarily why it is precisely the
most backward countries which can now play the *rôle* of the
shock-troops of the new spirit of the times; for not Russia and
Turkey alone are to be regarded as such, but Italy, too. Not
only had this country failed to reach the stage of industrializa-
tion of the other great western powers, it had failed in the
matter of civilization too. I refer the reader to the biography of
Mussolini: the Romagnoles among whom he grew up were
real savages; and no less primitive and savage are Mussolini's
own instincts. In countries with a backward civilization it was
easier than elsewhere to break through the framework of the
liberal era. And then the instincts of the inhabitants were
stronger. Finally, the masses in those countries offered the least
resistance to the leaders. From this point of view we can perceive why, at this turn of events, it was primitive Italy which
was able not only to skip several stages for itself, but in some
respects to set itself at the very apex of European development.

But all this still does not constitute an explanation. That

Italy can stand today where she does is due further to the fact that in *one* respect she has a direct psychological lead over the other nations: the great revolution which was brought about in the rest of Europe only by the World War passed over Italy with Cavour; to that extent the country is socially older by three-quarters of a century. Another piece of good fortune was hers: achieving little external success, she remained almost unnoticed during the entire interim between that time and to-day, so that the intimate forces of the nation were not prematurely consumed in external demonstrations. As a matter of fact the founding of the third Italy was no less thorough in its destructive effect on the Italy which preceded than the World War and world revolution were on Middle and Eastern Europe; it brought in its wake a fundamentally similar transformation and transposition of existing relationships. In the long decades which intervened between Cavour and 1914 there grew up, invisible at first, a new living balance of the national body and the national soul. Little wonder, then, that the furnace heat of the World War, which in the rest of Europe meant destruction, in Italy meant the exact contrary; it created the new synthesis. That, for the rest, certain so-called "accidents" contributed to this event, alters nothing in the state of things; no historic situation has ever been created without *significant* accidents. The accidents which came to the assistance of Italy were, indeed, exceptionally significant. The outcome of the war was such that for Italy, and for Italy alone, it meant an absolute justification of idealism, and this quite independently of the motives which impelled her to enter the war. Italy did indeed win, but not to such an extent that the impulse of brute power could become predominant in her; materially she gained little, ideally and morally she gained enormously; for in her case, no less than in the case of Germany at the time of the creation of the Prussian state, the mere search for self needed the recognition of ideal values in order to achieve satisfaction; and inwardly Italy was compelled to stress this the more because she felt that her attitude before and during the war had not always been ideal. *Thus it was only with the World War that the third Italy was born.* Everything that preceded it belonged to the embryonic stage.

THIS fact is of such symbolic significance that I cannot leave it without some additional general observations. It is not that the nations (if we begin by throwing light on that particular side of the problem) commit stupidities from time to time, then recognize these stupidities and turn back to better, earlier ways; a resumption of a way of life drawn from its earlier days becomes possible only *because* in the interim the people has lived itself out in other ways. The evolution of the soul is no less definitely a physiological progression of growth than is the physical. Just as emergent life acquires form by mutual interaction with its environment, while every definite phase, whatever it may look like from other points of view, represents the only possible state of equilibrium for the given moment—in exactly the same way the succession of historic states is unconditionally inevitable, and is not to be changed by any sort of ratiocination, if there is a definite succession of spiritual influences strong enough to change the psychological balance of a people. And on organisms capable of conscious thought, ideas produce the same compulsory effect of excitation as chemicals do on reagents. This explains why a single thread of meaning runs through all historical processes which involve intellectual development, and all nations which come under the influence of the intellectual complexes which emerge from each other in logical sequence must carry on a dialectic with them in order to maintain their biological equilibrium. Thus no European people was able to evade the ideas of the Reformation, of the French Revolution, of democracy, or of parliamentarism; the same will apply in an increasing degree to socialism and Bolshevism. But every people does of course react in its own way, in keeping with its disposition and the

stage and rhythm of its development. I do not need to enter
into an examination of the first consideration, for it has to
do with something which is for the time being a particular
constant. With regard to the second, however, the same influences must obviously evoke different effects according to the
particular stage of development in which a people finds itself.
Old peoples, which have already assimilated many ideas
(France, England) are immune to new ones which follow them
as sequels, to the extent that they are able to absorb them without a pathological disturbance of their equilibrium. The same
happy condition prevails among very young peoples (America,
some of the newly-risen nations which have resulted from the
World War) to the extent that the new ideas find no old
equilibrium to disturb, and can without opposition call out the
corresponding inner response. The worst condition prevails,
in this respect, among those peoples whose progress has been
one-sided to the extent that in some respects they have participated in the most recent development, while in other respects, having been artificially held back, they have not developed at all. The equilibrium of such peoples is constantly
threatened; if it is upset at all, a catastrophe must ensue. This
one consideration suffices to explain the fate of Russia, Germany, and the old Austria. Now when does a people outrun
the general development of a given sphere of culture? When,
for one reason or another, it can submit quietly, yet completely and swiftly, to the shift in equilibrium which is demanded by the assimilation of spiritual progress, so that it
comes out to meet the new influences not as something alien
but as something to which it naturally responds. On no other
grounds can we explain the fact that, in times of crisis, the
young man is always superior to the old man of equal gifts;
by no other means does the wise man anticipate and forestall
fate: since all possible conflicts are from the outset liquidated
internally by him, no external accident can threaten his
equilibrium.

From the foregoing considerations, it is perfectly clear that Italy occupies today a place of historic vantage. The disturbance of the old state of equilibrium had already taken place at the time of Cavour. Since that time Italy has remained open to all real influences without, on the other hand, having fastened on any set condition and become petrified in it. Thus the impulse of development carried on uninterruptedly. All the conflicts which in other countries had to find their abreaction in external dissensions were in Italy's case transformed into principles of education. Thus it came about that when the hour of Europe's destiny arrived, Italy could become neither socialistic nor Bolshevistic, nor could it relapse into a state of reaction, for its born leaders had inwardly transcended these phases. There now comes into play the principle that in Italy only the few ever count, and these few find a personal following such as is elsewhere unknown. The fact that the great Italian mass is in no respect in advance of the masses of the other countries was of no consequence: minorities, and minorities alone, counted. There was needed only the great "awakener of consciousness"—for which in reality all the natural leaders were physiologically ripe—in order that the new condition of equilibrium conforming to the spirit of the time, might be brought about. The external impulse was supplied by the "Red" phase which, from Italy's point of view, was a reactionary phase. Thanks to it, the first conscious leaders of the new day, i.e. the Fascisti, had a won game from the outset. In declaring that the modern development lay beyond such phases as parliamentarism, the party system, democracy, socialism, they gave expression to the people's inmost feeling and perception, for unconsciously, all Italians who counted *were* beyond these conceptions. Thus it was that the *rôle* of "Duce" became possible for Mussolini. He is not at all the "strong man" who subdued the trembling masses; undoubtedly great as he is—since Lenin's death the one statesmanlike personality of large mould in Europe—his significance is based on his evident representative quality. He is another vindication of the saying of Bismarck: "A man is only as great as the wave which breaks under him." The great Mussolini is possible because hundreds of little Mussolinis stand behind him, and, behind these, hundreds of thousands who recognize them inwardly as their spokesmen. The Fascisti are essentially heroic natures. That they will continue to rule Italy as long as they remain heroic is therefore certain, the more so as the typical Italian contrast between majorities and minorities is also illustrated here in the fact that the Italian mass is throughout uncourageous. The European prestige of the Fascisti, however, derives from the fact that a new heroic age is dawning everywhere, that democratic liberalism is everywhere losing its accelerating force. Thus, in spite of all particularisms, Italy can serve as a general European symbol in the same sense as Russia does for an awakening Asia (the reader is referred to the detailed exposition of this question in *The World in the Making*).

It is now clear why it matters so little what Fascism "actually" is. It really is none of those things which can be defined by means of prevailing concepts; it is *not* a program, it is *not* an abstract ideology. What constitutes its whole power is the fact that, following the law of historic counterpoint, it is supplying the counterpoint to the latest period; it is therefore anti-sentimental, anti-liberal, anti-quantitative, anti-abstract, etc.; to this extent it is at one in spirit with Bolshevism, which is the negative pole to Fascism, and which for that reason is the only other spiritual force in the political field with a historic future already manifest. In both cases it is a question of the defeat, by living forces, of the ideologies of the eighteenth and nineteenth centuries. In both cases the primacy of the idea has been replaced by that of the living person, for it is not its momentary, assuredly transitory system which makes Bolshevism an historic factor, but the new type of man whom it called to power, the proletarian ruler type. In both cases the basic characteristic is not reactionary but progressive in the most modern sense. But its basis was not an attitude of equalization, but an aristocratic attitude. Both Bolshevism and Fascism are striving by means of a temporary class rule to achieve a state without classes. Thus in the case of Fascism we have to do with the first positive expression in Europe of the new state of equilibrium, which has come to liquidate the old one, the intellectual content of which still derives from the eighteenth century. What it will develop into no one can say today. Since its chief value, in my eyes, is its fecundating force, it will some day disintegrate as every fructifying seed disintegrates. It will yield place to an unsuspected, unpredictable new phenomenon, if not in Italy then in the rest of the world, in so far as the rest of the world appears ready to receive its impulses.

NEVERTHELESS we can foreshadow, because of the unmistakable signs already evident, what the predestined *rôle* of Italy is to be in the complete structure of the Europe of the future. As always in its great periods, but this time more than ever before, Italy will embody *the principle of the paganism of antiquity;* the more so as the post-Christian era, which began with the World War, signifies in many respects a return to the soul of antiquity. It is only for this reason that the extreme expression of it, as presented by Italy at her latest, produces so widely convincing an effect. I recently read the following utterance by a young Fascist: "We need truth, assurance, and light. We must feel the ground secure under our feet, in our hands truths must be like polished swords of the hardest steel. So-called freedom of the spirit has been a most pitiful failure, for it gave us no certainty in the place of the truths of antiquity, and knew only how to create principles." This is exactly the judgment that the Roman of antiquity would have rendered on the liberal-democratic era. He was a man utterly devoid of problems. Truth had only one purpose for him, to provide a reliable basis for life, to furnish clear directives for all action. Truth was therefore nothing but political constitution and

juridical form, and to tamper with either was, in his eyes, sacri-
lege. His adjustment lay solely in the realm of the ethos (as
distinguished from the pathos). Judged from the point of view
of the spirit, he was *terre-à-terre* to a degree unknown by any
man before or since. For what were his very gods? *Numina*—
that is to say, more or less the things we today call abstractions.
It was therefore possible to have not only little gods, but the
very littlest, not only private gods, but the most intimately private: I allude to the Penates, the Lares, and the little god-
ling Strepitus. But on the other hand the spirit became flesh for
the Roman, more so than for any subsequent type; the premise
of the Christian discord between soul and body was a negation
of his very substance. True, Christianity did teach that the
Word had to become flesh, but only in the sense that the transcendental spirit had to find embodiment in an earthly form.
For the Roman the transcendental did not exist. He stood flat-
footedly on the hither side of things. Yet he was not, for that
reason, by any means superficial. He resembled no one less than
the modern materialist. He was simply the pagan as distinguished from the Christian. He was not irreligious; his religiosity was only of a special kind; the only parallel which
exists today is in Japan, where patriotism means something just
as deep as the relationship to God does to the German. The
pagan of antiquity was the man of perfect profundity incarnated
with perfect naïveté and unproblematic consistency in this
earthly life. This resulted in a minimum of spiritual experience,
but it led to a maximum of spirit-born action.

And the Italian has remained a pagan in this sense. He is of
course no longer the man of antiquity. His living relationship
to the classic age is very well reflected in the following from
Prezzolini's *Culture Italienne* (a thought-provoking book in
many other respects, too): "The classic culture has embodied
itself completely in new forms, as the features of the father
do in those of the son. We speak Italian, but we no longer
understand Latin; we no longer have any great jurists, but the

juristic spirit is widespread. The ideas that dominate among
us are the culture of the family, a solid sense of property, the
need for clarity, precision, a certain architectural quality in
ideas; all this is of antiquity. Another survival of antiquity is
the majestic grace with which the peasant woman wraps herself
in her shawl, or the man of the people in his mantle, which is
the counterpart of the toga." The Italian, then, is assuredly no
longer the real man of antiquity. But he certainly is still the
pagan. He knows nothing of religiosity in the French or
German sense. Spiritually St. Francis of Assisi was a Provençal.
The Italian has no understanding whatsoever for the problems
of religion, which explains why there have never been any real
religious wars in his country. He does understand that religion
may serve a political purpose, but not that politics can have a
religious content. Thus, again, all Protestantism in the sense of
the will to find a personal relationship to the divine is, in Italy,
nationally unthinkable. In Italy the man of independent
thought has always been either a free-thinker or a sceptic. Thus
the Catholics as such play hardly any *rôle* in the spirit-life of
the country. The same applies to the Church. From the Italian
point of view there is nothing anomalous in the fact that the
state lives outside the Catholic law: the same thing obtained,
more often than not, in the time of the Roman Empire. From
the Italian point of view, Catholicism is a purely political institution, just as pagan religion always was. If Catholicism in
Germany develops today a tremendous cultural offensive,
Rome as such does not participate. It acquiesces in that offensive,
because that kind of thing is good for Germany. But just as
one millimetre of motion in the spoke of a wheel is enough to
correspond to a movement of several metres in the wheel as a
whole, so Rome always takes the proper political measures at
the right time. The fact that this purely pagan institution—
this most authentic creation of the realistic spirit of Italy—
can acquire the deepest religious content outside of Italy, and
can retain this content, only goes to prove how *deep* the pagan-

ism of antiquity was. It is the pagan, and the pagan alone, who can demonstrate his religious depth in the form of a political being.

But today a new era has dawned, an era which is no longer religious in the Christian sense; the extent to which this is true may be learned from the last three chapters of my *Wiedergeburt*. The emphasis of importance has been shifted back from the field of the pathos to that of the ethos. Wherever the affirmation of the earthliness of life implies the negation of everything beyond, it leads to pure superficiality or to Satanism. For the pagan this division does not exist, since he has no theoretical life-philosophy at all. He believes neither in matter nor in spirit, let alone in the idea of a program; he simply *is*. Thus, for him, everything that is real is condensed into the personal. For him the great man, at the highest, emerged directly as God, or at least as the superhuman hero; for in the great man his entire background, too, found personal utterance. This explains the cult of the Caesars. But the same thing also explains the Italian idea of the Papacy. Hence, too, the position of Mussolini. This enables us to draw the sharp line of demarcation between Fascism and Bolshevism, both of which we placed, at first, on the same plane. Bolshevism is antimetaphysical, for the Russian is a man torn between two poles: at one end the animal, at the other God. At this time he has decided in favour of the animal. Hence his collectivism. The animal has only a group-soul, for it is only at a later period that man differentiates himself from the group. If Bolshevism today hypostasizes collective man, if it really hopes to replace personality some day by apparatus,* that is only a peculiar result

* The historian of Soviet Russia, Pokrowsky, in trying to describe to the proletarian masses the significance of Lenin for the revolutionary development of mankind, explained the communistic view of the phenomenon of Lenin, according to Fülöp-Miller, literally as follows: "We Marxists do not see in the personality the creator of history, because for us the personality is only the apparatus through which history works. The time may yet come when we will be able to produce this apparatus artificially, just as we build up our electrical accumulators today. As yet, however, we have not advanced so far, and for the time being these instruments through which history works, these accumulators of social processes, must be bred and born in a primitive way."

of the synthesis of pre-individualistic primal feeling with the
mechanistic way of thought. The pagan of antiquity embodies
not only the most perfect conceivable psychophysical equilibrium, but with it the most perfect equilibrium within the soul.
He, too, was no individualist. In times of antiquity the state
came before everything else, but the state was then neither a
herd nor yet a mechanism, but an organism within which every
individual lived of his own free will for the good of the *res
publica*. And when the hour came for the birth of modern
individuality, it had to be born first in Italy, the one land in
which the political spirit of antiquity still survived; for in
that country the equilibrium of all the elements of life was a
matter of course.

Thus the same spirit of the times which in Russia called
collective man to the place of power, called forth in Italy a new
organism. All justifiable mass-ideals shall be fulfilled as far
as they can be. To this extent Fascism does not repudiate its
socialist origins; indeed, whatever ideology it possesses bespeaks, more than anything else, the spirit of Sorel, the founder
of syndicalism. But the commonwealth demanded by socialism
will have to consist of individuals. Do we now understand why
Fascism, in spite of its many and great mistakes, in spite of its
barbarism, possesses such great attractive power? It is only in
the form of a partial rebirth of the state of antiquity, and only
upon that basis, that the ideal of the times may be realized
for the good. The new world in the making can avoid becoming shallow or Satanic only if, in turning from Christianity, it
does not perpetuate the discord, but brings forth a new unity
in man, like that of antiquity. Things are thus and under no
circumstances otherwise in Europe. The new Italy offers the
primitive primal form of the new ideal. It offers this form,
first, because there the new ruler type of the antique pattern
emerges in the form of the chauffeur; second, because the
Italian in himself is primitive. But it is for this very reason that
he provides the best symbol of what all the masses of the
western world need. The imperialism of the Fascisti, taken as

an external tendency, is of course an absurdity: it is only as leaders in inner politics that modern Napoleons can any longer be significant for the good. And under no circumstances would any people permit itself to be conquered and ruled by the Italians of today, for they are not a ruling race like the ancient Romans. No people can today be won through oppression—for this only intensifies the self-consciousness of the oppressed. It is not as the liquidator of liberalism as such, but as its continuation (just as children, however much they vary, are the continuation of their fathers), that Fascism has a future. But if the Italians still continue, in the form of Catholicism, to rule from Rome a great part of the world, this symbol of the rebirth of antiquity in modern flesh cannot but create for them a tremendous new prestige. May Italy only understand where her true task lies. May she always think more of Rome's *tenue*, her self-control and reserve, than of Rome's conquests. May her leaning toward sober common sense master her leaning toward the theatre. It is a great thing that a rebirth of the great soul of antiquity should be possible at all in the world of to-day. It is a great honour for a modern nation to be able to serve even in part as the body for this rebirth. May Italy never misunderstand this situation, never lose herself in romantic dreams. This could only lead to a most unhappy awakening. May she soon renounce everything that smacks of the theatre. May she learn to appreciate that when the new spirit, with its new state, shall have reached this point—the fusion of the modern re-embodiment of the life-form of antiquity with the general European picture—*she herself will never again dominate that picture;* for the form of antiquity was small, while that of the modern world is immeasurable, and this gives the advantage to new qualities; the spirit of antiquity is today only one gen among others. May she learn to appreciate that she can today fulfil one of the highest tasks which any nation of our time may fulfil for the best interests of all.

HUNGARY

HUNGARY

Long before I knew Hungary I was an enthusiastic lover of Hungarian music. This compensated, in my nature, for the spiritual austerity of the music of Bach, which responds to my spirit to the same degree. If I am on the one hand a man of the most severely spiritualized form, if my inner discipline and outward form derive from this, my relaxation lies in the Dionysian element. This is embodied primarily in the Russian side of me, for as an emotional and temperamental being I am a son of Russia. But not the Russian of the melancholy variety; the boundless brown plains and the distant blue of the horizon do not answer to my nature: what answers to it is that Dionysian element which finds its utterance in the Tsiganes. There is something very remarkable about this wandering folk. Its harmony and melody is of India; more than one sacred chant I have heard in India comes close to the Magyar *Zigeunerweise*. But in every country in which the Tsiganes have a share in the national life this peculiar element, alien to Europe, brings out the primary instincts of the nation much more clearly than does the music of the original race. In the Gitanos the passion of southern Spain emerges like an independent entity. This passion always appears controlled even in the case of Andalusians, but in the gipsy form it bursts forth with real primal savagery. I shall never forget how, in a cave near Granada, I once dispensed a little too much manzanilla to a group of Gitanas, and how they, in consequence, reverted into pure maenads; my guide had to spirit me away from the place: there was every possibility of my being pulled into a Bacchanalian reminiscent of Parnassus. The Russian gipsy is the most authentic embodiment of the Russian *dukh*, that tremendous emotional rush which again and again exhausts itself in melancholy void. In Hungary the music of the gipsy is the most perfect method of expression for the conqueror in relaxation. After a wild gallop, after a mortal struggle, after perilous battles on alien soil, a moment of brooding suspense. On the one hand an intimate, familiar note, on the other hand an individual variation of it, responding to every mood and every singularity—complete self-abandonment, utter dissolution of form; then again, catching itself up suddenly, reverting to the strictest rhythm, ending at times in a close-locked forward thrust, or in the scattering tempest of nomad horsemen in retreat.

What answers to my ultimate nature is not the Russian gipsy world, but the Magyar. This certainly rests on the fact that even in me, somewhere in the depths, lives the nomad chieftain. But it no doubt rests chiefly on this, more than anything else—that his music, and his music alone, strikes me as aristocratic. That alternate tightening and relaxation which is expressed in the music of the Magyar gipsies occurs only in the soul of the aristocrat; that is, of the man whose centre of being is organically superior to the polar tensions of his nature, the man who does not need the even and equable, essentially *bourgeois* things, neither in himself nor in others; the man who gives his affirmation with equal force, both to spirit and to blood, and whose inner tension is not to be snapped, Hamlet-fashion; the man for whom the problems of those who find life a burden do not exist, because to him suffering and joy, like death and life, are naturally corresponding co-ordinates. But the gipsy plays as the hearer would have him play. Just as the Magyar leader directs the manner of his improvisation by the eyes of the one who best follows him, in the same way the music of the gipsies everywhere reflects the essential nature of those among whom they live. In Spain it is the occasional outbursts of passion of the man of reserve; in Russia it is the aimless temperament, veering forever toward its opposite extremes, frivolity and indolence, but always with a background of the most imposing spaciousness; in Hungary it is the relaxation of the ruler. For the Magyars are the most aristocratic race that lives in Europe today.

THE aristocrat is of course before all else a distinct zoological species. That is why he can neither be justified nor yet deposed on purely abstract grounds. Even the question as to whether a man is conservative or radical is one of physiology, and not of superior or inferior insight. To this extent Lenin, whose aim it was to wipe out all non-proletarians, had a deeper understanding of the meaning of things than the Frenchman who looks for the ultimate victory of the democratic idea on the basis of the spirit of his great principles. Nor can there be, when men believe in the original equality of all peoples in the matter of worth and of rights, any intelligent discussion of the question whether or not aristocrats ought to exist "as a general principle"; the question whether a people can produce, demand, and suffer an aristocracy is one of original structure. This structure exists independently of the form of government, which in every instance has at one time or another been instituted by violence and has then encroached, in most cases, on any kind of strata. Thus, during the Middle Ages, all Europe *seemed* to be aristocratic, and thus today it *seems* to be democratic. Actually, however, every people which is to any extent self-determining organizes itself in the long run in a manner corresponding to its structure; that is to say, the emphasis of moral power is always laid on the right point even when the emphasis of the official and material power is laid on what is, from the point of view of the national structure, the wrong point. How little it is inevitable that the inner structure and the external order should correspond, as modern prejudice demands, becomes very clear from the following: wherever the intimate structure was itself the cradle of the form of government, it nearly always led to something other than what this structure would naturally imply. Aristocrats, for example, are always republicans for themselves; the normal state-form of peoples with an aristocratic culture is therefore the republic and not the monarchy, for the man who feels himself to be a master finds it very difficult to put up with another, who thinks himself a higher being, over him. If, in spite of this, many of the aristocracies of history have been headed by a monarchy, this was due to unconscious perception of the fact that the sovereignty of all would also threaten each one as sovereign; in this lies the meaning of the caricature presented by the old Polish kingdom. In the case of England the meaning of the stability of its development—as well as of its present state—lies in the fact that a people aristocratic in its tendencies and republican by temperament turned at the right historic moment to the democratic form of state, whereby the rule of the aristocracy remained assured; and that it allowed this republic of aristocrats—as it really was—to have at its head a monarch who yet played a purely symbolic *rôle,* thus all possible complexes (to speak psychoanalytically) were in the case of this people so met as to produce the maximum of benefit. The English people is not, however, aristocratic in the same sense as the Magyar. As we have seen in the chapter on England, the outlook of the entire race is essentially social, and to that extent not exclusively bent on quality, but, to a considerable extent, on quantity. Accordingly, England's ideal is that every one should be a gentleman. This ideal is a compromise between the demands of personal sovereignty and those of social equality; it denies all differentiations of type except that between the gentleman and the non-gentleman; it is therefore the aristocratic ideal of an age of belief in equality. As against this, it is exactly differences that the Hungarian people affirms. It does not envy the exceptional position occupied by its *grands seigneurs;* it is proud of it. It does not take it amiss that the antlered stag carries its head high; it demands this bearing of him. It is a country so organized that it consciously identifies the best that is in it with a specific representative ruling class. Its sons have the inner ability to acknowledge, for their own part, ideals which not every one can achieve for himself. They want the pre-eminence of the *aristos* who is recognized as such. With all the consciousness of self which any

believer in equality has ever known, they demand a hierarchy.
This gives us the fundamental characteristic of the aristocratic
outlook: the pride and the consciousness of worth of the aristocrat do not need external equalization with others. *This derives
from the fact that in the consciousness of the aristocrat the
emphasis lies on his uniqueness.* He does not make any comparisons at all; he *must* therefore be free from envy. Now we
understand why all periods of supreme human greatness were
periods of a predominant aristocratic outlook. Humanity *is*
qualitatively differentiated; no one man can be everything;
thus the demand for equality in all things betokens a cosmic
misunderstanding. In its practical application such a misunderstanding cannot but lead to evil effects. Furthermore, wherever
the demand for equality is in force, envy *must* be a decisive
factor; the only cure for this is the individual consciousness of
uniqueness, and it is only the aristocrat who, as a type, has
this. But above all, whenever an ideal holds good for everybody—be it even the ideal of the gentleman—no finest flowers
can blossom. These grow only where the unusual is encouraged
as it emerges; this explains England's poverty in the matter of
individual personalities who can be compared with the best
among peoples of a less social outlook. The finest flower of
humanity cannot come to blossom in times of equality. So much
for the cultural significance of the aristocratic outlook. But this
outlook alone is true to the idea of Christian love, according to
which one should love one's neighbour as oneself: and rightly
understood this means not a demand for equality, rooted in
envy, nor yet philanthropy, but a joyous affirmation of the
existence of the Not-Self and of the different.

But to repeat: not every one can be an aristocrat or feel
aristocratically. We are here confronted with as fundamental an
attitude as that which renders both the centralism of the French
and the parliamentarism of the English productive, and renders
them destructive when they are transferred to Germany (to
what extent this is the case has been demonstrated in detail on

p. 172 of *The World in the Making*). There *do* exist entire peoples in which there are millions of individuals who joyously find the highest outlet for their pride in their identification with some one else, just as the real Christian sees his ideal in the Saviour. Peoples of this kind need not be among the ones whose majorities have the noblest moral standards. Given the invincible inferiority of all that is average, and the law of enantiodromy (the shift to the opposite extreme), it would perhaps even seem a rule that among aristocratic races there must emerge, as a decisive factor, an unusual quantity of conceit and intrigue; among such peoples there is surely much more injustice toward groups than in democracies, for the aristocrat—his consciousness of self being a consciousness of uniqueness—sees the individual and the element of uniqueness, while the group sacrifices the individual to every majority. But peoples of aristocratic structure are under all circumstances the ones with the greatest inner multiplicity and the finest sensitiveness to rank and level, for which reason they do more justice than any other to the individual; thus mediaeval England made possible the rise of a much larger number of gifted men than does the England of today. The man of democratic outlook necessarily lacks the organ of perception for rank and level, for he who bases himself at all on the postulate of equality cannot understand any differences other than those of quantity. Thus Jews, who have suffered more than any one else from inequality of rights, are even eager to deny that there is any significance at all in differing degrees of talent.

There are many forms of a possible aristocracy. In India it is the caste of the Brahmins, i.e. of the wise—who must, however, remain poor—which is recognized as the crown of all the others. In ancient China the same applied to the "nobles" who had been recruited from whatever level it might be, as the Catholic priesthood is recruited among us; in that country nobility was not hereditary. Also in the case of modern England, which, half-aristocratic as it is, makes the impression of an aristocratic structure by contrast with most other modern peoples, there is no real aristocratic caste, for everybody wants to be called a gentleman; but there the aristocracy of merit and property perpetuates the picture of the old nobility, and its especial splendour is a source of happiness to all. In Hungary the state of things is such that a people which as a whole is of an aristocratic outlook and feels itself to be a nobility throughout, again and again exalts its traditional aristocracy upon a throne; and it is the absolute duty of this nobility to shine. This was true not only until the close of the World War: it is true even today. And how little it is necessary for things to be different even with the most far-reaching external democratization, is shown psychologically by a country closely related in this respect—Poland: the emergence of a *tiers état* since the time of the Partition has in no way shaken the moral position of its high nobility. All Poles would in fact like to be great lords. But, for inner and outer reasons, very few can be. The recognition of the ideal inevitably insures the proper prestige to its born representatives.

THE aristocrat, then, is first a distinct zoological species, and secondly, he embodies a certain all-human value. Thirdly, he is the product of special external circumstances: he must be placed, externally, in the position of an exception in order to grow and unfold. But this applies to every human group, without exception—even to the proletarian; every exceptional position makes of the man in question an exceptional being. The born proletarian can attain the perfection of his type only within the framework of the proletarian position in life. The born king is psychologically different from the "ordinary mortal"; his environment and his world of perceptions are of a special kind; many little and petty things do not exist for him, whereas even with a minor degree of talent he can envisage naturally great groups of relationships, which are otherwise

apprehended only by the most gifted within other classes. It
is much the same with the *grand seigneur*, the original model
of the aristocrat, except that he is a specialist in no respect.
*His special significance lies in the fact that in him the human
element as such finds its highest expression.* To that extent the
grand seigneur embodies a higher type than does the reigning
prince. With all his pride of family he is essentially *not* a man
of caste. There is no grotesque differentiation between his like
and the "ordinary mortal"—a differentiation which in the last
analysis converts the self-consciousness of the prince into pride
in himself as a rarity, such as we might conceive the okapi to
possess. He is essentially free, essentially superior. His ethos
forbids him to have any petty or even narrow trait. The fundamental device, *noblesse oblige*, is the really decisive factor in
his life, for the very possibility of his existence is bound up
with its rule. The gesture of the donor really predominates
with him, for the ability to make gifts is the sign manual of his
position of advantage. Private interests are not his last resort,
since, by very definition, he has no merely private life; even in
his private capacity he knows himself to be representative, and
that not in the same sense as the king, who, sundered from the
individual by an unbridgable gulf, represents "the people," but
as the representative of every man. Last, and above all, he is
essentially independent; he need reckon with no one, for his
worth consists in the simple fact that he is, whereas a reigning
prince must reckon with the susceptibilities of every single individual; of all human beings he is the one who must, on
occasion, put up with the utmost humiliations. What has been
said here is actually typical of the Hungarian *grand seigneur*.
Unfortunately, however—it may as well be said at once—it
applies to him alone in Europe among the born aristocrats,
for he alone enjoys the position necessary to his kind. To this
extent his class differs from no other more than from the one
which the *Almanach de Gotha* ranks with him or even above
him—the German baronial nobility and landed aristocracy of

today. The *Standesherren* were, as types, higher men, as long as they represented something greater than they themselves and their estates were; and the French historian who claimed that the only good foreign policy of Germany, down to modern times, was directed by that class, was probably right: political tact is only another form of peasant cunning; the best foundation for this gift is a traditional association with the soil, i.e. a personal identification with the land. The higher position gives one *ipso facto* a greater range of vision, not to mention the advantages of material independence; and the German, with his inner uncertainty, stands in special need of a higher hereditary position in order to give of his best. But this could apply to the whole class only as long as the hereditary idea dominated Europe, and membership in a caste carried, as such, the implication of greatness and effectiveness. Today the landed German high aristocracy is nothing more than a separate zoological species, the exponents of nothing deeper than the particular position which has descended to them. There is no doubt that they are something special: every family which lives apart long enough, interbreeding with only a few families of similar fundamental character, really becomes a special nation in miniature, which quite rightly sees in all others a different variety. But the only thing that actually matters is what such a miniature nation is worth. Unless its inward breadth and nobility of spirit bears an inverse proportion to its external smallness, it is worth less than the greater group. But this width of spirit can be sustained, as a race characteristic, only by means of a corresponding task. The *Standesherren* who are still called by tradition to the assumption of great tasks are even now, whenever they belong to talented families, men of a higher type. Still, they are in the minority; so much so that they by no means determine the type. This aristocracy, as a class, constitutes today a real ghetto, leading its special, particular life, guided by the narrowest private interests, unaffected by the course of world-affairs. If it did recently assume a *rôle* in the national life, a number of grotesque situations resulted. This is what happened in the years immediately following the *débâcle* of 1918; what frequently took place in these circles after the revolution was, I am told by reliable witnesses, a sight for the gods. During the period of the inflation, when forests brought in more than factories, there were some who planned a *coup de main* which was to restore conditions such as obtained not before 1918, but before 1815; those who had last governed were to be shown finally that they were nothing better than the mediatized princes. This sort of caste outlook is the very opposite of the aristocratic. The moment a nobility regards itself in any degree as one class among others, which lives for its private interests, it has lost its *raison d'être* and deserves to be overthrown. The only thing that justifies the position and the self-consciousness of privileged aristocrats is *superiority*. That is why such qualities as pettiness, meanness of spirit, narrowness of vision, party outlook, inability to respect an opponent, should, in aristocratic circles, be regarded as complete disqualifications; a bearer of one of the greatest German names who does not possess the superiority of the English gentleman ranks, socially and humanly, beneath him. The actions of the true aristocrat are never the result of compulsion or of lack of inner freedom, the dictation of the code or the standards which others expect of him; they are the result of nothing but free personal choice; where such freedom is lacking, there can be no talk of nobility. If family- and class-interests are to be the deciding factors, there is not the slightest reason why a family which goes back to the Carolingians should be ranked above one which is descended from Levi—the less so as the latter happens to be older. The man who is inwardly a peasant, big or little, a low-class *rentier*, a shopkeeper, a drill-sergeant, or a petty official, is not a nobleman. Today, at any rate, the idea of a nobility as a separate class has lost all meaning. And this is not only because the age of privileges is past; the claims of the geese of the Capitol have lost all validity since the whole world awakened to the eugenic idea, for before long every man will know his line of descent, and in the new world-order no one will think differently of the hereditary high German aristocracy than of any other line; from now on only one thing will decide, namely, what particular quality has been perpetuated in the succession of generations. No; the German nobility as a whole can, unfortunately, no longer be regarded as an aristocracy. If it is to grow into its position of privilege, in the sense of meeting the demands which the world has a right to make of it, it will have to renew itself from the foundations up. In Hungary, however, the high aristocracy is still really a high aristocracy; that is, it still fulfils its proper function. And its spirit sets its stamp upon the whole nation; the whole nation is correspondingly noble. However numerous their faults, the fact remains that for the whole nation the ideal is magnanimity, generosity, and the spirit of sacrifice. Every Hungarian has that consciousness of uniqueness by which the aristocrat as such stands or falls.

However, before entering in more detail on the subject of Hungary, we should examine more closely what it is that differentiates the virtues of the aristocrat of Hungarian stamp, that is to say of the *grand seigneur*, from those of the mere gentleman. His peculiar type is scarcely understood any longer. A French noblewoman once observed to me, in connection with one of the society novels of Paul Bourget, that the writer, in spite of a long life spent in the heart of the Faubourg St. Germain, had not yet learned to understand the very first elements of its spirit, for he was too different from it; the same applies even more strongly to all the German writers that I know of; it applies even to Nietzsche, noble in soul as he was. He did indeed happen to be noble-minded, but not in the aristocratic sense, for the latter idea of nobility implies superiority of being. As a being Nietzsche was the typical product of a pastor's home; there was in him a longing after greatness which his nature did not permit him to achieve in person. And particularly today, when, as Börries von Münchhausen once put it, even the "decent man falls between two stools," there is hardly any feeling at all for true nobility. For today it is unfortunately the *writer* who gives the tone, and among writers the decisive element is the journalist, and in eighty cases out of a hundred he is, unfortunately, a creature filled with resentment; with the result that those things which have a positive meaning only in terms of freedom are understood by him in terms of thraldom, and the modern youth thus grows up in an atmosphere of distorted ideas of this kind. A great degree of blame attaches, again, to Nietzsche, however pure in heart he may have been personally: he suggested it as a principle that one should look behind noble motives for the base, and since with most scribblers a search of this kind is bound to uncover a veritable treasure-house, they compete with each other in pulling the higher things down. If things were as they ought to be in the matter of the distribution of power, the law would be that only the man with the soul of a *grand seigneur* would be allowed to exercise the profession of journalist; that is to say, the thoroughly generous and unenvious person whose thoughts and acts are dominated by the highest point of view. This was what Leopold Kalckreuth meant when he once said that all painters ought to be counts; because of the great instability of the artistic nature, the gyroscope which is in the blood of every real aristocrat is especially needed in his case. It is just for this reason that in India—as Rabindranath Tagore recently pointed out—all the greatest men were not Brahmins but Kshatriyas; from this same source derives the incomparable greatness of such spirits as Plato, Montaigne, and, recently, Tolstoi. How completely all standards of worth have been transposed by the fact that the tone is given by the scribbling pygmy is made especially clear in the case of modern German literature. In it the envious man, of all persons, is exalted as the highest type. This and nothing else is the "silent one in the land," who, instead of fulfilling the one task to which God appointed him—which is to keep silent—makes virtues of his necessities which the whole world must recognize as its standards. He looks down upon the great of this world, because their life is mere vanity; in every gesture he sees presumption; in the generous radiations of a great spirit, avarice, in freedom, insolence; for him every person of substance is inferior. But in this, such people merely establish the presumption of their own greatness, and then all values are inverted. Their reserve is not nobility but arrogance, their apparent humility a grudging spirit. What finally unmasks them and shows their true face is a loathsome exhibitionism in regard to their sufferings. Naturally, the deeper and more sensitive a man is, the more he suffers; but the higher type of man does not linger over it. For him the tragedy of existence is a tacit premise, like the tension of the strings which makes music possible. It is here, then, that the ultimate ignobility of the ideal of the resentful scribblers emerges with final clarity. Under certain circumstances the noble one is ready to relinquish his life, for inwardly he stands above it. It is just for this reason that he cannot possibly suffer life's difficulties in the manner valued by modern literati as the sign of a high humanity. I really cannot read about this type of person without being seized with disgust. If they were seen to be what they really are—cases of arrested development, poor, sick weaklings, one could certainly have sympathy for them. But as exemplars . . . Seldom has any age seen true values so distorted.

For some time yet there is nothing to be done about it. We are fated to see, for a long time to come, a continuous descent of the level of public opinion. Not because mankind is becoming irretrievably abject, but because, in the main, the historic duty of the immediate future will lie in the lifting up of the general level. The consequence of this will be that the existing level must first sink further still, until a general abreaction of suppressed envy has developed. Things can improve in a large

way only when such external conditions have been created for
the whole of mankind as will bring forth, in every aristocrat
whose heredity is not inferior, the unfolding of a finer soul than
in the plebeian. On the other hand, however, the period which
immediately follows the turning of the soil by the plough is
the period of sowing. This is the very moment, then, to prepare the way for the best type. To this end it would be well
to examine in still closer detail what constitutes not only the
absolute positive in the *grand seigneur*, but also his absolute
superiority of value—a superiority even as compared with the
gentleman. The best method, because it avoids all uninten-
tional misunderstandings, is to take as our basis the definition of
his physiological limits. There is no doubt that the state of the
grand seigneur is dependent on an external position of special
privilege—and it may be thought that no one is entitled to this.
There is no doubt that to a certain extent his type develops at
the expense of others, just as the giant tree does at the expense
of the underbrush—and the man in the street may be valued
more highly than the great lord. There is no doubt that, as a
representative type, he is an extravert, and one may accord to
the "silent in the land," with their subjective experiences, a
higher value than to any world-conqueror. Further, there is no
doubt that the *grand seigneur* is, as an extravert, inwardly limited in a special sense. The possibilities of his type stand and fall
by the inward distance which he maintains between himself and
all others. Hence his extreme courtesy to all who are about
him; he has no direct man-to-man contact. His acts and
thoughts are involuntarily directed by intentions of an historic
or otherwise far-reaching nature. Yet in the case of this kind of
structure, one which Alfred Adler, the founder of individual
psychology, would like to do away with and practically ex-
terminate, as being simply pathological—in the case of this kind
of structure, we are dealing with nothing more or less than
the structure of every leader of great calibre, in whatever field.
Every large perspective implies, before everything else, dis-

tance; only the principle of distance, in contradistinction to that of intimacy, makes leadership possible at all. That is why no real leader can be found wherever democracy is literally interpreted to mean a man-to-man understanding between every one and every one else along a mean line—as is the case in the latest German politics; co-operation in the spirit of colleagues will fail to kill off initiative only when extreme inner distance is there to offset external intimacy; which is the case in England. Fundamentally the saying of my grandfather applies everywhere: the co-operation of more than two persons has as seldom resulted in a reasonable idea as in the making of a child. In the realm of the spirit only autocracy is creative—it is only the sphere of self-rule which must be delimited in each case in accordance with its meaning; for since all initiative derives from the substance of the unique, it follows that only the inwardly lonely can create.

Now if that distance which makes the great leader is to be maintained, as a matter of history, independently of the accident of talent, it must be helped along by the maintenance of external distance. In this lies the meaning both of the military hierarchy and the etiquette of courts. And it is actually possible to help things along externally in this regard. Tradition can replace talent to a very large extent. This explains the absolute superiority of the *grand seigneur,* whose inward growth corresponds to his position, to all other types—types, be it noted, not individuals. This is true, in its historic connection, even where the *grand seigneur* is of inferior substance, as long as he is otherwise gifted; which is demonstrated, for all times, by the symbol of Talleyrand. His superiority, rooted as it was in descent and in historical and political instinct, and developed into organic form, enabled him to remain the leader throughout all revolutions. He was not a man without character; he stood, much rather, above that which constitutes character in limited circumstances; he embodied nothing less important than the spirit of the continuity of history. I deliberately mentioned at this point the great gentleman against whom objections can most easily be sustained; I admit all his faults. But what matters is that his advantages were *absolute* advantages; they implied superiority plainly and simply, because it was superiority over man as such. Man as such is, once for all, the premise of all special thought and action. Seen not only from the high point of vantage, but from the point of view of God Himself, mankind looks like what the *grand seigneur* judges it to be. The *grand seigneur* is, in fact, the highest expression of man, not in the sense of a specific ability, but simply as man. The world of antiquity knew this, and so did the age of the Germanic heroes and knights. And now we can make clear why this is true in spite of the specific limitations of the seignorial type, and for this purpose we cannot do better than set it in direct contrast with the ideal which was erected by Jesus. Why was it that Jesus exalted the weary and the heavy-laden, the unimportant and the silent in the land? *Because he had in mind only the introvert:* he had to do this, for his kingdom was not of this world. The introvert is actually adapted to external life only in the form of humility; his structure being what it is, he cannot conquer life. But for that very same reason he must not set the tone for this world. He may do it for the beyond—*à chacun son tour*—but in this world he is subordinate to the one who radiates life out of himself. The type of the latter alone can give body to the highest conception of man.

That the *grand seigneur* actually does this is demonstrated by the particular approach of his type to that of the sage. The sage sees the world just as the *grand seigneur* sees it. But the latter has the advantage that he can see it thus without any special talent. A few examples of the agreement between judgments of values as rendered from the viewpoint of absolute truth and from the viewpoint of the typical *grand seigneur:* Schopenhauer abused Hegel, naturally, for "objective reasons"; in this sort of thing the *grand seigneur* sees nothing but the quarrels of prima donnas; in reality there never is, nor can

there ever be, an objective reason for insulting anybody personally; the concept of "objective pathos," which is invoked
for the purpose of justifying this situation, is always evidence
of the most contemptible meanness of soul. Just as little can
deeper reasons ever be found when one man tries to dispute
another's metaphysical substance. There is, of course, a hierarchy of spirits; this is based on the degree to which the man
is personally and consciously rooted in his metaphysical being,
as well as on the degree of his power of expression. But substance, "in and for itself," stands back of every man; "in and
for itself" no root-quality, and no form in which it manifests
itself, is superior to any other, for every variety and form is
dependent on external circumstances; one can achieve the same
depth being centred in will, or spirit, or intellect, or power, or
contemplation, whether one is turned inward or outward. This
is known instinctively to every true *grand seigneur*. Furthermore: in the struggle for power he is as relentless as any one
can be; under certain circumstances he admittedly desires the
death of his foe. But if any man lacks the courage of a clear
will to kill, and yet makes an attack, he becomes the object of
the *grand seigneur's* contempt, if his criticism is not made in a
fundamentally positive connection, i.e. if he does not compen-
sate for the negative things which he has to say by a correspondingly strong emphasis on the positive. If an opponent does not
see the positive side, or if he ignores it, the *grand seigneur*
takes it as self-evident that the cause lies in ill-will; respect for
one's enemy is the first law of chivalry. On the other hand, the
grand seigneur is incapable of overrating anybody, in the
fashion current among people of small calibre. No man is more
than a man; he judges even the greatest on the plane of the all-
human. Oh, there are many more things which he knows out of
the wisdom of his blood! Even without psychoanalytic training he knows that any man who exalts another to divinity, and
is all the more impertinent to others, only means himself. He
knows that it comes to the same thing whether one is derided as

a charlatan or deified as a classic; in either case the actual intention is to reduce the phenomenon to unreality. He knows that whenever a man is universally and unanimously acclaimed, it only means that those who acclaim him do not really consider him superior to themselves—which explains why they can bring themselves to deify him. He believes that it is only among demonstrably great men—not merely great minds—that personal motives are not the ultimate deciding factors. . . .

But these examples must suffice. What is the source of the *grand seigneur's* sense of justice? It is the expression of his primal consciousness of uniqueness. This consciousness develops, if the hereditary strain is at all good, from his mere position itself. Of course the *grand seigneur* is quite naturally unassuming in the true sense of the phrase; that is to say, he does not assume that he is other than he is, whether he be great or small. It never occurs to him to compare himself with some one else; he therefore can and must give each one his due on his particular level; he is psychologically incapable of envy. For he knows that no one can take away from him his one true essence, his uniqueness; he knows that under all circumstances this lies beyond the reach of comparisons. Thus it is that the *grand seigneur*, whenever he comes to power, is by his nature bound to see all things in their right relation to each other, and can therefore master them and direct them to good ends. And if he lacks external power, no external events can affect him inwardly. It is true that he must do many things that small people do: he, too, must fight, judge, even destroy. But then he does all this on the basis of a superpersonal equilibrium. In the words of a man whose hardness was often misunderstood: *Je ne connais ni le ressentiment, ni la vengeance, mais je connais l'exécution capitale.*

What I have pictured here really answers to the ideal likeness of the sage, i.e. of the man in whom the metaphysical core guides and determines all his external life: the cardinal point is that this likeness seems to be realizable as a type only in the body of the distinct species of the *grand seigneur*. It is only in this formation that the emphasis is laid primarily on uniqueness, and only within its dimensions that all values, without exception, find their place. Any one who makes comparisons at all, who sees values at all in relation to others, as Christianity already knew, is incapable either of seizing or of realizing these values.* Of course there is such a thing as achieving superiority in the form of lowliness. But this, as we have seen, cannot present itself as earthly power, and can quite certainly not be cultivated. It may really be that, as Christian doctrine teaches, the All-Highest finds in the semblance of earthly slavery His most expressive manifestation—perhaps the pure spirit postulates a state of tension with external powerlessness, for all power is of this earth; but however this be, human greatness as a tradition within the framework of the earthly order of things has never existed save upon the heights of life, and until the end of all time will continue to exist only there. Confined to cramped conditions of life, nature is crippled; that fact cannot be changed. Superiority presupposes self-assurance, and only the most sovereign soul can achieve self-assurance without external buttresses. This, then, is the place to demolish that most stupid prejudice of the ignorant; namely, that the aristocrat is essentially heteronomous because his function is to represent. Everybody, the very great exception excluded, must have some sort of framework in order to hold firm. But no one needs as little external support as the aristocrat. If it be demanded of him that he keep up appearances, the thing to be emphasized is not the judgment of others: what should be emphasized is the fact that he should, under all circumstances, direct his life from within, that he should, under all circumstances, guard his bearing, his *tenue*—conditioned as that is, purely from within—out

---

* Cf. the development of this idea in *Wiedergeburt*. A particular aspect of this circumstance which has especial value as a supplement to the above is treated in the essay *Von der wahren Selbstachtung* in Section 14 of my *Weg zur Vollendung*.

of self-respect. What matters is not simply the recognition, as such, of norms (every ideal, once objectified, is to that extent a matter of externals); it depends on the question of *which* norms apply. In itself the discipline of the code of honour means nothing more and nothing else than the discipline of the soldier or of the religious ascetic. The *grand seigneur* is actually the one type of man with whom it suffices simply *to be*, who needs no proof of the value of his uniqueness. It is for this very reason that he himself acknowledges as a matter of course the rights of others to be what they are.

Under these circumstances, has it any meaning to resent the fact that certain classes exist, or rather, existed—for as far ahead as we can see, they are everywhere, with the exception of Hungary, dying out—within which the highest type was bred out? Is it not much rather a happy circumstance that such a thing should exist at all, as a polarizing example for others? Assuredly the ideal would be to lift *every one* to the level on which only the privileged aristocrat has stood. If the world some day becomes so rich, and so happily organized, that favourable living conditions can be provided for every one, it is certain that a large part of the meanness which now reigns will be wiped out; with regard to this point, historic materialism is in the right. But a time will never come when every one will have the seignorial mentality, and that for two reasons. In the first place, this mentality depends to a large extent on the hereditary blood-stream; and because of the self-sacrifice and attrition of the noblest, there is, unfortunately, an enormous preponderance of bad over good blood. But then man is a creature of differentiations. Since it is only as a function of the unresolved tensions of his soul that he can be a living personality, a *cosmos humanitatis* is thinkable only in the contrapuntal balance of mutually complementary types. A man, whatever he is, can be this or that only if others are something different. Wherever this law is ignored, retrogression sets in. This may be seen in the ghastly standardization which the democratic ideal is producing over the whole world; humanity is really becoming more and more "a manufactured product," as Schopenhauer called the average man. But above all there must be differences for two reasons: first, be it a question of leaders or of other specific types of being, only the existence of these differences creates the tensions which give rise to differentiations of quality. And then because a recognition of differences which is free of envy is the first premise of a higher type of man, for that recognition alone is capable of creating an authentic consciousness of uniqueness. It is in fact a basic misunderstanding to make equality the foundation of a system; it is only *uniqueness* which provides an intelligible foundation.*

Now every unique individuality belongs to a type, so that there is indeed some meaning in fusing it with the representatives of that type. This explains the inner truth of the mediaeval hierarchy based on differences of occupation and position in life. It is the only sensible system, but it must be so elastic that considerations of heredity and of origin shall not carry more than a reasonable weight. It seems to me that these brief reflections should suffice to justify the existence of a special aristocratic order. It is only where "lords," ruling types in contradistinction to others, are given the opportunity to develop, that we have any ruling types at all. Accordingly all great periods were periods in which the *grand seigneur* was the determinant factor. Nor did any great age ever resent the fact that the *grand seigneur* frankly outshone every one else. Today, true enough, matters are otherwise. Alfred Fabre-Luce has written so pregnantly on this subject that I cannot do better than reproduce him here: *Dans les sociétés démocratiques, tout l'art des ambitieux est de créer d'abord les sentiments populaires qu'ils seront en suite obligés de suivre. Ils doivent appliquer leur volonté à la dissimuler; nier leurs grands desseins, même quand ils se réalisent, car la franchise romprait cette*

* Cf. the development of this idea in the essay *Vom falschen Gemeinschaftsideal* in Section XIV of my *Weg zur Vollendung.*

vague unanimité qui est la condition de leur réussite; chercher plûtot à favoriser, dans l'interprétation de l'histoire par la nation, les contresens, féconds générateurs de haine et de docilité patriotique. Ils doivent sembler n'avoir pas les intentions des grandes choses qu'ils font. Ainsi toutes leurs actions se trouvent dégradés d'hypocrisie. Today, if any man wishes to exercise power, let him for heaven's sake avoid any legal title to it; the man who wishes to govern with dictatorial powers may, at the utmost, style himself General Secretary. Best of all, let him deny completely the significance of personality, as Lenin did. In this denial the latter was, by the way, undoubtedly quite honest. In general the contrary applies. The more a man ignores in his statements such things as influence and effect, the more certainly may be deduced, in his case, a hypertrophy of the will to power.

L ET us now turn to the objection which is most frequently brought forward against the type of the *grand seigneur,* and this will lead us back to the special case of Hungary: that is, the objection relating to its element of playfulness; this is supposed to indicate a lack of seriousness. There is a German-Hungarian proverb which sets us on the right track:

> Every man can be intelligent,
> Reason is the privilege of the hussar and the nobleman,
> But wit belongs exclusively to the magnate and the higher clergy.

What is actually meant here by "wit," as an essential trait, is lightness of touch. This, precisely, is the one certain exponent of inner superiority in the same sense as gracefulness alone shows a complete mastery of the laws of gravity. I am sometimes irritated to tears to hear certain men, intellects who otherwise do deserve to be taken seriously, speak in this wise: "What I say here is not lightly said, I have wrestled with this problem"; or when others rate a work high because it shows evidence of hard work. An outlook of this kind proves absolute inferiority, if only from the point of view of the mere ethos of work; as Pater said, only work can efface the footsteps of work. But it proves inferiority chiefly because it elevates the labour of the navvy above achieved mastery. The man to whom things come hard is under all circumstances and in all respects inferior to him who snatches at them lightly; when critics reproach a free spirit with having mastered the results of painstaking research as if he were playing a game, it amounts to the same thing as if they were to reproach Bismarck with having created the German Reich with a few playful gestures while his poor cook had to perspire in the kitchen in order to keep him in good health. In exactly the same way, and quite as unconditionally, are deadly earnestness and humourlessness evidences of inferiority. Dean Inge is surely right when, speaking of God, he takes it as a first premise that He must have a keen sense of humour. But the humour in question does not happen to be of the English variety, which is a middle-class virtue (in this kind of humour a man acquiesces in what annoys him on its own plane, but transposes this acquiescence into cheerfulness; its foundation is therefore essentially social); it means instead the divine laughter of the man who is inwardly superior to all those things which men take, among themselves, with such fearsome seriousness. That which is understood under the word "wit" in the Hungarian proverb is actually an echo of that divine laughter. An example of the descent from the divine to the human has been furnished by Pope Leo XIII., who, having to deal with a certain member of the higher Catholic aristocracy, an *enfant terrible* who insisted on thinking everything out for himself, in his own head, took the latter aside and whispered to him in German: "You make as if you were dead, and then I'll make as if I were a saint." If the heavy-footed, respectable middle class could only understand how lightly all really serious decisions come to truly superior persons! It is not only on occasions that the really serious man has the heartiest laughter; it is a primary law with him that he finds it utterly impossible to exhibit to others that which has the deepest significance for him. At the right time, he does show it externally, but in as impersonal a connection as possible; and where necessary he exerts his personality, too, in this form. But never does he take either himself, or the question in hand, as seriously as do the seemingly profound, those who peddle their profundity. That which is deep must remain in the depths, and produce its effects out of the depths, if it is to remain deep; in this way most so-called deep speeches and deep books of spiritual experience are not merely indecent but also flat; if that which is deep is brought up to the surface, it becomes superficial itself. That is why a certain *enjouement* was characteristic of every truly deep personality, even of Goethe, who in other respects was surely pedantic enough. Thus the external lightness of the French people is actually the exponent of its moral force, and the easy gliding of the English over what is most profound is the sign of the deep roots of their substance. Now for the aristo-crat, inward discipline and self-assurance are basic norms. It is just for this reason that, externally, he is playful. The fact that among the majority the negative side of this characteristic is much commoner than the positive is only a special expres-sion of the circumstance that unimportant people greatly out-number the important.

But the foregoing is not the only root of the trait which we have examined. Playfulness is the normal expression of a per-sonal assumption of risk, and in this—as I have demonstrated in *Wiedergeburt*—lies the true meaning of freedom; but in the case of the gambler the emphasis is wrongly placed; that is, it is laid on accident as a fact, and not on the mastery of acci-dent from within. Fundamentally, then, playfulness is nothing other than the sign of inner superiority to the world of fact. This, too, is why children play. And thus again, only the man who plays with death—an attitude which is demanded by the standards of the nobleman—stands in the right relation to its seriousness. I was for some time intimate with a certain occultist who, as far as truthfulness and sincerity can decide, really knew of a life after death, and who seemed to be quite at home in other, spiritual worlds. Over and over again he told me of the state of blessedness, of the difficulties of the path which lay beyond, the path which to every great spirit appears peculiarly hard. All that one needed to do, he said, was to accept sweetly the order of things as God ordained it; then everything would be easy. Finally I asked him: Is it impossible for you to understand that he who throws away his life out of sheer earthly courage and honesty can, under certain circumstances and for the same reasons, take upon himself spiritual death and the agony of the beyond? Is it not clear to you that to one of noble mind, considerations of happiness are of the least importance? Do you not see that *every* higher man has naturally taken upon himself that risk which you seek to belittle, that the very worth of humanity rests upon the possibility of being responsible for oneself? Actually every noble spirit is a Don Quixote to the extent that the personal, spiritual world means more to him than things as they are, more than all accepted norms. Finally, playfulness is a demonstration of superiority to the whole world of things. No *thing* should be taken seriously; that seriousness is reserved only for the living person; here, once more, the norm of the nobleman coincides with the norm of Christianity. The fundamental motto of the aristocrat is that everything depends on the *who* and not on the *what*—not even on good and evil, right and wrong, life and death as such. This, then, explains the duel; there should not be an objective decision who is right and who is wrong—where is the man whose decision would be valid?—but, once a conflict arises, let it be fought out, man to man, so that he who is in the right shall run the same risk as he who is in the wrong.

IT is out of the deepest conviction that I have sung the Song of Songs of the *grand seigneur*. And it is out of the deepest conviction that I do it, precisely in this book about Europe, in connection with Hungary. For everything that has ever made Europe great has its roots in the aristocratic spirit which today animates Hungary alone, as a people. The Hungarians came to us as conquerors, but all European peoples began as conquerors; the ethos of the conqueror is after all the ethos of the European. All honour to the ethos of work; the question whether some should work and others not does not exist for the future; there is nothing more to be said for exploitation. But the final triumph of the ethos of work by no means constitutes the ideal of the future. All work as such is subordinate; nothing essential has ever been brought about by work; all important decisions have lain beyond the borders of the mere possibilities of labour. No essentially creative spirit was ever essentially a worker. It is obvious that he, too, had to work—that is, once for all, a matter of destiny, just as the heart must keep on beating all the time; three quarters of all life must unavoidably consist of routine. But never, in the case of the creative spirit, has the emphasis lain on this. Indeed, he frequently works more than the sterile individual; but he does it as though he were not doing it. He knows that whenever work does not mean simply execution, it actually prevents the essential from working itself out. And even execution can disturb inspiration. Granted, leisure in the Greek and English sense can hardly become once more a general life-form; the background of possibilities for the free life has become too complicated for that. But on the other hand, such work as is necessary will call for less and less attention. In this fact, and not in the possibilities of greater and cheaper production, lie the blessings of mechanical invention. A higher humanity can develop only there where man feels himself the master and not the slave.

We may, thanks to the machine, reach a point, externally, where slavery altogether ceases to exist. But before the discovery of the machine the ethos of work could only be the ethos of the slave or of the oppressed. That is why it was the Jews who discovered that ethos. That is why, before modern times, it was only in theocracies that it was inwardly accepted by the general masses, as in Egypt and Peru. The modern glorification of work, at its loftiest in Germany—it is only in Germany that the definition of the man of intellect as an "intellectual worker" is current—fails to be a sign of decline only if it is regarded as a transitional phenomenon; it is leading the unfree—and this applies today to the vast majority of those whose grandparents breathed their last as faithful subjects—by slow transitional stages to a state of freedom. In the premodern world the possibility of freedom existed only for the born lord or for him who could attain to this position. That is why all cultures hitherto have been founded by conqueror peoples. In fact only he who is a lord can admit the right of others to be as they are; it is only he who can find it in himself to acknowledge quality as such; only he is unfettered by the compulsion of convention. Where all are oppressed there inevitably emerges the mentality of the ghetto, i.e. the triumph of the ideal of the sardine-box, where all are laid side by side in equality, or where, if it happens that one is laid on top of another, it means nothing. When all are free only in the sense in which the Swiss first were, and in the sense in which freedom reigns in most of our democracies, i.e. when all are offered the same opportunity to work their way up, it is inevitable that envy should be the ruling passion, that quality should be suppressed, and that what is barely normal should, of all things, occupy the highest place; under such circumstances even the great man receives recognition only to the extent that he is normal, much in the sense indicated by the official who, at the funeral of Alfred de Musset (it had to be just De Musset!) remarked pathetically: *Il fut non seulement grand poète, il fut un honnête homme.* A mentality of this kind, which denies all personality, all the more naturally looks to money as the decisive measure of worth. First of all, money is without quality; every one can have it—which cannot be said of moral quality

and culture. But above all, the labourer is accustomed to re-
ceiving wages; and he therefore measures the worth of the employer by his ability to pay. This brings us to the particular case
of America. In that land of the free, where all lordship is
denied, the wage-payer is intrusted as a matter of course with
absolute powers within his particular sphere—and that applies
even to matters of conviction. But, before all else, one thing
in America conclusively proves the absolute superiority of the
man who is *basically, fundamentally* free; in that new country,
which was first settled by poor refugees who, because they were
refugees, interpreted freedom to mean not lordship, but the absence of the fetters of overlords—in that new country, in spite
of the independence which every one otherwise enjoys, no
human type has arisen which is inwardly free. In that country
normalcy is becoming more and more the ideal; woe to him
who outgrows the average! There standardization plays the
same *rôle* as exclusive quality did in old Europe. The fact is
that the man who is inwardly un-free feels himself secure only
when he is like "every one else" and "every one else" is like
him. From this springs the conventionality of the American,
which outdoes the conventionality of the European a hundred-
fold. Well, the ideal is no doubt that every one should become
a lord. But the above-mentioned examples show how lengthy
this process must be. The unconscious in us is governed by our
remote ancestors. Thus Hendrick de Man has demonstrated, in
his *Psychologie des Sozialismus,* that it is precisely the socialist ideal—the *super-bourgeois* ideal—which is, throughout,
the exponent of psychological demands which originated in the
feudal age. One should not, therefore, talk about qualitative
progress if he bears in mind the liquidation of the aristocracy
by democracy. Democracy can *prepare* the world for a state
which shall be absolutely higher, by removing the external
basis of the slave mentality: but that state can be *attained* only
when, thanks to that democracy, all men shall belong to the

ruler type; that is, when all men shall have become the very thing from which democracy fancies it is leading mankind away. And that can only be achieved with the utmost slowness, for to attain this it is necessary—to put it paradoxically—that all should become privileged in the same sense as the aristocrat used to be. The more aristocratic a being is, the more special are the conditions of life which it needs; it is just the best man who cannot work himself up.

Little wonder, then, that all culture hitherto has been established by conqueror races. They alone could, on psychological grounds, be masters. It is quite true that the element of inadequacy in all cultures that have existed hitherto derives from this. The small man, or the man in the street, could never have become an ideal if he had not for a time been unworthily treated. To correct what is evil in this state of affairs is the positive task of this transitional period of belief in equality. Yet in the future, as in the past, it is the ruling races which will embody the ideal. Were it otherwise, it would have been impossible for the English, the laziest of leading European peoples—a nation which, one might say, was able to develop the characteristics of the ruler largely because it did not work— to have acquired the greatest attractive power. Yet the true ideal of humanity is not embodied in that fruit of compromise, the English gentleman; *that* is to be found only in the *grand seigneur*. This is the only type in whom the sense of uniqueness is a decisive force. He is the only one who, out of "the bestowing virtue," loves his neighbour for his own sake. He is the only one in whom the essential being dominates all external appearance. That is why the predominance of his ethos is the only safeguard for any true culture in any sense whatsoever. —Is it now clear why I have given so high a place to Hungary? It is the only country in Europe in which this thing of highest value is still the decisive element. It does not play that decisive *rôle* in an ideal embodiment; far from it. But that decisive *rôle* it does play. And since only visible ideals work creatively, it is of the highest importance for Europe that Hungary should be recognized at her true worth.

Now, finally, let us turn to the special problem of this country. I have treated it hitherto as a symbol, and I have indicated that the reality represents the ideal only to a certain limited degree. And after the foregoing I am even compelled to make further modifications, against my personal inclination, in order that the reader should not involuntarily misapply the fundamental principle to particular states of things. In the modern world feudal Hungary, with all her absolute advantages, does naturally represent a state of arrested development, and many things will have to change very greatly before the country can become what it is capable of becoming. Wherever a people does not recognize specific types as representative, or wherever their quality as representatives no longer corresponds to the spirit of the times, the position of representative always implies—and this is true even in the case of the highest personal or group value—a physiological retrogression; this may be taken either in the sense of petrification, the inability to understand any longer what is going on, or in the sense of degeneration. The most tragic instance of this kind is supplied by the Balt aristocracy, for this aristocracy believed that it represented the "land" when it represented it no more—the "land" in its historic sense is not the soil, but the human group which predominates upon it—and continued, up to the moment of its overthrow, to fight for ideals which were historically dead, and thus showed itself incapable of recognizing in time the new duties of the hour. The state of things is altogether different in Hungary, for there the aristocracy actually represents the land, the general population has the aristocratic outlook, and, furthermore, the political instinct is so powerful that even during the period of the revolution no errors were committed, in a general way, which could be fatal to the aristocracy as a whole. But in the new world the old aristocracies, as such, are no longer the born leaders. That is why their representative function no longer has, on the whole, the pathos of ultimate responsibility; accordingly, the purely playful element becomes increasingly preponderant in their inner disposition. The peculiar position of ruler which belongs to the Hungarian aristocracy, and which for the last time corresponded to the general situation in the seventeenth century, has, in accordance with this latter fact, retained its primitive spirit. Just as slavery does more harm to the slave-owner than even to the slave, so the mere fact that one is able, under certain circumstances, to administer a thrashing to a servant, can obstruct development toward that superiority which distinguishes the *grand seigneur* as the highest type even without any privileges. The soul of the Hungarian magnate, with all its high intellect and its magnificent temperament, is in this sense astoundingly primitive. And this primitiveness, as much as their lost feeling of ultimate responsibility, explains the extremes to which their gambling instincts run. There are times, even today, when these instincts go almost as far as those of the *Mahabharatam* age in India, when princes used to gamble away their wives. Precisely this explains the frequently fantastic quality of their politics—the fantastic leads to the phantasmagoric when its spirit-born imaginative faculty has not yet developed far enough to be able to fuse organically with reality. An extreme example of both is furnished by Michael Károlyi. As a politician he played *va banque,* taking the most unlikely chances. And he did this chiefly for the sake of a woman. The particular character of Hungarian legitimism is, for its part, born of the spirit of unreality. Again, the Magyars show the spirit of the old-fashioned and the outlived in their preservation of the duelling code, which reminds one of the *bretteur* period of Russia, and they show it equally in the fact that they are more parliamentarians than politicians; debate can be an end in itself only in countries where the system of things has been established once for all and where nothing of an essential character is under discussion. This explains the remarkable poverty hitherto of this highly gifted nation in the matter of important personalities; these do not develop; to such an extent does the inessential pass current as the essential that original creativeness either remains in obscurity or else is overwhelmed, so that it never becomes a determinant power in conformity with its best particular qualities.

But in spite of all these flaws it was proper for me, I repeat, to make Hungary the occasion for my remarks on the absolute value of the seignorial type. Let things be as they are today; the fact remains that within this thoroughly distinguished people the seignorial type can, by evolution, find renewal, and become seasonable. Here the state of arrested development does not, on the whole, signify liquidation, but rather historic youthfulness. The Hungarians are essentially an unexhausted people. All that they have behind them, up to this point, is probably their early middle age. Were the *bourgeois* age to continue in the ascendant in Hungary, there would be reason to fear that the country would long have to remain in the shadow. But now that age has passed. In all ranks, and by no means last in those of the proletariat, there is a longing for a new aristocratic ideal. Hence the possibility that the Magyars, like the Russians and Italians, but along different paths, may overleap several stages and find themselves on a higher plane than they have ever known before. Their geographic-political situation is a consideration of some importance. They are superior to all their neighbours. They are just as much rooted in earth and as stolid as any of them, and no less shrewd. To this must be added the fact that they carry in their blood a tradition of parliamentarism, that is, a modern political experience, which is even older than that of the British. They are a politically mature people; such ripeness is possible at all stages, for were it not so, there would never have been any politically mature nations before the moderns. Nothing, then, is more comprehensible than the fact that the Hungarian people should have been unanimous in regarding it as an insult when their lot was cast among the oppressed peoples; they *could* not take it otherwise—one might as well expect the English to take it otherwise under similar external circumstances. I have treated here only of the high aristocracy. But what applies to them applies fundamentally to all authentic Magyars. In all ranks the same spirit reigns, the same ideal; it is only for this reason that the high aristocracy is accorded its position. Thus, regarded from the point of view of internal politics, Hungary is seen to be in much the same condition as England was in the time of Robert Peel, and that is a disadvantage only if one look backward; if one look forward, this condition simply indicates that the country has not been used up. The Magyars are therefore *bound* to rise again. And they are doing it even today, with gigantic strides. As far as external politics are concerned, the advance must certainly be slow. It is a small people, bound hand and foot by the oppressive treaties imposed on it. But how swift is the inner advance! During the last year I was a frequent visitor in Budapest; with every visit I felt streaming toward me a stronger, more vital atmosphere. Thus I cannot doubt that in the not remote future Hungary will play a more important *rôle* in the Middle East than it has ever played before.

THIS, then, would be the right place for some remarks on the matter of blood. As I see it, the superiority of the Magyars is due to a large extent to their admixture of Turanian blood. Throughout all history, the Turanians have shown themselves the race which brings forth the greatest ruler types. The Aryans, who can compete with any stock in the matter of blood-thirstiness and destructiveness, have never produced anything like the tremendous types of Attila, Genghis Khan, or Tamburlaine. And whenever Turanian blood has mingled with the blood of any other high-bred race, there have emerged individual personalities of unique superiority. The West has never brought forth a man to compare with Akbar, that cross between the blood of the Timurs and the Rajputs. Whenever a human type of mighty will has been revealed, one might say almost without exception that its character bore the trace, however remote, of the Mongolian blood-stream; this applies, in most recent times, not only to Lenin, but to Clémenceau too. It is much the same, in this respect, with peoples as with individuals. Wherever there was a successful infusion of Turanian blood, there emerged races of nobility and beauty. The Turks who came first to Asia Minor resembled the Kalmucks of to-day; the Byzantines could not find epithets enough to describe their repulsiveness. But for a long time the real Turks have been not only one of the most distinguished, but one of the handsomest peoples. The same applies to the Magyars in comparison with those who first descended on the Puszta. But the particular virtue of Turanian blood exhibits itself primarily in strength of character. If the Russians are a great people, they must thank for it, not their Slav part, but the Mongolian blood which they have absorbed to a degree which surpasses, in quality as well as in quantity, all the other Slav stocks; thus was created that splendid tension between soft soulfulness and hard masterfulness which has lifted the Russian to so high a level. It is a similar power which distinguishes the Magyars from all the peoples with whom they have lived for centuries, the peoples whose borders they touch and with whom they have mingled; in the case of Turanian blood it seems that the slightest admixture suffices to transmit its fundamental advantages; the Hungarian magnates have always intermarried with Austrians and Germans, and yet have remained wholly different in their strength; as for the Turks, they have always taken wives from anywhere they chose, and have nevertheless remained a pure ruling race.

There is no doubt that, on the other hand, the negative side of the Hungarian character can also be traced to Turanian blood. Not only is their love of splendour often Oriental in the worst sense; not only is their vanity Oriental in the unpleasant sense of the word—for some reason or other, this vanity grows with every step one takes from Central Europe toward the Bosphorus; so much so, that the old Turkish code of courtesy forbade a person even to think, in the presence of another, of anything which might displease the latter, and every Greek waiter exhibits the self-consciousness of an Alcibiades: that undeveloped state of the soul which I have described above is surely explained, in part, by the fact that there is a certain inborn soullessness. When the German speaks of "soul" the Magyar instinctively interprets it as heart, or temperament, which is exactly what the German does not mean. All Turanians are matter-of-fact, unmetaphysical, thoroughly of this world. Throughout the entire course of their history they show themselves soulless not only to the extent that they are men of action and therefore to a very small extent men of spiritual experience; their natural disposition is one-sided in its warlikeness and masterfulness, which has this significance: they are men of fantasy and will, but of undeveloped feeling. Every human type is one-sided; he who is impelled to overrun countries and conquer peoples must, save in the exceptional case of the genius, lack that fund of sympathy which belongs to the emotionally gifted man of pathos. But even among the ruling races the matter-of-factness of the Turanian is something of a special kind; that is why it must find itself such a fierce Dionysian compensation. We shall arrive at the best definition by comparing the Magyars with the racially related Russians of Tartar origin and with the Turks and Esthonians. The Russian peasantry, with its admixture of Finnish and Mongolian blood, has no idealism in the Western sense of the word. In Russia it was only the aristocrat, whose blood was preponderantly Slav with a Germanic admixture, who was idealistic. But even Tolstoi was able to assert that a pair of boots was more important than all art. In Bolshevism today, it is a pure Turanian spirit which emerges; the world of Bolshevism dispenses with every emotional component, with all understanding of values which are not practical. The Turks were never great except as masters; in matters of the intellect and the soul they ranked below the conquered races. In the case of the Esthonians, this Turanian sobriety goes so far that other than practical questions are simply not understood; they have no ideals at all in the Western sense. We can now understand why the Turanians have always played the *rôle* of the carriers of the principle of evil (we have only to think of the sagas of Iran); they, more than any one else, really lack what passes, in our world, for soul. But, as I have shown in *Wiedergeburt*, the so-called evil principle is on the other hand a positive factor in the world's totality of relationships. It is nothing other than the principle of the Eternal Nay, of limitation, of change and renewal. If it is the principle of destruction, of death, it is at the same time the principle of rejuvenation, of rebirth; that is why all progress began with Cain; to that extent force, if it is to be exerted at all, can only be exerted in the spirit of evil. Thus, whatever the prejudices of the weak may be, the races which are by their nature "evil" are *ipso facto* the predestined ruling races. He that has not the courage to deny, to say No, bringing death thereby, cannot give form to things, for every affirmative has its correlative negative. We have thus been carried, beyond this digression which was to have justified the actual oppression of the Hungarians, to a justification of the position of advantage which they should in reality occupy. The Hungarians are born rulers. None of the neighbouring peoples, with the possible exception of the Serbs, are such. How should it be possible for the Hungarians not to be playing again, before long, an important political *rôle?* They resemble the Turks more than any one else in this respect, that they have a sure sense for immediate possibilities. Where necessary, they can be extremely opportunistic; that is, unless it is just their imagination which runs away with them.

It is, of course, improbable that they will produce anything of all-human importance in the realm of the mind and the soul. As far as I can see, it is only the formally juristic which is with them an original gift of the mind; and this also is characteristic of the ruler nature. And it is hardly likely that the soul of Hungary will ever attain the differentiations of the soul of the Slav. But no one is capable of everything; the ruling nature, too, has its defining limits. As against this, rulership is something absolutely positive. It is ridiculous for all the peoples of the world to desire to be equally capable in the same fields; in the best of cases they can only supplement each other.

THIS brings me back to the problem of the Hungarian aristocracy. If the Hungarians should succeed in overleaping entirely the *bourgeois* stage of development, if they should succeed in bringing to birth once more a type of determinant *grand seigneur*, on a modern basis, they could become the exemplars for the whole of cultivated Europe, to whatever extent the latter may have an aristocratic bias. They can achieve this, as it happens, on the very grounds of their partial foreignness; a symbol of meditation must be composed of elements to which the mind is not accustomed if it is to capture the attention and interest of the unconscious. Whether it will come to pass in this fashion, I naturally cannot tell. A number of circumstances make it possible that the opportunity will be missed; the Magyar nation is both small and in imminent danger, the gulf between the magnate and the peasant is still much too wide, and the guardians of intelligence, the middle class, have fallen, as a result of the peace treaties, into an even more ruinous state than the middle classes of other countries. But if it can be born anywhere at all, that class of *grands seigneurs* which was the ruling and determining element wherever the noble outlook prevailed in Europe, will be born again in Hungary. For let us repeat: democracy, if it is not to destroy all value, can only amount to a passing phase for Europe—a phase which derives whatever meaning it has from the fact that it is laying a broader basis for aristocracy. It is ridiculous to see in the aristocratic view today a reactionary outlook; on the contrary, this view represents the only progressive outlook. It is quite impossible to define progress or retrogression without taking into consideration the time factor. When the old class-system had outlived itself, democracy represented the element of progress. Since the World War it has become a reactionary element, for from now on, only the rule of quality can save Europe; the idea of quantity has exhausted its *rôle*. There was a time when, in my own country, I passed for a "Red." During the Wilhelm period I was, as far as Germany was concerned, an extreme democrat. But, lingering in Berlin after the outbreak of the German revolution, I saw one acquaintance after another change his traditionalism overnight for socialism, and when I was asked where I stood, my answer was: From now on I stand for aristocracy. Naturally Germany must and will be democratic first, during a certain period, for in many good respects which can be advanced by democratic institutions, the country is still in a backward stage. But as far as principle is concerned, the problem may be regarded as solved. Precisely because of the triumph of democracy which has been sealed by the Versailles Treaty, it follows from the law of historic counterpoint that all future progress can come only through the idea of aristocracy.

SWITZERLAND

No other people, so far as I know, offers such an example of intimate tragedy as does the Swiss. The tragedies of the intimate are more oppressive than any which unfold in the open, for in the case of the former there is not that positive compensation to reality which is found in imagined experience, one's own and that of others, and in the appeal to emotions of sympathy and wonder. And such tragedies produce their worst effects when those who suffer them are not conscious of them and even feel happy in their lot. For then the clash between imagination and reality inevitably leads, by reason of psychological law, to the emergence of objective facts which are all the more disagreeable. This is the reason for most of the psychic, no less than the physical, deformities exhibited by the oppressed; the contented among these are not the finest type, but on the contrary the worst, for positive hate can become positive love, whereas resignation to a servile condition never bears within itself the seed of possible liberation. The Swiss are, indeed, not an oppressed people. They belong much rather to those inhabitants of Europe who were the first to achieve self-determination. But what is both characteristic and tragic is the fact that, thanks to a specific complex of circumstances, the thing which is good "in and for itself" has produced upon the greater part of the people—or at least upon the most visible part of it—the effect of oppression. A right understanding of the condition of the Swiss is therefore of importance for all; granted the progressive pacification of Europe, it is possible for all European peoples to fall into the same condition as the Swiss.

First, as regards natural features: as a permanent environment this magnificent mountain country is, to all appearances, not favourable to man. In the period following the year 1918, when everybody saw in Switzerland the model of the Europe of the future, I was, for my part, engaged in a study of the

historian Johannes Müller; and when I congratulated a famous
Swiss scholar on the fact that his country had demonstrated a
devotion to reason so much earlier than the others, he retorted,
with that grim smile of the Swiss: "You seem to forget our
endemic cretinism." There is no doubt that nature must be
blamed for much. It is not only the famous goitre; the extraordinary absence of good looks in this people must certainly be
traced to a large degree to nature's influence. Nature, too, has
certainly played a part in the production of the Schwyzer
Dütsch dialect. Many non-German dialects may have been
spoken on Swiss soil in the course of the last few thousand
years—the tone and accent were assuredly already there in the
time of the lake-dwellers. And they are terrible. Why ugliness
should be characteristic of this particular mountain people, instead of beauty—as in the case of the races of the Caucasus—
is something which, on the surface, cannot be explained. Probably the primal complex of things is the same here as among
the Tibetans and the other hill tribes at the foot of the Hima-
layas. As we descend to the plains, the characteristics of the
Swiss hill stocks fade out; but the impossibly broad back,
caricatured in the uniform of the Confederate gendarmerie,
the visage, now stony, now gnarled and knobby, the stiff cater-
pillar-walk, the general absence of grace—these, too, proclaim
unmistakably a physiological relationship to the landscape. The
authentic mountain Swiss, who form the core of the race, have
in them something of the gnome and the troglodyte. It is
surely the very oldest blood that flows in their veins, just as
Mime was racially older than Siegfried.

Wherever these people have persevered in the state which
was originally proper to them, they produce, as all races do
under similar circumstances, an effect not merely of authenticity,
but, in addition, of lovableness. The old Confederate spirit,
which I have so often felt in the mountain villages, that spirit
of independence, of inflexibility, of obstinate labour, of readi-

ness to help, of unpretentiousness, is a thing of absolute beauty. But, like every expression of life, it preserves its beauty only in the proper setting. I know a self-made man who, with all his commercial ruthlessness, was not only decent, but actually like-able—as long as he lived in a three-room apartment; no sooner did he own a whole house than he began to demoralize, and eventually became positively Satanic. Thus the Swiss world produces an impression of beauty only where the traditional spirit has conserved the frame which properly belongs to it. And that frame must be narrow, extremely narrow, like some mountain gorge.

But unfortunately, this authentic Switzerland has long since ceased to be the one which Europeans have occasion to observe, except on mountaineering trips. This real Switzerland, which lives on in the heart of all good Swiss, and which, I repeat, belongs, in its proper framework, to the most lovable things in Europe, now plays scarcely any *rôle* in the Switzerland which concerns that continent. Of European significance are only Zü-rich, Geneva, the Swiss institutions, Swiss neutrality, and the humanity which bespeaks the spirit of these things—all matters which, from the national point of view, are not essentially Swiss. Today the significance of the Swiss does not reside in their history or in their special national character; its resides only in the extent to which *new* "Swiss" can arise. This might actually happen; just as the Jews are, on the one hand, as-suredly a race, but above all a social type which under similar circumstances would again reproduce itself, so the Swiss of today are primarily a psychological type. This alone suffices to explain why even those who settled in Switzerland in their childhood can become as authentically Swiss as Europe feels that race to be, just as immigrants to America become Ameri-cans. A hundred years ago, and less, this was not so. Today it is. It is under this psychological aspect, and under it alone, that I wish to draw a picture of present day Switzerland as I see it.

I COMPARE the Swiss of today, as they appear from a distance and as they possess significance for the modern world, with the Jews. Actually both peoples are characterized by the fact that they are what they are less because of race and physical environment than because of the psychic circumstances which surround them. In the case of the Jews these circumstances are on the one hand internal, and, on the other, external. The inner effect is produced by the claim to be the Chosen People. The Jews have withstood the terrific pressure and the incredibly unfavourable conditions to which they have been largely exposed almost throughout their entire history, because their religion demanded and sustained an inner adjustment which made it the first principle of their national being that they remain true to themselves and endure in spite of all. Thus they have guarded their law ever since the time of Moses, and the spiritual tension which this called for is the real *raison d'être* of their tremendous life-force. In this particular case the spirit is even the foundation of their racial particularity; the East European Jews were only partly Semitic, and even apart from the influence of environment, intermarriage was frequent enough from the beginning to destroy the national characteristics, had not the spirit been there to prevent this. Externally, again, the psychological influence of the parasitic position of the Jews among the other nations has worked, in a like sense, toward the production of a specific type. Thus one may really say that the Jews are primarily a psychically conditioned people. This is exactly why they so easily degenerate, not only morally but even physically, as soon as they cease to be true to their Law or find themselves in a position to which they are not adapted. As the most conservative of all peoples, the truest to law, they are bound to decay as soon as they cease to be Jews in the strict sense. Turned into a type by thousands of years of persecution, they resemble those chemical bodies which can only be produced under high atmospheric pressure; once the pressure is lifted, they lose their special capacities and disappear.

In the case of the Swiss, the forces which have built up the type lie wholly outside themselves, since they do not possess any great idea which they represent. For the freedom and the constitution of the Swiss can scarcely be compared with the significance of the Old Testament, that Magna Charta of ethos on earth. At this point, then, enters that element of intimate tragedy which I mentioned at the outset. The rest of the world does not see in the Jews a chosen people, but the Jews are inwardly adjusted to this. It is only the rare romantic among them who would ascribe to Jewry a great national *rôle* among the other nations of the world. The Jews are, for the other nations, more or less beneficial parasites; either they further the interchange of material, as middlemen, or else they destroy. The Swiss are not at all suited to their actual position. Not only do they feel, both for the past and for the future, that they are important as a land and a people, in the same sense as the Germans, the English, and the French; not only do they honestly cling to the belief—in a manner which is really pathetic—that, both for the past and the future, the old traditional confederacy idea stands above everything else; they consider Switzerland, both as nation and idea, an exemplar. But in the eyes of every one else in the world they exist only as a host people and a host country in the broadest sense, just as the Jews are considered middlemen. The real European significance of their country lies in the fact that it can serve as the ideal neutral meeting-ground. And it cannot be otherwise. The fact that the Swiss live at all visibly for others greater than themselves not only serves to misplace the emphasis of significance for the former; it produces a distorted situation which in the long run has a deforming effect, just as the discrepancy between the self-consciousness of the Jews and that of their host peoples has developed ugly characteristics in the former. The Swiss national character calls for so narrow a framework that every extension of it, even every departure from it, destroys the positive element in the original form. That which is good in the Swiss

world is inextricably bound up with the soil. Thus the Swiss
who has in one way or another torn himself loose inevitably
produces an unpleasant effect; what is good for a mountain
guide is no longer good for a minister to Paris. If the Swiss
often succeed in achieving a European reputation not only as
hotel managers, pastors, and doctors, but also as presidents,
world secretaries, auditors and arbitrators, this is due to the
fact that in the case of these offices we have to do with specific
functions for which a certain stock may "by accident" be peculiarly suited. Thus the Swiss also provide the largest percentage
of born attendants and debaters at international congresses. But
here I must immediately modify what I have said above with
regard to Swiss lack of adaptation: the best Swiss (I use the
word always in its European, not its Helvetian connotation),
who are the best because they have been set longest in their
type—the Swiss, that is, who are hosts or inn-keepers in the
widest sense—the pastors, the doctors—know that their modern
rôle derives from their office, and not from their national connection; that the latter is, as it were, a private matter of theirs.
They are, correspondingly, men of inner freedom; they are unquestionably a valuable component of the European commonwealth. I include Hans Badrutt, for instance, of the Palace
Hotel in St. Moritz, among the important personalities of our
time. In the same way many Swiss doctors and many clerics of
international reputation are Europeans in the best sense. They
assuredly do not represent an aristocratic ideal, and since the
latter is higher in the absolute sense, they can be of equal spiritual rank with good Europeans of other countries only when
the specifically Swiss element seems to have been overcome; but
they are just as good as the best native (not Europeanized)
Americans, whose type is also that of the peasant and provincial. We might also mention in this connection those Swiss who
live themselves out in social welfare work, that is, in the spirit
of the Red Cross, were it not for the fact that, just as among
members of orders, this has to do with a special vocation, which

may be found among all peoples, and not more among the
Swiss than among others. But in contradistinction to the Jews,
psychological adaptation is unfortunately completely lacking in
the majority. This, then, is the reason why the Swiss, as a national type, have no position at all among the other nations—
again I mean *not* the native villager, but the Swiss who is known
outside the country, who has entered into larger relationships;
he bears the responsibility for all, exactly in the same sense as
every people, as such, must quite naturally pay for the short-
comings of its government in case of defeat. If this does not
accord with public opinion as a whole, we may ascribe it to the
fact that there is hardly one representative European to whom
it ever occurs to consort with Swiss, while they, in turn, are instinctively reticent; they feel that their style of life lacks every
attractive force. Yet there is hardly a single foreigner who does
not recognize that the public institutions of the Swiss are excellent, if not positively exemplary, and who is not happy to spend
a holiday or to take a cure in that beautiful country. How, then,
would it be possible for the discrepancy between what they are
in their own eyes and what they are in the eyes of others—
particularly when the latter remains unknown to them—not
to lead to the most unfortunate repressions?

Now the most significant and also the most tragic fact is
that in the new world in the making, this discrepancy must
inevitably be intensified. Among the best of the Swiss youth
there is a movement toward the renaissance of the authentic
Helvetian spirit. But in the far-reaching relationships of today, how can that spirit continue to live, or even be awakened
to new life? If a people has once fitted itself in a certain
specific fashion into the surrounding world, and if the surrounding world is mightier than the people itself, the same thing
must happen as in the case of the individual; it adapts itself not
only outwardly, but inwardly, too. That the spirit of the time
of the oath on the Rütli, or even the spirit of Gottfried Keller's
Fähnlein der Sieben Aufrechten, should continue to assert its

sovereignty except within the most intimate circles, is utterly out of the question; before long the national celebrations in honour of this spirit will have as little meaning as the memories of the legendary era. In the new world the Swiss will have to become more and more a purely host people; that is, if they desire to maintain their independence; the foreigner industry in its widest sense does happen to be their divinely appointed vocation; whatever else they may do in addition is in the large sense meaningless. That little country which, thanks to specific circumstances, has carried over into the modern world a mediaeval free state, cannot, in an inwardly interrelated Europe, mean anything more than any other particularly well-administered city. It will probably mean even less, for, as the international meeting-ground which it happens to be, it will experience increasing difficulty in developing a spirit which shall be really its own, a spirit, that is, which shall be native and original. For to repeat: in a wider complex of relationships the spirit of the time of the oath on the Rütli is not exportable. Furthermore, the larger world is absolutely superior to the narrow in suggestive power; there has never been a case where a village has transmitted its spirit to a metropolis. For instance, what other destiny can unfold for Geneva than to become the one gigantic central bureau for international organizations and international employment agencies? How can the unceasing expansion and internationalization of Zürich help leading to the break-up of the old traditional Swiss way of life? How can that which takes place within the little cantons have any international significance? The original national type of the Swiss will have to yield, functionally, in an ever-increasing degree; first of all, the new situation will inevitably increase the influx of foreign blood—it is already large—and naturally more and more of those foreigners who find the Swiss position and mentality congenial to their natures will become naturalized. And, typically, these foreigners are no longer heroes of freedom. Naturally the Swiss peasant, the Swiss cowherd, the Swiss mountain guide, will remain what they were. The peasant never changes. But not he will be the one to determine the spirit of future history.

It was in a not dissimilar fashion, I repeat, that the Jewish type arose. And if we recall that the Jew, too, has predominantly unpleasant characteristics, we can understand why the same applies in such a high degree to the Swiss. There is an extraordinary resentment among them directed against all those who have a greater degree of inward freedom than they. But in this case it is, unless I am very much mistaken, even greater than the well-known resentment of the Jews; it is bound to be greater, for in the case of the Swiss, external pressure has hitherto failed altogether to produce a corresponding inner adaptation. Thus, in the collapse of the old world, the victorious French suffer more from the breakdown of the old world than the defeated Germans do. In the case of the Jews the recollection of ancient glories is after all mere romanticism; they are too long past, and at that, the national glory never did amount to much. Orthodox doctrine even teaches plainly that God chose the Jews because of their badness, in order to be able, by means of that badness, to manifest the needed tension of infinity between God and man. The Swiss can really look back upon a great history. They actually were among the very first to realize the political and social ideals of modern mankind. The very fact that for more than six hundred years they have maintained themselves against overwhelming odds on every side merits the admiration of the world. Furthermore, they are today better balanced not only politically and socially, but also morally (using that word in the sense of the French *le moral*) than many other peoples. And yet they feel that they do not, and can not, play a *rôle* of any importance at all in the modern world. They feel this—but they cannot understand it.

L ET us now examine the position of the Swiss from a higher point of vantage, and let us take as our basis the spiritual condition not of the Swiss peasant, but of those Swiss who feel themselves European leaders. There is an extraordinary number possessing this feeling; in fact it is common to all of those who attract attention outside of the country. This applies first of all to the majority of Swiss journalists. The unpleasant aspects of the state of the Swiss also prove once again that a movement which has once triumphed is thereby liquidated. This continuous beating of the drums of freedom when the ideal has become common public property sounds, in the ears of others, like the cackling of the geese of the Capitol. The history of culture does not follow a straight line, but moves in cycles. It follows from this that a straight line can have a meaning-content only in two cases; first, when it is drawn on a plane above organic evolution; second, when it lies within a given cycle; and even then it possesses meaning only for certain stretches of its length. As soon as a new cycle has set in, the principle of progress no longer resides in the old which has survived, be it ever so perfect, but in the new, be it ever so barbarous. Thus, at the close of the period of antiquity, progress lay not with the Alexandrians, but with the Germanic peoples. This is the reason why all the understanding spirits of the West are rejecting in increasing measure the concept of progress which has been carried over from the last century. It was not always a false concept, but it possessed meaning only as long as it was the symbol of a rising life. As such a symbol it still serves most of the nations of the Orient, who can therefore use to advantage the very categories which are failing us. In the West this symbol no longer possesses meaning, because it no longer represents any principle of living growth. Within the meaning of the ideals of the nineteenth century the most progressive countries, next to the Swiss, are, as far as I can judge, New Zealand and Sweden, for it is in those countries that the largest numbers are guaranteed "the most progressive" life; in those countries, too, there reigns the most firm-set social morality. Yet in New Zealand, where social well-being has reached its highest point, there is no sign of further initiative; as far as the well-being of the inhabitants is concerned, there is nothing more to be desired. In Sweden the nation has attained such perfect inner balance on such a high level that the dynamic has been transformed into the static. In Switzerland material conditions may vary as they will; the fact remains that institutionally and morally the country is so completely saturated that for the inhabitants of the country the very idea of progress, in the large sense, beyond their present condition, is in direct contradiction to sense. They have remained inwardly stationary since the time of the Reformation; all events since then have failed to implicate their sympathies. Now the Swedes and New Zealanders are in the same happy state, able to go on living in their traditional way as far ahead as can be seen; they are "self-supporting," as we used to say in war-times. Thus, if they are hostile to change, they are so without resentment; their self-contentment is not an aggressive self-righteousness; they are Phaeacians and not Pharisees. Switzerland is not "self-supporting"; that country must depend on being the middleman, in every sense of the word; if she is to live, she must share in all the changes in the condition of the world. But she does this only outwardly, not inwardly. Thus, with all her belief in her exemplariness, she feels essentially uncertain of herself and of her value. Out of this, then, arises that world-famous Swiss self-righteousness.

This brings me to the element which seems, to every non-Swiss, to stand out as the chief characteristic of the Swiss who does not live in a narrow complex of relationships and who has not been reduced to type by the functions which we have examined. There are no worse Pharisees in this world than the propertied, the educated, and—in the first line—the literary Swiss. We need only read the lectures handed out in the Swiss newspapers, as from some lofty tribune, to the nations of the world; we need only hear them declare, as in a fiat, that Zürich, or Geneva, has no faith in the possibilities of Russia; or read how the Geneva papers reject, in the most arrogant fashion, the claims of despoiled minorities—but consider it very creditable in the latter that they have shown, by the tone of their memorandum, a deep regard for the judgment of Geneva. Now the Pharisee is the *one* man for whom there can be no advance. There cannot possibly be any advance or progress, because he is completely muscle-bound; in essence he is nothing more than a barbed-wire defensive system; he is thoroughly and completely a psychoanalytic case. A thoroughly ludicrous demonstration of this truth once came within my personal experience. Part of the material which appears above was already published, under the title *Fortschrittliche und rückständige Völker*, in the *Weg zur Vollendung* in 1926. Naturally no New Zealander, and certainly no Swede, took any of my observations in bad part. But the *Berner Bund, per contra*, reacted with such incredible coarseness, with such personal offensiveness, that I took advantage of the opportunity to conduct—while remaining personally impassive—an experiment in national psychology. Though I never, under any circumstances, respond to attacks, this time I wrote a thoroughly courteous reply. The letter was promptly printed, but with an even coarser commentary. I wrote again, even more courteously. The answer was coarser still. Thus it went back and forth for quite a while. The material which was brought together in this fashion is rich enough to permit me to regard the results of my experiment as conclusive. In the first place the *Bund* wrote from the outset as the protagonist of Switzerland, protesting that I had drawn general unfavourable conclusions from individual cases; the paper was, therefore, authorized to speak for the country. And then the tone of the reply most certainly appealed to its thousands of readers. Not a single Swiss came out openly against its procedure. Instead of this, the little provincial newspapers also set to, and produced even juicier specimens of journalism. But above all I have to thank this controversy for a whole flood of private letters, from the pens of Helvetians personally unknown to me, letters of a kind which no enemy of any other nationality has ever written me; the tone and the phraseology of these letters sufficed to overcome the last doubts as to the significance of the situation. I had to do with something wholly pathological, the abreaction of an extreme inferiority complex. But for any one trained in psychoanalysis, this pathological aspect can be wholly explained by the tragic position of the Swiss and by the failure of this position to find realization in their consciousness.

THIS would be the right place for a few observations on the national element in the Swiss. It is certain that this inward cramp would never find such external expression were it not for the fact that the Swiss are German. So German are they that national Switzerland can best be described as a caricature of Germanism. For it was the German Swiss who supplied Switzerland with this type; the French and Italian Swiss who joined the Confederation later are only Latins with a Swiss veneer. The World War and what followed demonstrated this. Nowhere does Léon Daudet find so large and so enthusiastic a public as in French Switzerland, and about Lausanne the quip is current: *Peut-être que Paris pardonnera un jour aux allemands; Lausanne—jamais.* The French Swiss are in essence French Protestants from a particularly narrow province who, in the fusion with the essentially German Swiss, have lost in fineness and grace, acquiring instead a goodly share of coarseness and pompousness; thus they produce today the impression of the very worst French *bourgeois*—the worst, because they are the most uncouth and the most obtrusive; they feel certain of themselves neither as French nor as Swiss. Switzerland is in every way a caricature of that Germany which will inevitably arise if the prevailing democratic order within, and the tutelage of the Great Powers without, should persist. For then Germany, too, will have to remain unconditionally neutral in order to keep alive. This neutrality will in turn bring with it an enormous material gain. And then the type of the "neutral" will become the determinant national factor. To recapitulate: the spirit of the cantons is the caricature of German particularism. The Swiss attachment to the land is the intensification of the general German feeling for the *Heimat;* in the case of Switzerland, attachment to the land means almost as much as citizenship meant in the ancient republics. Switzerland's perpetual neutrality is the extreme expression of the worst consequences of German objectivity, the complete triumph of the idea of equity over the idea of justice. The demand for equity does, indeed, always mean the negation of the idea of justice, for it premises equality of rights independently of merit. Where the idea of justice prevails, the man in whose hand the decision lies must have the courage to take sides; that is to say, he must side with what is qualitatively better. Should a conflict arise between a saint and a blackguard, it is consonant with "equity" that they should meet somewhere on a middle line, so that the interests of both should be safeguarded; the only just solution would be that the blackguard should be rendered harmless. From the point of view of equity, the highest function of an arbitrator or a judge is to find a compromise between two groups of facts, independently of their worth; his decision is not bound up with any risk, for every judgment which he utters can be motivated by "objective" considerations. Here the decisive element really is impartiality, but with it goes cowardice and, in the last analysis, meanness. What is becoming evident in Germany since the Treaty of Versailles—I will not say that it is constantly on the increase, but it is unfortunately very much in evidence—is, in the case of Switzerland, a firm-set national characteristic. And circumstances have brought to pass, in that country, an actual hypertrophy of impartiality in the worst sense. Switzerland has always had to steer a middle course between mighty powers; she *had* to do business in order to remain alive, whatever the situation might be. From this there inevitably ensued a complete lack of moral standards in all matters where they might endanger personal

or national interests. Neutrality, in and for itself, is actually
lack of moral standards. As the great ethicist Albert Schweitzer
recently stated with such refreshing emphasis, neutrality is, in
itself, unethical; a very thin line divides the neutral from the
profiteer. And if, examined from the point of view of unconscious motivation, this neutrality has its roots not in an inborn
talent for arbitration, but in the urge toward personal profit,
then it is bound to have a deforming effect which will inevitably
make itself increasingly felt from year to year. Naturally, in
the case of Switzerland, it is circumstance which is to blame.
But even the tapeworm can make that same plea. And if the
Swiss are so much the more upright in other respects, if they
show so much the more idealism where their interests permit
it, if they tend to objectivity and equity in the best sense—
e.g. in the matter of political refugees, prisoners of war, etc.—
it does not alter the fact that there is another side to the story;
the less so as all this is a good heritage out of a past which was
different, and that it therefore has little chance of surviving
in the new complex of circumstances. Here again we have a
demonstration of the fact that all Swiss virtues premise a
narrow framework of life. If, in a struggle between the cities,
the individual mountain village remained neutral, this could
not be made the subject of reproach, for the horizon of the
villager actually does not reach as far as the city; in his case
the deciding principle is the fact that, when necessary, he would
defend his native soil to the death. But even in earlier days,
things were already different with the patricians of Basle, of
Zürich, and of Berne, and they are altogether different in the
Switzerland of today, which, *quā* neutral, has almost achieved
the status of a great power; they are altogether different, too,
with the individual Swiss, whose psychological structure should
make it impossible for him to take the "respect" of others as an
ultimate motive. In a Swiss mountain village I recently read
the following inscription on one of the houses: *Der eine
betracht's, der andere acht's, der dritte veracht's, was macht's?*

—"The first looks at it, the second respects it, the third despises it—what of it?" In the case of the educated man, or the man of higher social position, an outlook so free from any idea of value means, quite simply, lack of moral standards.

But if German equity and objectivity find their caricature in Switzerland, the same is also true of German "personality" (in the sense of taking things all too personally), which everywhere is the compensation to predominant objectivity. In Germany, where everybody talks only of objective matters and objective values, it is in reality the personal motive—to a much greater degree than in France—which is the deciding factor; this is most evident in politics and in the feuds of scholars. In Switzerland the same things may be witnessed, grotesquely intensified. I quote an article, "Three Years of Switzerland," by Herbert Schäffler; I judge from the fact that the worthy *Berner Bund* printed the same in its columns, that its contents were not objectionable: "I have gone through a series of elections—elections of pastors in the press, elections of teachers in my so-called professional world. And as a democrat I have been terrified by the people. There was such talk of trickery, of dishonesty, petty jealousies, self-interest, that, quite unexpectedly, the entire picture was darkened for me. Suddenly the sovereign will of the people was transformed into the will of a bowling club, the will of a glee club, of a party committee, of a neighbourhood clique or a Freemasons' meeting. Even this would not have terrified me if I had not at different times felt that in the last analysis scarcely a word was ever uttered from the objective point of view. A number of Swiss with whom I discussed these matters supplied me with even more striking instances." And again:

"Another question emerges for the thoughtful observer in connection with post-war developments. The Swiss people is not strong in numbers. And it is being steadily drawn into a larger number of international enterprises and missions of all kinds. It is fusing itself, as no other people is doing, into the

world, with the organizational forms of the League of Nations (thus I became aware, through a scion of the Geneva
aristocracy whom I examined for his high-school graduation,
that there is in Geneva such a thing as a 'League' career,
which the young begin to prepare for in their middle high-
school years). If the course of development should continue
to follow this line, which is becoming more clearly defined
from year to year, then Switzerland will be transformed, to an
increasing degree, into the arbitration court for European
problems and even for world-problems. And at this point, one
who loves Switzerland must ask himself whether a very heavy
destiny is not being laid on shoulders which are perhaps not
broad enough. This question arose for me, for the first time,
on a winter evening some three years ago, when a certain Swiss
confided to me, innocent as I was, that the international possibilities were helping to solve the problem of the higher Helvetian Federal officials, who suffered from inadequate salaries
and, above all, from inadequate pension allowances. I was
somewhat bewildered by this view of international matters
which were of serious import to me, and decided that this
expression of opinion was purely personal. On other occasions,
however, the opinion I had here heard expressed was supple-
mented by statements to the effect that the director of such-
and-such an international bureau really had very little to do,
and that the work was really being carried on by the men
'lower down.' Now one may say, in all modesty, that the
world hardly regards the Hague, Geneva and Berne, and the
other international offices, as social welfare organizations. So
that the real question is this: Will Switzerland always be able
to do justice to those great world-political tasks which await
her? Will there always be dozens of able, energetic personalities to fill those positions on commissions and in bureaus which
are constantly increasing in importance? Or will such a situation as this develop: 'Now that So-and-so got that job, it's time
for the law faculty of another university to land something.'

These are serious matters, and the more one loves Switzerland, the more importance one must attach to seeing the country properly represented from every possible point of view."

And just as the Swiss people presents a caricature of the German in the matter of objectivity and equity, so it caricatures it in the matter of its *bourgeois*, middle-class character. It is the prototype of a people of the petty *bourgeoisie*; it is absolutely typified by the small man. The German majority, too, lacks aristocratic instincts; but at least it always recognizes the aristocratic as of higher value. In Switzerland, historic development has willed it that the best elements in the inhabitants, their consciousness of freedom and their manly courage, should unfold in forms utterly opposed to everything that is fine and distinguished. Thus plebeianism is the ideal of that country today. Among the small and the poor, and among those who occupy inferior positions, this, as we have already noted, does not result in ugliness; for in their case, meaning and expression harmonize. But among those who stand higher it does result in ugliness; and this explains why no man of finer type can like the Swiss as such and why it is only Swiss who have fallen away from their type who can give the impression of "Europeans" in mentality and form. For a long time I have paid particular attention to the way in which the Swiss express themselves, for this affords a deep insight into things. Where the German of the better kind uses *überlegen*, the Swiss says *pfiffig*. Where, in the worst case, the former would use the word *Gemeinheit*, the latter would use *Niedertracht*. He says *ruchlos* where the German would say, at most, *hässlich*. What the German would call *lässige Freiheit*, he would call *Liederlichkeit*; and for him *Schroffheit* is *ruppig*. The general coarseness of the German achieves a fantastic intensification in the Swiss. But this does not, as in the case of Holland, lead to a culture of ugliness; it remains pure, i.e. cultureless, ugliness. But enough of this. Any one who knows Switzerland will find many other parallels in illustration of my contentions. I only wish to adduce five of the more harmless instances of similarity between Switzerland and Germany. In Germany, too, the higher type of man is necessarily isolated; there is not, as in France, a recognized group of the *élite*. But in Switzerland he must actually bury himself alive, so great is the envy and distaste felt in that country for human superiority. In Germany, too, there are differences of caste. But they lie visible on the surface, so that membership in a caste or extrusion from it does not create inward repressions. As against this, the *gens bien* of Geneva, the upper "four hundred" of Zürich, and the patrician families of Basle, officially deny any consciousness of inequality, but for that reason they actually seal themselves up all the more hermetically; and this frequently goes so far as to result in spiritual asphyxiation. The important German, too, is fundamentally not representative, as the important Frenchman is; on the contrary, he is a contrast-product to the majority. But in Switzerland this applies to such a degree that not only the important Swiss, but even the attractive Swiss of the higher classes produces so exceptional an effect that every one instinctively regards him and judges him outside the framework of his people. (This would be the right place to remark that I exclude the distinguished and attractive Swiss whom I know from the above characterization. There is no doubt that even outside of that professional class which is creating out of itself a Swiss type of European standing, there are many Swiss who stand comparison with every other European.) The German, too, is a born innkeeper. Wherever he settles, he maintains himself in that character. But the Swiss must be defined as a nation of innkeepers in the same sense as other peoples are defined as warrior peoples or seafaring peoples. And finally: the German, too, readily enters the service of the foreigner. But in Switzerland the profession of the mercenary soldier has always been a national business. The Swiss Guard of a Pope who no longer governs is the most amusing piece of persiflage on the Swiss spirit.

WE turn now to the symbolic significance of Switzerland in the general European complex. Here I must refer to the ideas expressed in the last paragraph but one. Among all the peoples I know, the Swiss have the extremest resentments; their resentment goes even deeper than that of the Jews, for they are psychically unadapted to their modern position. They still feel themselves, with regard to their past and their future, the pioneers of freedom, of progress. They are that no longer. For the freedom which they desired and stood for has since become common public property; they are to that extent their own classics. As I have pointed out in connection with Italy, liberalism is today devoid of any accelerating momentum. Thus the pride of the Swiss in their condition must have a deforming effect. And their pride is altogether extraordinary. The fact that their pride relates to what they call their *Schlichtheit* (unpretentiousness), their *Gediegenheit* (soundness, genuineness), or their *Gleichheit* (equality), changes nothing in the psychological fact itself. But the principal effect of their anti-aristocratic disposition today is an immediate deadening of the soul. In the time of Gessler that outlook had, of course, a lofty sense. Today, when feudalism has been completely liquidated, and when the struggle against the principle of nobility in life is not a struggle for external freedom, but against inner freedom, the same outlook signifies nothing better than a struggle for a base mentality as against a high one. And since every Swiss with some intelligence naturally suspects the real state of affairs, there ensues an extreme spiritual ugliness. In the case of the majority, this is externalized as jealousy and coarseness. In the case of the better individual, it expresses itself in a peculiar lack of sincerity. In the last analysis, even the best type of Swiss lacks forthrightness. Only too naturally! During my journey round the world, I once appeared at a masquerade ball in the costume of an Oriental despot, with my features made up to suit. Despite the fact that it was merely a masquerade, six female representatives of Swiss "liberty" positively jumped on me, upbraiding me furiously with: "Such a thing wouldn't be permitted in our country." Assuredly every kind of nobility—and I mean just the true kind of nobility—is, in the eyes of the majority, something to be penalized. A Swiss of distinction must carry on in secret in Switzerland, much like a monarchist in Russia. It is in Switzerland that the curse of all democracy stands out most clearly today; namely, cowardice in the face of public opinion. In America, too, public opinion serves as a sort of divine court of appeal; men who are in other respects honourable throw down their weapons before that opinion as a matter of course, even when the most crying injustices are involved. The fact is that every man, with the exception of the hero, instinctively thinks first about his own life. In the case of the Anglo-Saxon, this does not produce a general effect of ugliness, because he (the Britisher primarily) is essentially social; i.e. in his case, the common good does honestly—that is, from his own inner springs—supersede the individual will. The Swiss, as a German, is asocial. Thus his hostility to what is noble is simple ugliness.

And in this respect, Switzerland emerges as the immediate warning token of that which an inwardly inter-related Europe may easily become in other countries, too. It was of set purpose that I put my observations on Switzerland right next to those on Hungary; I did not want to repeat myself. The noble is something absolutely higher than the ignoble; the mentality of the aristocrat is absolutely superior to that of the *bourgeois*. Should Europe ever become like Switzerland in this sense, then that principle which has from the beginning made Europe great again and again will be done for. Let us once more, and this time from another point of view, examine the psychological picture presented by present-day Switzerland. The Swiss is moved by resentment to a greater degree than any other people, because his self-consciousness does not correspond to the real situation. Switzerland believes herself to be the land of freedom, but today she is in reality the land of extremest

narrowness, and that in the inner sense which ultimately
governs all values. During the Middle Ages the little state
was the common external life-form; it found compensation in
universalism, in the sense of Goethe's "outwardly bounded,
inwardly boundless"; that applied to Switzerland, too. Today
the inward state corresponds to the outward. Accordingly Switzerland is in *all* respects a province. This is the immediate result of democratization. It was precisely Switzerland which,
until the time of Napoleon, had one of the most aristocratic
national structures; man being what he is, only the ideal of
width and distance can sustain a broad spirit in him who, externally, is narrowly confined. In modern Switzerland it is
precisely the ideal of narrowness which reigns, for that coincides with the ideal of the little man. This is assuredly the
foundation of what passes for the political exemplariness of
Switzerland; a common understanding can most easily be
reached in the most elementary matters and on the basis of the
elementary; for, to put it plastically, it is not in their root that
men differ from one another, but in their blooms. But this
exemplariness is, on the other hand, obtained at the expense
of the possibilities of a higher and freer mankind. For in the
last analysis it results from the fact that the individual and
unique abdicates all importance in favour of the majority. Now
all human values achieve realization only through the instrument of the unique. To that extent the social mentality is, as
the last word, an unconditional proof of inferiority; it may and
should be the *first* word; it is a first premise that man, that
"political animal," should live in as favourable an environment
as possible. But after that, every emphasis should be laid on
the unique, for, as Jesus first recognized, it is only the dimension
of uniqueness which distinguishes man from the beast. But let
us turn back to the social-political problem. He who is capable
of insight should learn one thing definitely from the example
of the Swiss; the man who has become typified in a narrow
framework of life and who then reaches out into a wider

relationship must inevitably deteriorate if he is incapable of inward breadth. The independent Swiss villager who was the deciding factor in the days of Gessler, and who still lives on, is in his unpretentiousness and modesty of needs unquestionably a higher type. But the man who has retained that psychology and has become a wealthy *bourgeois* is not. In him the inherited virtues are transformed into vices. The neutrality which has been practised for so many generations has made the upper classes in Switzerland rich, in some cases inordinately rich. And since it is material power which everywhere is the deciding factor, it is on these classes—whatever the constitution may say—that the real emphasis of importance rests; in the case of Switzerland it must be so if only for the reason that these classes alone are in a position to share in international life by other means than the foreigner industry. But, measured by their mentality, these rich Swiss are the most middle-class of middle classes. Here the curse of the original Calvinistic spirit takes effect. This applies not only to Geneva, where the inheritance of the Calvinistic spy-system, which compelled the well-to-do to dissemble their wealth, still causes many millionaires to live practically without servants; it also applies to Zürich, a happier town because animated by the spirit of Zwingli. Hence even the rich Swiss live in a pinched way. But all the more do they live for their wealth. They are not Calvinists in the sense of the Pilgrim fathers, who were indeed forbidden to enjoy their wealth, but who therefore put it out to all the greater usury for the glory of God—their thoughts and their feelings belong to the stocking-hoard of the little *bourgeois*. "Solidity" is their one ideal. They have no understanding at all of how to spend money. Now the only meaning that money has is—to be spent. Of course one must first have it, or earn it. In this material world no ideal can be realized in a large way without material power; that is why external want deforms the soul in any man who is not a born ascetic. And with a few rare exceptions complete inner freedom belongs only to the man who is not merely free outwardly, but actually possessed of power. This explains why the *grand seigneur* represents the highest human type. If the *grand seigneur* possesses, it is only in order to give; if he is a householder, if he increases his possessions, it is only that he may be able to give the more. If money-saving passes as a virtue with the little man it is only because, still a child, socially speaking, he must first of all learn how to keep house, in order that he may later develop within himself an equilibrium equal to a wider complex of relationships. To spend money sensibly is, indeed, much more difficult than to save money; that is why, out of millions of honest money-savers who simply live out the animal urge to hoard provisions, there are very few who know how to spend properly. But as a matter of fact saving always has, from the point of view of the soul, a devastating effect. In the first place it intensifies the instinct to security, which always acts as a brake on the road to inner freedom; for inner freedom stands and falls by the will to run risks. And finally it inevitably leads to miserliness, that meanest and most godless of all vices. Thus even those democracies which have in one way or another developed a higher type of man have always been beyond the stage of the middle-class money-saving ideal; in America it is a fundamental principle that one must spend what one earns. It is obvious that money should not be squandered as long as there is poverty. But however paradoxical it may sound, occasional extravagance and a feeling for this kind of prodigality hurts a people much less than excess of respectability. If anywhere at all, it is here that the sinner is better than the virtuous man. Whosoever has money, his first duty is to *spend* it intelligently. If a man does not know how to spend a large income, it is he, and not the prodigal, who is not entitled to it. And in the Swiss there are many millionaires who act as though they had less than three thousand *Fränkli* a year to live on, and the entire people count it as a virtue. They save, save, save, save—interminably. They lack the slightest understanding of the ideal of generosity as a virtue. If you ask a young Croesus of this kind why he does not permit himself this or that, his answer will be, "I haven't yet come into my inheritance." Later he saves for his children.

And this "virtue" is the profoundest reason for the moral ugliness of the Swiss type of today. Yes, unfortunately it is true: the Swiss are today the unaristocratic people *par excellence*. Provincial narrowness regarded as human worth, the petty *bourgeoisie* regarded as an ideal, will never yield a higher humanity. And least of all in a modern world which has become very wide. The age of the middle class is no more. And though it is true that only the spirit of the *grand seigneur* can lead to greatness, even the proletarian spirit is always better than the middle-class spirit. The *bourgeoisie*, thrust back into a corner, is becoming correspondingly smaller and uglier. In the case of the Swiss the process may be observed from beginning to end with classic clearness. Thus only a national psychoanalysis can help them. They must become *conscious* of their real condition. In the case of those Swiss who as types have already adapted themselves to the real Swiss situation, we observe even today no essential ugliness. These must become the norm. Swiss self-righteousness must be transformed into real modesty. The Swiss will have to understand that even on their ancient soil the old times have passed, and that they must renew themselves. They will have to understand that they must look forward, not backward, that they must base their pride not on their past, but on their will to a higher future.

Will this come to pass? I cannot tell. But this much I can say: if it should come to pass, then, and then only, will Swiss humanity again become beautiful. Then the Swiss pride in attachment to the soil will no longer be narrowing and deforming in its effects, as it is today. Swiss humanity was indeed beautiful as long as it interpreted its mission in terms of its true being. Until now the Swiss have been the race of little people. If they are that still, they must desire that which is suitable to little people; and as such they really have a mission to humanity. A very great part of the human world belongs once for all to this type. To plead for the rights of this type is the special vocation of a nation which in its entirety belongs to it; above all, its vocation is to stand up for the weak against the strong. This is needed today more than ever before, and it is a very sad circumstance that precisely in these days of oppressed minorities, public opinion in Switzerland is generally on the side of the great and the mighty. . . . Or else, on the other hand, the Swiss are no longer little people: in that case they must educate themselves up to new norms. Under all circumstances, if Switzerland is to blossom into new beauty, the Pharisaism of democracy and of the social outlook must come to an end. To repeat: if it should come to the point that Switzerland can achieve inward renewal, then, since she must and naturally should remain the geographical-political entity that she is, she can undoubtedly become, in new ways, a valuable component part of Europe. I can best make clear what I mean by an analogy, which every one may translate into his own personal language. Not long after the German revolution, Richard Strauss once thundered, in my presence, against the possibility of a union between Austria and Germany: "Then the last German art-country will become Prussianized!" I retorted: "I see the matter in a totally different light. It is only then that Vienna can become purely an art-city. For then all the official bureaus of the German-speaking countries will be concentrated in Berlin, where they properly belong."

A FEW words, in closing, on the particular character of the individual Swiss of importance, who has hitherto been an isolated and special phenomenon and who, in the long run, will, it is to be hoped, become the national exemplar. For since Switzerland can no longer remain inwardly narrow without sinking into a more and more rancid provincialism, she too must set before herself models taken from the higher levels of humanity. Unless she perceives without delay that the average

Swiss citizen is no model for her, her *rôle* as a cultural factor is ended, and she will continue to exist for the sole purpose of fattening Philistines in a secure little neutral world. From now on, Switzerland must take as her polar focus the type which is today best represented by Carl Gustav Jung. Even the individual Swiss of importance is fundamentally man in the raw, a bear, a cross-product between the primal rock and a surly peasantry. But he is at the same time distinguished in his own particular way. He is independent, modest in the true sense, and genuinely unpretentious. Above all, he is free of envy. He bears only a mild resemblance to the best European types. But he resembles all the more the best representatives of the old, now moribund America. And this is comprehensible. The American is the product of the transplanting of an originally narrow type into a landscape of tremendous sweep. The generosity of his outlook originally arose as a polar reaction against the feudal form of nobility. His riches were created by the spirit not of the knightly conqueror, but of the Puritan. America and Switzerland are therefore inwardly related, to the extent that in both cases the national type took its stamp not from free rulers, but from free peasants; and in each case people with middle-class traditions, with corresponding norms and ideals, later became rich. Thus the Swiss are not off the track when they seek the exemplars needed for their new inner expansion in America. Outward and inward breadth of life are proportionately related to each other. The man of inward superiority is physiologically akin to the man of external wealth. For this reason the littleness of Switzerland does not stand in the way of a process of Americanization under its good aspects, if only the important man, i.e. the man of inner width, serve as the national exemplar, and not, as hitherto, the narrow-minded man. This close kinship with America no doubt does, in its turn, set narrow boundaries to Swiss possibilities of development. The real America is the land of the small town in the same sense as Switzerland is that of the *Kantönli*. The truly

noble attitude is unknown there as a type. Thus a rich exfolia-
tion of his nature, and the perfecting of it in the European
sense, is hardly attainable by the American. The sole reason
for this is his belief in equality, the deciding factor with him,
together with its ideals of standardization and normalcy; man
becomes whatever he believes himself to be; differentiations
presuppose a recognition of differences; culture accordingly
presupposes the recognition of the exception and not of the
rule as the model. But to grow and expand out of his original
quality and out of his original format till he bursts asunder his
primal form is given to no one. And every soul seeks out for
itself the body which befits it.

THE NETHERLANDS

I N many respects culture is unquestionably hostile to nature. In the long run old races become diminutive and ugly. In England a very large proportion of the dukes must wear beards —that is, if they have any aesthetic sense; today it is among the people that the traditionally beautiful features, clear-cut, may mostly be found. The younger we take them, the more frequently do we find among the upper classes faces that are pig-like, with receding chins and noses the opposite of aquiline. Wherever a process of breeding is in course, it seems as if nature—as though in malice or resentment—deliberately sets out to intensify whatever is inferior. It is because she does not succeed at once in this (for in the beginning it is the inherently best which breeding enhances) and because mankind prefers chewing the cud of memory to exerting itself to reckon with the new, that the culturally old always has the advantage, without reference to time-limits. The truth is that the Habsburg lip, taken as a symbol, signifies what is always normal in the long run. Beyond a doubt this fate may be counteracted to a considerable extent in the physical as well as in the spiritual and moral fields, in which the same law is at work, but under more favourable conditions; I mean that families retain their decency and their good sense, as a rule, much longer than their physical beauty; there is even reason to hope that this anticipation of fate will succeed, in the future, in ever higher degree, for eugenics leads us to give a more complete attention to the laws of heredity than any previous system of breeding. But it will be impossible to suppress fate wholly. Spirit is essentially not of this world, and only when managed with the extremest tact and understanding does Nature permit it to carry on. Even the various breeds of pigeons, left to themselves, sooner or later either die out or revert to the wild pigeon; even the fine breeds of horses and cows survive only under the constant vigilance of the highest human knowledge; and even then they lose their powers of reproduction as compared with the species ruled by Nature and not by the spirit; if these lower forms of life are subject to this law, how much more does it apply to the species Homo Sapiens, on whom the spirit works not only externally, but also from within. The last man will in all probability be the greatest ass that ever lived. Rejuvenation can never be effected except by fresh blood. If the majority of the very great talents emerge without eugenic preparation, this is chiefly due to the fact that only a virgin Nature, not used up, can stand the pressure of spirit. And if, on the other hand, few of these great talents leave their like behind, this is due to the fact that Nature never stands or tolerates spirit for long. In this we may glimpse the eternal significance of undifferentiated lower strata; if once the possibility of rejuvenation out of pure Nature becomes exhausted, there will be an end to any possible manifestation of spirit on earth. A cultivated stock has of course this advantage over a stock close to Nature, that it is better immunized against the dangers of civilized life. But unfortunately the best immunized families are, with very few exceptions, also the stupidest and ugliest.

So much for this side of the problem. On the other hand ugliness, that product of nature's vengefulness, does at times feed one of the most important psychological roots of the cultural form. Some kind of lack is always necessary if man is to strive upward out of things as they are. Not the least reason for the superior dress of the Frenchwoman is the fact that she is less well built than any other European woman. Instances could easily be multiplied in support of this interpretation of the fact. Yet I know only one cultural sphere in Europe—the word is used in a wholly general, wholly unorthodox sense; that is, not as Frobenius uses it—where there is a culture *of* ugliness; this sphere is that of the Netherlands.

IN order to make my meaning clear at once I shall begin with Volendam, that curious fishing-village which lives on the foreigner industry. There the costumes of the age of the

great painters are still worn, but the inhabitants seem to have
set themselves with the utmost refinement to the task of accen-
tuating not what is pleasing but what is ugly; impossibly large
feet, impossibly wide hips, impossibly narrow shoulders, impossibly small heads. To this is added, as the result of an
unparalleled consistency of inbreeding, a refined grotesqueness
of features. What emerges is not something unaesthetic, but, on
the contrary, a highly aesthetic totality. We see here that
beauty presented as life which once emerged as art on the can-
vasses of the Netherlandish masters. For they, too, always
showed a preference for the ugly. Even Rubens, acquainted
as he was with all the beauties of foreign countries, did this
quite definitely; otherwise he would have painted, at least
sometimes, feminine bodies less repulsive than those which
regularly adorn his pictures.

But the important fact is that no Netherlander of whom I
know has ever attained to the counter-ideal of the *beauté du
diable*. The culture of the Netherlands is really a culture of the
ugly norm. And this is quite comprehensible just because the
Netherlanders are a cultural people. A culture founded on
natural beauty presupposes that the latter is normal. No people
will endure as a representative picture of itself a form of life
which gives consciousness to its own inferiority, just as no voter
cares to go to the ballot for a parliamentary candidate whom he
feels to be his superior. This explains the naturalism of the
unlovely nineteenth century; this explains the glorification of
the chaotic by the Russians. It was my experience with the
latter people which first made clear to me with how objective
a reality we are faced in the case of beauty; during the Revolution the peasants turned first with unerring instinct to destroy
whatever was most beautiful; they could not bear the sight of
it. But if Russia is hostile to culture by reason of her ugliness,
the Netherlands have created a high culture on the basis of an
even greater ugliness. To this extent they are the land of an
even greater triumph of the spirit than Greece was. Since only
the ugly seems to be natural here, the artists of the country

have taken natural ugliness as the basis of their intensification and stylization. Thus they attained a highly spiritual beauty. Whatever is really beautiful in the culture of the Netherlands, from the works of Teniers, Breughel, Höllenbreughel, to Rembrandt's latest pictures, has its basis in the culture of ugliness.

The statement that the natural basis of the Netherlandish type is ugly applies, moreover, all along the line. The psychic equivalent of their outer unloveliness is a sort of brutality which is none the less striking because it stands in much the same relation to Prussian brutality as a "Kermess" by Teniers does to a military parade in old Potsdam. Even nowadays, the Dutch harbour mobs are among the ugliest in the world. Satan himself would think twice before approaching a Dutch street-walker. Never will I forget how, in Aden, I once saw a Dutch colonial of mammoth-like proportions lay hands on a negro because he had dared to ask too much for his ostrich feathers, and simply pitch him overboard; and when the unfortunate wretch, thrown down the gangway, nearly had his neck broken, the Dutchman stood by smirking with satisfaction and declared that this was the right way to deal with coloured people. Nowhere did hatred toward the foreigner manifest itself in uglier form during the World War than in Holland. Even among themselves, the uneducated Dutch trust each other out of sight less than the inhabitants of any other country; the old English couplet still holds good:

> In matters of commerce the way of the Dutch
> Is giving too little and asking too much.

If subordinates are still addressed by the familiar *du*, and if the title of *Mevrouw* is used, as a form of address, only for members of the aristocracy and the upper classes generally (all others are addressed as *Juffrouw*, the equivalent of *Fräulein*, or Miss, and would think they were being sneered at if addressed as *Mevrouw*), this clearly shows, in a democratized and highly civilized country, a natural and original crudeness of character. In the same way I have encountered, among highly educated Dutchmen, outbursts of boorishness which would have been unthinkable in the same classes among other peoples, and which would have misled me completely if it had not been clear that the ugliness of the Dutch is something basic, for which God alone is responsible. And what can one say about their language? The German who knows it only superficially is driven to believe that it was once invented at a stagparty around three o'clock in the morning. Its basic character is loutish. How deep-rooted this loutishness is, may be seen from the special way in which they speak or write German badly. The fact is that in the case of ugliness, too, we have to do with an objective reality, for even little children know instinctly which words are improper and take a special delight in using them. But out of this intractable natural material the Netherlanders have, I repeat, created a high culture. Whatever may be the numbers of those whom that culture has not touched—it exists. And that is what matters.

N ow as to this culture itself. That it represents, in its particular way, something of general human significance, is of course beyond question. The Netherlands are a Germano-Latin frontier country; culturally they therefore belong to this broader complex. They can have a special significance only in the same sense as an exceptional individual personality in the midst of a uniformly educated cultural class. At this point we must for the first time distinguish sharply between Belgium and Holland, for within the Germano-Latin complex the emphasis lies, for each country, on a different point.

Let us begin with Holland. The first thing to be said about its culture is that it is essentially what one calls *cossu;* this adjective is used by the French to characterize cloths which are of great worth, but which are discreet, not showy. He who has never had the opportunity to share in the life of the patrician families of Amsterdam—I speak of them because they alone represent the culture of Holland; the aristocrat, who means nothing in that country, does not—sees in the country little evidence of refinement. *Per contra*, he who has been admitted to their midst has become acquainted with an atmosphere in which the art-patronage of Holland's great age immediately becomes comprehensible, for without this patronage there might indeed have been great painters, but there would never have been a great Dutch art. These patricians are unintellectual, free from problems, worldly in every sense, and yet cultural types throughout; everywhere, and in every respect, the material appears artistically formed. This gives the impression of a particularly high culture for the very reason that the material is in its original nature especially crude, so that only a strong spirit could have bent it to its will. But the peculiar character of Dutch cultural life does not lie in this; it lies in the fact that its form is Latin. This fact is the key to the Dutch cultural problem; the spirit of this essentially Germanic people is Latin and in its present form bears the stamp of that arch-Latin, John Calvin. Given the natural rudeness of this people, the result is an unusually powerful tension. All the productivity of Holland is based, in the last analysis, on this tension. It was this tension which formed the great character of Netherlandish Protestantism (in this connection it occurs to one that the English character should, in the same sense, bear a predominantly Latin stamp); it is the reason for the Dutch sense of form. If even the Greeks were consciously Apollonian only because of the ever-threatening Dionysus within their bosoms, then the Dutch cult of the beautiful means essentially a defence mechanism against inner loutishness.

What occupied my mind particularly, for various personal reasons, during my several visits to Holland, was the significance of her present state in connection with the position among the great powers which she once occupied and has since lost. For this loss has not made the Hollander as provincial, as narrow, as exclusively interested in private and personal gain, as was to be expected from his unfavourable basic character. On the one hand this is undoubtedly connected with the fact that Holland still has colonial possessions. Her people has thereby retained a wider outlook, as compared with other small nations, just as the Hanseatic merchant has a wider outlook than the inland shopkeeper. Another circumstance to be taken into consideration is that the Hollander is German in this, that his element is the small sphere and not the wide. In the days of its greatness, Holland was extremely particularistic; it was almost a land of determinant clubs and guilds; thus the element of spaciousness never represented its best essence. The circumstances enumerated above certainly have some bearing on the situation. If the loss of her position as a great power has done Holland so little harm, however, this is due primarily to the age of her culture. Here, then, we have something which may serve as an exemplar, something which, in view of what I said at the beginning concerning nature's hostility to the spirit, and concerning the particular uncouthness of the basic Netherlandish disposition, awakens a new hope in me for the future of the human race. This culture is one of the oldest on earth. The great wandering of the nations left this land- scape untouched. Even in Roman days the Batavians already belonged to the most civilized of the barbarians. Thus the Netherlanders are possessed of fixed emotions and cultural instincts which make them largely independent of external accident. This brings up one correction in the observation at the beginning of this chapter. If the spirit becomes flesh to the extent that the impulses of the spirit have built themselves into the emotions and instincts, then the cultivated man is superior in the absolute sense to the man of nature. On this circumstance is based the universal superiority of the aristocrat. The very same thing is true of the superiority of authentic Jewry. The

Jews, too, are anything rather than one-sidedly intellectual—
that description applies only to those representatives of the
race who have become uprooted. The Jews really owe their
vitality to their absolutely correct evaluation of the blood
element and the spirit element in their best mutual relation.
No Western aristocracy has ever known more exactly than they
the virtue of blood. At no time have they lost sight of the
spiritual values bound up with blood. No people has spoken so
frequently of "the seed." But at the same time this people
knew better than any other that in man, biological heredity
functions along two lines simultaneously: the line of blood and
the line of tradition. Thus Jewish life was governed by spiritual
laws as no other life has ever been. The *Goy* has not even the
remotest idea of the rigid discipline of form to which the most
miserable Polish Jew submits. I had to bring the Jews in so
as to envisage the problem in all its width; if the Jews still
exist, and if they have not yet degenerated in spite of the
heavy pressure under which they have lived for thousands
of years, it is one more proof, and this time the extremest and
most striking proof, of the fact that blood in a cultural sense
can be an advantage. It is an absolute advantage wherever the
spirit has become flesh. On the other hand, it is only where
this has taken place that the word "cultural" can be used at all.
Now the surest measure of culture is the degree of good and
evil a man can stand; of good: only the *born* ruler type can
stand elevation to great power, only the sage can endure fame;
of evil: only a highly cultivated people like the Jews could
endure thousands of years of slavery without being broken.
During the world-revolution the aristocrat everywhere sustained ruin much better than the *bourgeois*. But above all it is
only the traditionally cultivated type which can stand defeat
—defeat, which, seen from the cosmic point of view, creates
as normal and as positive a form of life as does victory—for
his consciousness of self does not depend upon the opinion of
others. Thus Spain was able to sustain, in the most magnificent

way, her decline from world-power; and so was Holland. And
if we look at Germany from the viewpoint of the foregoing,
it becomes very clear how young that people still is—or has
become again. . . .

H OLLAND is primarily interesting because of the tension,
essential to her, between crude nature and refined culture.
This tension naturally finds embodiment in the habits and
customs of the various classes. Before I became acquainted with
the best carriers of culture, I knew, like all foreigners, only
of the fat, materialistic type of Dutchman. Among the people
this type does indeed play a great *rôle,* and the same is true of
the aristocracy. But among the educated classes the first thing
that struck me, by way of contrast, was how little they eat and
how frugally the table is set; the noonday meal consists of
almost less than usually comes for the first breakfast in northern countries; the evening meal, too, is more than frugal.
One day I was informed that the naval heroes Ruyter and
Tromp used to eat meat only once a week, and in general lived
almost like ascetics. And then I understood the meaning of
the Netherlandish still-life paintings—for it was in Holland
that this *genre* was invented; people were shown in the form
of pictures what was withheld from them *in natura.* . . .

This brings me to Dutch puritanism. The age of a productive
puritanism has everywhere passed away. No longer is any one
sustained by a great faith; he cannot be, for a broadened and
deepened insight into the correlation of things has restored
in principle that freedom of outlook which was last possessed,
in the Western world, by pagan antiquity. Thus the rule of
puritanism, wherever it still endures, is based either on hypocrisy, conscious or unconscious, or else on petrification, or, finally,
on inward cramp. In America, where puritanism emerges in its
most constrictive form, it bears all the earmarks of that reversion to the primitive which is the fate of every psychological
function which has lost its meaning within the whole; in order

to understand the moralism and fundamentalism of small American towns, one must bear in mind that the actuality of the youngest generation's life is best mirrored in Judge Lindsey's *Revolt of Modern Youth*. Among the English, given the fortunate nature of this nation, puritanism really survives only in the form of external conventions, which actually bother no one. In Holland the situation is, in keeping with the natural bent of this people, grotesque—grotesque as the figures painted by the Dutch artists are grotesque. Among a race with so ponderous a character and so ancient a culture as the Dutch, the extremest kinds of petrification are unusually frequent, and these petrified forms stand in the same relation to the petrified forms of other countries as a mastodon to a humming-bird. In a land of such great contrasts between nature and spirit there also occur, with unusual frequency, cases of inner constriction— there are perhaps few Dutchmen of intelligence who are not psychoanalytic cases—and their abreactions immediately evoke the symbol of the *Klabautermann*. As puritans, the majority of male Dutchmen are impostors. The best symbol may be found in one of the tax laws: all silverware exposed in a show case is subject to tax; but if it is hidden by a curtain, it is tax-exempt: I cannot think of a more pointed application of the idea of the fig-leaf. No; with very few exceptions the Dutch male can no longer be taken seriously as a puritan. By contrast, however, the puritanism of the Dutch woman is all the more serious. Her extraordinary lack of charm leads her instinctively to adopt a life-philosophy which makes a virtue of necessity. Those principles by virtue of which every Netherlandish culture had to be a culture of ugliness also explain why the Netherlands never possessed a culture of love except in the form of licentiousness. Aesthetically, drunkenness and repulsive women belong together. But debauchery never appealed to the *bourgeois* wife. Even the *Regentinnen* immortalized by the brush of Frans Hals do not betray the slightest comprehension for *les charmes de l'ivresse*. Seen as a whole, then, the life of the women of Holland is, in the absolutely final analysis, a fulfilment of duty in the most appalling sense of the term. Fulfilment of duty toward the race, toward property, toward society. A Dutchman, Adriaan van der Priel, who surely ought to know, wrote recently that the sole purpose of woman's life in Holland is motherhood and maternal duty. And he adds: "A crisis of womankind, such as Gertrude Baumer has indicated in her work *Die Frau in der Krisis der Kultur,* is out of the question in Holland, and always will be. There is a crisis of the generations in Holland, as there is everywhere else. The novel *Die Frauen der Coornvolts,* by Jo van Ammers-Küller, does portray masses of women in revolt; but the revolt is directed against the limitations imposed by convention, not against those imposed by personality. There is, in the nature of the Dutch-woman, that is to say in her physical and nervous structure, a heaviness to which she does not even desire to be untrue; she is as remote as possible from the promiscuous passions of the Slavic woman and from the erotic play-instinct of the Gallic; this does not imply that she is more virtuous than they as a result of reflection—as compared with the two types mentioned, she simply has the advantage of a greater spiritual massiveness. This may be interpreted in the negative sense as a lack of feminine graces, but it does keep her far from the Bohemian type and in all cases assures her a smooth, safe *bourgeois* life. She possesses the instinct of security in the widest sense. She wants security for herself, for her husband, for her posterity. As wife or as sweetheart, she will never spur the man on to dangerous enterprises, and should he plan some audacious stroke, she will assent to it only if the outcome promises to add to the security of their lives. She has no feeling for the unusual as such, and she thus undoubtedly has the effect of a healthy restraint in man's life, or she would function as such if he were ever involved in anything extraordinary. But man and woman are mutually complementary; both are creatures of duty. Respectability and dignity are cardinal prin-

ciples with them, and their contempt for the fallen can take on
hard and even cruel forms. Dutch society may some day be
turned inside out politically and socially, but its sexual morality
can never be convulsed as Russia's has been. And for this we
have to thank essentially the healthy Dutchwoman, who hun-
gers for nothing but purely positive, material things. Her
share in the structure of national life is accordingly unusually
large. Regarded from without, the effect may be but slightly
visible. In the Dutch Parliament there are only three women
deputies. But throughout the entire complex of relationships
there runs, strongly, tangibly, that feminine influence; it does
not express itself, as in France, through domination, nor as
in Russia, through incitement, but through a motherly co-
operation and sympathy, which is not concerned with high-
flown phrases. The feminine literature of Holland has nothing
revolutionary in it, but quantitatively it is considerable. In
proportion to her population, Holland probably has more poet-
esses, more women novelists and women critics in politics and
the arts, than Germany. Quite a number of women lawyers
are now established in the courts; child care and hospital work,
the peace movement, athletics for the young, are carried on by
the sober, the motherly enthusiasm of the Dutchwoman. Like
the men of the middle class, the women know at least three
languages, and through their correspondence with relatives
overseas, they learn of the latest literary events in Italy or in
North America sooner than their sisters in Germany or in
France. But the most exciting detective stories, too, are read
here without emotional over-excitement. Dostoievsky or Piran-
dello are taken up for information's sake, not as romantic
guiding-stars; one is never swept off one's feet; one remains
unshakably anchored in oneself; one remains a woman of Holland, one who has achieved motherhood or awaits it."

All of which is about as healthy as it possibly could be. But it
is awful. It gives the collective life a keynote of Philistinism,
banality, and lowness. For Holland lacks—there are excep-

tions, of course, but nowhere are exceptions rarer—tne essentially free "sweet girl," as the English put it, who in the last analysis is only hedged in by the similar morality of the English middle class; nor does Holland possess a national ideal of aristocracy. In that country simplicity is an end in itself. Thus the spirit of puritanism, after having spent itself as an heroic or accelerating principle everywhere on earth, may yet find in Holland the permanent security of feminine incarnation—for never has a female population been wiped out—and for many thousands of years lead a life of unshakable Philistinism. The national Dutch type of woman will no doubt become the ultimate earthly expression of what once resembled the Islamic conqueror in its austere greatness.

L ET us now turn to Belgium. The Dutch-Belgian contrast mirrors in miniature, within the framework of a family, the German-French contrast; hence its sharpness. That is why the northeastern Netherlands had to separate finally, in the last historic hour, from the southwestern Netherlands. In the Belgian and even in the Flemish nature the French element predominates. He who fails to see this forgets that Pantagruel and not Voltaire is the primal French type, and that the migration of the Franks into this country and their fusion with the Gallo-Romans made French, and not Germans, of the latter. I really cannot think of a single difference between the essence of the Belgians and that of the Dutch which does not repeat, in miniature, one between the French and the Germans. If the Hollander is brutal, the Belgian is cruel, unforgiving, vengeful, filled with chicane. If the Belgian painters of the great age surpassed all others in their portrayal of torments in Hell and on earth, it was only in Belgium that the greater part of the people, the patriots, refused for fully ten years after the War to grant an amnesty to those who had not shared the opinions of the victorious majority. If the Hollander is reserved, *cossu*, the Belgian is noisy, showy, colourful. The full magnificence of the colours in Flemish art can be appreciated to the full only by contrast with the art of Holland. The culture of Belgium, too, is a culture of ugliness—but if the Hollander solemnly exalts necessity into a virtue, the Belgian laughingly aestheticizes the clumsy into the grotesque. Recently, in a Belgian hotel, I had occasion to learn by personal experience how very much alive that joyous rudeness of the national taste still is, such as it has been revealed in Flemish art. Some clams which I had eaten in the hotel gave me a very unpleasant attack of ptomaine poisoning. Instead of being alarmed for the reputation of their house, the entire personnel was delighted by the *bonne farce* and proclaimed joyously, "Eighty per cent. of our guests always get sick in the same way." Looking at Belgian life, I was really reminded, again and again, of that Belgium of the East, my Baltic homeland, as it was in my boyhood. In my student days I went through this experience: We had been drinking heavily in a village tavern, and after a time I fell asleep. I was awakened by a curious shaking motion and the sound of a choral chant. When I opened my eyes I saw that my fellow students were carrying me on my bed to a blazing funeral pyre, in which a part of the furniture of the tavern had already been burned. Without their noticing it, I slipped out of the bed, which was then actually consumed in the flames, to the unceasing accompaniment of their chanting. . . . A *bonne farce* of this kind would surely have been after the heart of Belgian students, too; in any case no one in Jordaens's time would have thought it anything out of the common; for what, after all, was the Netherlandish war of liberation, at its start at least, if not a sort of Fronde among barons resembling those of the Balts? I repeat: looked at from Holland, Belgium really is essentially French. And never was there a more striking demonstration of the political incapacity of the Germans than their attempt to impart a German political orientation to this occupied territory on the abstract basis of the Germanic racial idea. Even Holland, which by blood is

Germanic to the core, would have risen like one man against such an attempt on the part of Germany. What is essential for the Netherlands is that they are a Germano-Roman *border-country*, and consequently have a particular soul of their own. From this we should obtain the most important data on the Germano-Roman frontier question in particular and on the nature and the limits of the national idea in general. Linguistically, Alsace-Lorraine is for the most part German—but the French element is so strongly mingled in the national soul that even today nothing but a separate Lothringian state, like that of a thousand years ago, could provide a final solution to the problem. There is no longer any prospect of this. But if some day war between France and Germany should become impossible, because outlived as an idea—nor is this day very far off—then the regionalist idea, combined with the idea of cultural autonomy, will, in one way or another, recall to life the meaning of that state. What applies to Belgium and to Luxembourg applies equally to Alsace-Lorraine.

And now as to the Rhineland. When the French tried to make politics out of the Rhenish separatist movement, they were out of step, as they so frequently are, by something more than a century. *Before* 1815, when Prussia annexed this country, it might not have been impossible to make of its northern half something similar to what Belgium has become. This would have become increasingly German in culture in the same sense that Belgium has become increasingly French, but that would not have prevented it from growing into a separate living organism. For the North-Rhinelander was more closely related to the Fleming and the Burgundian than to the eastern and southern German, not only in the days of Lower Rhenish art; he is so even today. For a German, he is fantastically unintellectual. Both in his materialism and in his carnival spirit he resembles the Belgian. But since this Rhinelander does happen to be essentially German, those elements which in the Belgian find positive expression of one sort or another, yield inferiority in the completed picture. What is missing is the power to shape the visible. If the Belgian garden landscape is pretty, the landscape around Cologne is mostly tawdry. It is apparently not without significance that the main railway station of Cologne almost runs into the Cathedral; the latter lacks atmosphere. The national spirit of Cologne is the sheerest profiteer-spirit I have met anywhere in Europe. It is only where the Rhineland of the eighteenth and preceding centuries still manages to survive that we have some sort of culture. Otherwise this rich strip of country is as culturally barren as East Prussia, the more so because there are memorials which still bear witness to days of greatness and beauty. The character of the Lower Rhineland will acquire—or rather recapture— a positive form *only* when it has become purely German. And thanks to the stupidity of the Powers which now occupy the country, this will happen in a decisive way before long.

But for all that, the Rhineland could, up to a hundred years ago, have evolved into a separate state. It thus becomes clear how, from any one-sided point of view, we seem to be dealing with the "accidental" not only in the case of political, but also in national structures. It is neither race nor yet culture which decides. To my knowledge the best that has been said on what builds nations is still to be found in Renan: *Une nation est une âme, un principe spirituel. Deux choses qui, à vrai dire, n'en font qu'une, constituent cette âme: l'une est la possession en commun d'un riche legs de souvenirs; l'autre est le consentement actuel, le désir de vivre ensemble, la volonté à faire continuer valoir l'héritage qu'on a reçu indivis.* This definition not only explains all of the past, it shows the way to the constant creation of new nations for thousands of years to come. On the basis of the tremendous events of the World War, new nations are undoubtedly emerging. In part they are the ones which the treaties created, however artificially. In part they were never intended at all; Greater Germany will some day look back upon the Treaty of Versailles as its cradle. Nothing but the incredible inner and outer isolation through which it lived from 1914 until . . . ? could have fused this people, which on the one hand derives its character from the pathos rather than the ethos, and on the other hand is a-national, into national unity. The situation is not very different with the new Russia and the new Italy. Many, many things can yet become very different, and that many, many times. No national structure is a final quantity. I do not indeed believe that in the new world in the making the little nations will, as such, acquire a special importance. On the Mid-European continent there are actually only two great cultural forms, the German and the French; the creations of the little races with different languages will therefore represent, to an increasing degree, variations of dialect. If Belgium was at one time not only an independent but a determinant cultural centre, today, in the larger complex of relationships, she is inevitably being absorbed into the French sphere of culture. But as modifications of dialect, the little races are all the more important. They alone are capable of sustaining that which can live only in a regionalistic and particularistic framework. Today there are many who await the coming of a new mediaeval era; the character of the old Middle Ages was determined entirely by the particularist principle. Thus there is something fine in the idea that in the new world in the making, Belgium and Holland have every prospect of enduring. For if provincialism always has a sterilizing effect, regionalism, *per contra*, is always creative.

SWEDEN

I HAD hardly stepped down from the rostrum in the gaily decorated lecture hall of the Stockholm Grand Hotel, which was filled by the highest Swedish society—the pick of the court, the government, and the aristocracies of birth and intellect—than my ears were greeted by the music of a guitar. I turned round, and there was a street-singer holding forth lustily. A German friend of mine flared up: "Let's get out of here! After such a deep and earnest lecture, *that!*" My answer was that we knew nothing about the customs of the country; if we did not like them, we had no business to come. I asked him if he had seen the bill of fare. I had one handed to me, and there, sure enough, it was printed: "Lecture by Keyserling. Street-Singer X. Supper. Dance."

"There you are," I said; "I happened to be the fish. Other courses to follow." During the supper I gradually slipped into this picture, so new to me. Speeches of tremendous seriousness were delivered about me, or to be more exact, were read off from typed manuscripts. Then I struck another mood, recalling first of all the closing scene of Plato's Symposium, where Socrates and Aristophanes, the last of the revellers, awaited the dawn, debating meanwhile whether or not the true tragic poet is not also the best fitted to write comedy, then leading to the general conclusion that tragedy must always be followed immediately by the satyr play. The hour had come, then, for the latter. All restraint was cast to the winds. That evening was followed by others, each better than the last. It was the very spirit of Gösta Berling, reincarnated, which came down to join us. I recall fantastic scenes in an old underground inn, where we roystered by the light of tallow candles, to the accompaniment of the Bacchanalian lyrics of Bellmann; one guest, following a mass of shattered crockery, tumbled headlong down the length of the stairs and fell at our feet, whether alive or dead I no longer know; no one paid the slightest attention to him.—And, again, I remember a night ride in an open sleigh, to the sound of bells, up to a castle among the hills; in honour of his guests the Count had lined the snowy way with blazing torches for a distance of nearly a mile; we seemed to be riding into a world of stars. I entered very easily into the spirit of this land and this life. For I soon grasped that it is one spirit which embraces the whole territory from Sweden across Esthonia to Ingria and St. Petersburg. It has nothing to do with Germanism; it is a distinct and separate Nordic spirit, differing very little in expression whether its embodiment be North-Russian, Balto-German, or Swedish. In spite of their slowness, the Swedes possess, in their moments of jollity, what the Russians call *Dukh*, that tremendous emotional drive which distinguishes the Balt so radically from the German; they have absolutely nothing in them of the *bourgeois* Philistine. On the whole, they are indolent and frivolous; and if they are frequently reproached with irresponsibility, the impression is due to the fact that no one expects to find this sort of mentality in the heavy blond type. And then many people who do not understand the Swedes do not appreciate to the full their lack of intellectuality. Their spirit repudiates all "significance." Much as in Vienna, though in another sense, the clever and far-sighted man would be considered *fade*— insipid. Accordingly, the national hero is not Gustavus Adolphus, but Charles XII., the man without a single aim which could be taken seriously, who planned nothing right, and whose life was, from beginning to end, one *Podrett*.* And the Swedes are not only unintellectual; as a mass they are assuredly the least spiritually gifted cultural people in Europe. This is not contradicted by the fact that they produce so many excellent actors; on the contrary, it has something to do with it. For actors are only mediums; except in the rarest instances they should not think for themselves.

* *Podrett,* a word of Russian origin, was in use among the students of Dorpat; it meant a wild and senseless outing, making the rounds of the country inns.

On Germans of deeper intelligence the effect produced by
the Swedes is often nothing short of uncanny; the reason lies
in what has been said above. And the situation becomes perfectly intelligible when we remember that in Sweden the six-
teenth and twentieth centuries subsist side by side. From the
point of view of its institutions and the frictionless social life
of its inhabitants, Sweden is beyond a doubt one of the most
civilized countries in Europe. But on the other hand the life
itself has hardly changed at all when compared with the uncomplicated state in which their—and my—forefathers lived in
the period of the Reformation. This is particularly noticeable
in the case of the women. The high-bred among them produce
the effect of Valkyrs. They are healthy, strong, beautiful, in
soul as well as in body. But they are incredibly uncomplicated—
a simplicity which, thanks to their natural freedom, produces
an effect of nakedness, so that I often said to myself: This is
how it would have been in Paradise if Adam and Eve had ever
entertained company. Intellectual nuances are, of course, beyond the reach of Swedish women. Yet even in the sphere of
the soul, where their gifts are high, they lack all romantic
complexity. Things happen as simply as among animals; and
this, precisely, cannot be called immoral. Among the lower
middle classes, I am told, it is no uncommon thing for a girl to
say over the telephone to a young man whom she has seen only
once, "I long for you"—meaning just about everything that
one can mean; and if she happens to be out picnicking with some
acquaintance—not necessarily a very intimate one—the same
thing is considered part of the dessert. But this behaviour, too,
produces an effect of essential innocence, not at all as in other
countries. But as regards the higher classes, there is much less
demoralization among them than in post-war Europe as a
whole—not as a matter of inward discipline, but from a self-
assurance born of closeness to nature. When women are moved
by the immediate impulse of nature there is always something
bafflingly sure and clear in their actions. In a conversation with

a subtle-minded and high-bred Austrian woman, I once happened to say about a certain girl that she would unhesitatingly undress in front of a man if she were asked to do so; to which the reply came, without premeditation, "But of course, if she felt that the man really meant business." Thus most women will, as mothers, play the Almighty; they will lie or tell the truth, they will give or withhold themselves, according to their instinctive evaluation of the situation. This is precisely why the very women who twenty years ago were ashamed to show their ankles blush today if they happen to be wearing too many clothes. In different situations, one thing and the other actually mean the same. But when women are both as high-bred and as uncomplicated as those of Sweden, there results a picture of almost primordial weirdness. The Swedish women are so healthy that they think it ridiculous for a man to fall ill. They are often fantastically strong; should circumstances demand it, a Swedish woman can without ado treat a man as Brunhild treated Gunther, and then, in the singsong speech of the country, recount it as a matter of course. I am alluding to what the Nibelungen saga expresses in these lines:

> She took up nail and hammer
> And hung him on the wall.

It would be hard to find anything which Swedish women would not take as a matter of course. Even the women of Boccaccio's days were not so buoyant. I do not know whether they have ever "had" that love which was created by our Middle Ages and to which romanticism gave the last polish; I am inclined to doubt it. As against this, one should not be too prudish when visiting in the castles of Sweden; the practical jokes which the ladies are inclined to play in the night are indeed of an Eden-like innocence, and yet primitively tomboyish.

But should the impression have been created that the Swedes are "wild," like the Russians and the Balts, it would only be right to correct it at once. They are essentially not that. They only happened to discover their definite form of life in a wild age, and they are so incredibly healthy that they have continued to carry on in this manner until this day. The essential element in Sweden is an unaffected good nature, frequently transfigured by a rare beauty of soul. As often as I think back on Sweden I see in it the symbol of *light*—far more so than in the case of ancient Hellas. The free, wide spaces, the glowing primary colours of the dresses, the open-hearted laughter, and, by no means least, the whole wonderful cult of singing—nowhere, except possibly in the South Seas, is life so essentially melodic, nowhere is there so much singing, nowhere is song so necessary a part of life—all these make up the basic picture. And if anything is to be effective in Sweden, it must fit in harmoniously. Their demand is that life should be good and beautiful. In the complete absence of feeling for intellectual nuances, this is bound to lead directly to what the German can not possibly understand. My experience at the lecture may be very simply explained by the fact that in Sweden everything is judged, if not solely, then primarily, by whether it pleases, i.e. whether it raises the pitch. Under these circumstances one may really find the most curious things side by side without any feeling of incongruity, exactly as at a dinner. Unless I am mistaken, the adjective which the Swede generally uses when some positive emotion has been roused in him—whether it has to do with a bottle of good wine, a fugue by Bach, redemption through the death of Christ, or a wild night —corresponds to the German *hübsch*, "pretty." This does, of course, produce an uncertainty in judgment of intellectual values. But on the other hand the most impersonal thing is judged by its human value, and that is beautiful; it is the basis of a wonderful tolerance coming straight from the heart. Poul Bjerre, the psychoanalyst, arrived at the conviction that the Ten Commandments issued by God are a failure, and he opposed to them ten better ones of his own. He did this more than once from the pulpit. Archbishop Söderblum does indeed shake his head, but he does it with a smile, and he never so much as thinks of protesting. This is what makes it such a pleasant experience to mingle in meetings which are devoted in Sweden to intellectual pursuits. There exists in Stockholm a society—I forget the name—which meets once a month, and which brings together all classes of society to listen in on intellectual matters. Thus a thoroughly difficult lecture on the theory of relativity was delivered there by Svante Arrhenius, and besides the prominent intellectuals, there were present representatives of the court, the mayor, the police commissioner, and the heads of the fire department, the chamber of commerce, the local garrison, etc. The vast majority certainly understood not a word. But after the lecture the secretary rose and performed his duty—which was to subject the lecturer to a running fire of witty persiflage. Here everybody was at home. And I have seldom heard such free and hearty laughter. The general impression was simply delightful; to the extent that they stressed the human side in intellectual values, they really did draw nearer to them. Even intellectuals find this the only way to endure one another. That is why the symposium was the typical framework for the philosophizings of the ancient Greeks. That, too, is why I am introducing more and more a similar style at Darmstadt. If men of value are to live together without any encroachment of their feeling of independence, and without permitting their external incompatibilities to stand in the way; and if, in addition, others are to benefit by the interplay of their minds, there must be created a special plane on which they can meet; from the point of view of their external incompatibilities, this must be a neutral plane, on which the lines which otherwise divide them are dissolved, so that it becomes possible for each man to become ironical toward himself without offence to his self-respect. In Sweden it is just because of this exclusive accentuation of the "purely human" that important individuals can unfold. And they do so to an unusual degree, which seems to contradict the assertion that the nation is unintellectual. Actually there is no contradiction; in the case of the important man the intellectual side, as such, is the last to receive attention. The great simplicity, forthrightness, and human friendliness of this people even finds room for that most eccentric of eccentrics, the man of genius. If he be the cause of good—e.g. if he brings honour to the country—it even honours him; not because it understands him, but because the question of understanding scarcely enters at all. This absence of understanding, in its turn, has a creative effect. Lastly, the same circumstance which enables the German of unusual gifts to become particularly great, also proves a special spur to the talented individual in Sweden; the contrast with others works itself out creatively.

In this accentuation of the human element, Sweden approaches England, which, in spite of its rigid idealizing of the norm, makes more allowance for the eccentric than any other country—provided he is tactful and does not run up against the ultimate, immovable barriers of convention. In fact the racial kinship between England and Sweden strikes one at every turn. The English, too, are entirely unintellectual. With them, too, the chief advantages are those of human nature. They, too, recognize the right of every man to be as he is. That is why they are able to rule others. That is why pride of caste and pride of race are tolerable only in them. The English gifts, too, are essentially gifts of the soul. The same applies to the Swedes, except that their souls are simpler and more primitive. If they were not psychologically gifted, they could not write detective stories which, next to those of England, are the best in the world.

YET, on the other hand, the Swedes are altogether different from the British. That is because their character is utterly devoid of tensions. For a long time history has skipped over Sweden. In that period it has been largely fortunate—beginning with the fact that most Swedes live beyond their means, while the circles to which they belong seem, for some mysterious reason, never to grow any poorer, and ending up with the accidents of history. Thus there has developed in Sweden a truly Phaeacian style. In my opinion this description fits Sweden better than Denmark, to which country I have frequently heard it applied, because the Swedes have a freer and nobler basic character. The Phaeacians were essentially *not* Philistines. Yet they were certainly materialists. And in Sweden the emphasis unquestionably lies on the material element. In no other place in the world that I know of do people eat anything like as much—and digest it so well. The true Swede can with perfect safety eat a heavy meal and then immediately go for a swim in the cool sea to get up a fresh appetite; anybody else would die of heart-failure. It frequently happened that I was invited out to dinner twice in the same evening, and was actually expected to eat on both occasions, for the first dinner began at seven, and the other at eight. To refuse would have been considered impolite. The only thing you can do is to say "Yes" and then "Thank you." It is quite possible that in the matter of their digestive organs the Swedes differ from the rest of humanity as the deep-sea fish does from the ordinary fish; it would probably be worth while to conduct some research along these lines. This materialistic basic disposition is also symbolized in the national dances of Sweden—their primary purpose is to let off steam. Thus they easily run to excess in other materialistic respects. The sons of many lands proudly display their stars and ribbons of royal orders. But Sweden is the only country where I have ever seen any one wearing large numbers of them simultaneously around the collar, so that the distinguished possessor begins to resemble a pouter pigeon. Yes, the Swedes are undoubtedly not unmaterial. But all this earth-heaviness is, I repeat, animated by an extraordinary friendliness. And this, for its part, is the expression—this links up again with the opening of this paragraph—of a complete absence of tensions in the Swedish character, so that the visitor is never quite sure that he is not dealing with angels. The only tension which I ever observed in Sweden is the one between a state of sobriety and a state of intoxication. This absence of tensions explains the survival, in a land which otherwise is supermodern externally, of institutions dating back to the earliest times. A member of the aristocracy complained to me that his class had recently been deprived of its last privileges. And what were they? The nobility had been permitted to beat its servants and had been exempt from the jurisdiction of certain courts. I was speechless; special rights of this kind have long since disappeared from all countries with a similar degree of civilization. In Sweden they could survive because nobody misused them. Thus, too, the style of the court, in sharp contrast with that of Spain, produces an effect not of reality, but of pleasing make-believe. Its effect is similar to that of the French cult of a polished society life, which still survives in Sweden—though in attenuated form—in the sense of the eighteenth century: as an accentuation of courtesy. A modern democracy with a constitutional monarchy—and this is what Sweden is, more than any other country—certainly makes a pleasanter first impression on the visitor than does a republic. In this connection it occurs to me that, from the social point of view, France, too, has remained monarchistic. If she no longer has any princes of her own, she needs their existence elsewhere all the more. What will the French do when all the foreign kings necessary to her life-style will have been dethroned?

Bᴜᴛ to return to the Phaeacian character of Sweden. In spite of her model social institutions, in spite of all system and all discipline in individual matters, Sweden is fundamentally Phaeacian; it is precisely good hotels, devoted solely to comfort, that need the strictest management. Again I am reminded primarily of England, which resembles this country in so many respects. There, too, the original Nordic character, untroubled by life-problems, has survived. There, too, good living is an

end in itself—but in England it means both material blessings
and a state of inward happiness. In that country, too, the latter
aim is ennobled by the basic disposition of a free manhood.
But if in Sweden that same attitude has something more charming, it is because no emphasis is laid on possessions as such:
Sweden's ethos is essentially not that of the merchant; in that
country freedom has in it something of the age of fairy-tales;
the peasant really does feel himself the equal of the King, only
God has called him to a different position; in English pleasant-
ness the tension of the imperial will is always latent. In England only the home bears that character which in Sweden is
proper to the state, and this cult of the home is touched with the
implication of a haven for the man of many adventures, or
the man weighed down by responsibilities. In England life is
essentially historical, and to that extent it is, even if unconsciously, tragic. The expression "the white man's burden" corresponds to a true inner experience; the pathos of the phrase,
civis Britannicus sum, is authentic throughout. If the Englishman seems only to skim the surface of serious problems, if he
is impatient with the insistent person, this is due to the fact that
the man of real pathos and of true inner discipline finds the
serious discussion of intimate matters intolerable. Thus the true
warrior is very reluctant to speak about mortal danger. The
man who insists on discussing first and last things with deadly
solemnity and fulness, after the manner of German writers,
the man who wears his so-called "objective pathos" on his
sleeve, can certainly not be regarded as a man of inner and
essential seriousness. This kind of pathos is altogether absent
in modern Sweden. And how could it possibly be otherwise?
The founders of England, the Danes and the Normans, as
well as the conquerors who preceded them, came from these
parts. It was typical of Scandinavia that her great men have
always gone forth to found new kingdoms. What remained
at home was sediment, those who lacked the characteristics of
the Vikings. Out of that mass the latter-day Swedes are

principally descended, and only in the rarest cases, and even then without aim and purpose—I am thinking, again, of Charles XII., the national hero—did that original spirit burst forth into a brief renewal of life. But then, *per contra*, the positive element in the modern Swedes also springs from the same root. The great pacifism of the country is due to the circumstance that all her warlike sons went forth, and sooner or later the purely warlike races must die out completely. That is the one reason why "the meek shall inherit the earth." The rich soulfulness of the Swedes is explained by the fact that only the soulful remained at the hearth. *This* characteristic was wholly lacking in the Normans. They were a hard robber-tribe, not altogether unlike the Huns of an earlier time and the Bolsheviks of today. They were an extreme expression of the psychological law that the will to power cannot exist side by side with emotional sensitiveness, that the extraverted type can never possess the virtues of the introvert. They were men who lived life: they were not men who received it as a spiritual experience. . . .

There is as a matter of fact something very remarkable in the centrifugal element in the Nordic. At his most typical, he has at all times been a nomad; it was only when he became fused with a matriarchal population that he ever produced a culture genuinely attached to the soil. It was thus primarily in France. If he entered a country in insufficient numbers, or if he happened to belong to an extremely nomadic stock, he was almost completely lost in the conquered population; his presence was felt only as a ferment or through an occasional reversion to type, just as Sicilian and Neapolitan nobles now and again exhibit purely Nordic features. The Normans, as such, have never founded a state. A particularly favourable fusion of blood, tradition, geographic position, and accident enabled the inhabitants of Great Britain to transmute this robber-admixture into a cultural ruling power. In Italy all the Germanic types vanished in the Italian; it is ridiculous to emphasize their *rôle* in the phenomenon of the Renaissance, rather than that of the rejuvenated Etruscans. In Spain they have meant almost as little as in Africa, where one still meets from time to time, among the sons of the desert, the features of a Sigurd; they have never even succeeded in founding a real feudal state. The same applies to the Germanic stocks which were co-founders of the Chinese culture in Chinese Turkestan, as is evident from the frescoes which have been brought back by LeCoq. As far as they themselves are concerned, what they did was—to use the phrase which Otto Franke coined in answer to a question of mine—to "rake in the shekels and raise hell." And what is the situation with regard to Germany? The great German, too, is essentially centrifugal. That is why Leopold Ziegler does well to call him the eternal wanderer. In all ages the great German has always left whatever he was born to, to seek out something else. If he was a man of the spirit, he exiled himself into some personal spirit-world of his own. If he was of the ruling type, he created for himself and his nearest a higher class of their own, or else he passed over into some already existing class of similar origin. And it is typical of Germany that every class seals itself hermetically against every other class. This sort of vertical emigration is peculiar to the German; as far as I know, it belongs to him alone. But the most energetic types, the true men of action, have always seized the first opportunity to migrate to some distant land. This explains the Wandering of the Nations. That is why we have in North America a repetition of what took place in France two thousand years ago. We need only examine the skull-shapes and, more than that, the bespectacled myopic eyes of the new American types; this is the German mass-heritage. Among the Europeans the German alone has an hereditary tendency to short-sightedness. Thus one may say much the same thing about the German cult of soulfulness and home as about the Swedish. It is the cult of the "silent in the land"—the very concept of which, combined with the emotional stress which accompanies it, shows that we are dealing with something which arose as a reaction against other types, unconsciously recognized as superior. But nowhere, I repeat, does this character of the earth-rooted Nordic culture emerge with such clarity as in Sweden. That country entirely lacks the spiritual and historical complex of problems which, because of a blood-admixture which has resulted in inner tensions, has predestined the Germans to be philosophers and the English to be world-rulers. The general condition of Sweden today is exactly what it was in early times when the fighters had left the country on a Viking raid. At home there was singing and story-telling, expectation and hope. Everything was seen to, that the returning warriors might find the home-coming really pleasant. And today the only thing that has any meaning for the Swede is the possession and the exhibition of this good humour.

THE result is that modern Sweden is uninteresting. The foreigner who visits the country does so only to enjoy a rest. And at this point, again, something affirmative enters; there is not a cheerier country to be a guest in (assuming that the guest does not collapse physically, trying to live up to their idea of a good time). Yet in a certain sense Sweden is interesting all the same, because it is symbolically significant; to the extent, namely, that until very recently there was a fundamental possibility of conquering the Phaeacian character from within, and the opportunity was allowed to slip by. In one of my last lectures in Sweden I was asked to say something addressed directly to the Swedes, and I tried to refuse, with the remark that perhaps my honest opinion might not be altogether pleasing; for like all Phaeacians, the Swedes are an extremely self-satisfied people—in a very pleasant and distinguished way, to be sure, not at all like the Swiss, but rather like some fully contented and simple woman, who has no desire for anything which she has not got—but for all that, self-satisfied. After I had been assured that I had their permission to say whatever I wanted, and that no one would take offence, I developed the following train of thought: You are not a little proud of the fact that you stood aloof from the stupidity of the World War. I grant you that in this your cleverness has stood you in good stead. And yet: it is not well to stand at the door and smoke cigarettes while the Last Judgment is in session. In maintaining her neutrality Sweden has actually failed to link herself up with the new history of Europe. (This surely applies, more or less, to all countries which remained neutral, with the exception of Spain, which, not really a European country, did not need to share the common experience; but through the World War Sweden could have acquired for herself a new historic future.) For the new Europe is, in fact, the child of the World War. One had to pass through the World War in order to acquire new significance—and with regard to this point, it is of no importance on which side one fought. In this sense, Sweden has not participated in European history since the Thirty Years' War; for the Great Northern War was nothing more than the cleaning up which followed a stupid blunder. But now Sweden has permitted the decisive moment to pass by. This can hardly be made good again within a visible stretch of time. For the experience of the World War was not something external; there was created in every participant a new soul, non-existent till then, a soul which is alone adapted to the new complex of circumstances. That is why, from 1914 to 1918, I remained uninterruptedly in my Baltic home, though there was nothing to prevent me from leaving it. I felt that if I did not take the destiny of the war upon myself as a living person, I should be an *émigré* if not in space, then in time. And the *émigré*, if he does not become assimilated into the new nationality, is a national suicide. All that remains to Sweden today, as a land and as a people, is to co-operate in the institutional management of history, through the League of Nations, through the Court of Arbitration, by helping to solve the problem of the white slave traffic, etc. But she cannot again co-operate as a living factor. She has remained behind *organically*. The fact is that in the last analysis the World War was *not* a stupidity, not somebody's crime, but a psychological crisis which was bound to come. A better future is possible only on the basis of the changes which the experience of the war has brought about. Theoretically speaking, these changes could conceivably have been brought about on evolutionary rather than on revolutionary lines; but it came about thus and not otherwise. Thus everything that the Swede thinks is, with very few exceptions, no longer representative of Europe. His thoughts are like those of a retired *rentier* in the midst of an heroic race of founders. . . .

H ISTORICALLY, Sweden's good fortune is actually her mis-fortune. As far as I can see, her future European task can only consist now of two things; first, the production of important individuals of international significance. A politically neutralized *milieu* provides for such people (*n.b.* if they happen to be born) an atmosphere especially favourable to their rise and development. Thus at one time Alexandria, and for a long period the Netherlands, were the typical birth-places of important individual spirits. The great non-political spirit needs, before all else, security; he must feel external life, with all its cares, as little as possible; in contrast with all others, nothing is less propitious in his case than what is generally called a life rich in experience. Archimedes carried on his calculations with special intensity in order not to become aware of the siege of Syracuse; during the battle of Jena, Hegel was writing *The Phenomenology of the Mind*. . . . The second European task which, as far as I see, may fall to Sweden, is to cross-breed with other peoples. At this point I can join hands with the Nordic fanatic. It is true that the Swede today lacks entirely that inner tension which quickened the blood of the Vikings. But on the other hand the tension between their pure Nordic nature and the essential character of the other Europeans is so strong that a cross between the two can bring about a creative tension. We are too prone to forget the actuality which inheres in the concept of race. Things long separated from each other become estranged. That is why the crossing of royal with plebeian blood so often produces gifted offspring. For the same reason, the admixture of Catholic with Protestant blood is even today proving productive in Germany. Now as a rejuvenating ferment, the Swedish blood-stream is one of the best, if not altogether the best, in Europe; not only in the sense of purity, but also in the sense of the spiritual disposition which it transmits. Thus its infusion into the blood of any other race can be similar in its productive effect to the crossing of the Gallo-Romans, the Italians, etc., with Nordic blood. For there is one thing which I forgot to say, or to be more exact, which I have not yet said clearly enough. Like the English, but to a higher degree than the English, because they lack their snobbishness, the Swedes are a people of innate nobility. They are, as such, aristocrats by blood. They are without envy, free from resentment, both reticent and open. And they are open in a sense fundamentally different from most present-day Germans whose blood cannot, unfortunately, be characterized as "noble" in itself. Only when openness means an absence of cunning on the one hand, and on the other hand an absence of obtrusiveness; only when it maintains a proper distance from others by means of a particularly distinguished courtesy, does it mean a virtue. The German who is rude out of his sincerity does not rank ethically higher than the Levantine braggart; whenever such a one begins a sentence with "To be quite open with you," the first thing I ask myself is whether I ought not to have a horse-whip handy, not in order to defend myself, and certainly not in order to become aggressive, but simply for the purpose of teaching a Thersites good manners. One never stumbles into a situation like this in Sweden. Now inner tact, inner distance, are undoubtedly dependent to a large extent on the blood. That is why the addition of Swedish blood to the mixed races of today—there are no other races in Europe—would be a blessing. I say Swedish, and not Scandinavian at large. The Danes, for their part, are a mixed race; even the addition of French blood, in however light a dose, has co-operated in the production of their type. As to the Norwegians of today, they, even more than the Swedes, can be called the dregs of a race. So consistently have the best stocks always migrated from the country, that today everything in Norway is typically small-scale—a thing unheard of in the North. Moreover, this Nordic race has itself received an admixture of blood from some prehistoric stock. The weird quality in the heads of Ibsen and even of Björnson derives from this. I have seen Norwegians who are immediately suggestive of trolls; others, again, remind one of dwarfs. This very fact explains their spiritual importance as reflected in their literature; they have within them tensions which the Swedes lack. If they are reserved to an unnatural degree, that is undoubtedly bound up with the fact that they have much, very much, to hide. In any case the Norwegian blood-heritage is nowhere nearly as good as the Swedish. It is only in special and individual cases that I could recommend a European to seek a wife in Norway. But as against this I would make it a principle to recommend marriage to Swedish women. I do not believe that, as consorts, they are easy to live with. The gentle type of South German, in particular, who should happen to make this choice would do well to follow the counsel which an Englishwoman once gave me in my young days: "If ever you marry, obey; it is the only way." But the offspring of such a marriage will be good.

THE BALTIC STATES

I N the summer of 1920 I was allowed for the first time after
the war to return to my homeland, Esthonia. I found nothing outwardly changed in Rayküll. Everything was still standing in my house as when I had left it in 1918. The same
household again welcomed me, more warmly than ever. All my
habits were known and respected.

How could it be otherwise? It was only a year and a half
since I had left the home of my fathers; I had lived there without interruption throughout the World War. And yet a strange
wonder fell on me. And in a very few days this wonder was
changed into horror. *I had returned to my home as a ghost.* If
I was received in all friendliness even by those who before the
revolution had maintained a different attitude, this was the
fact that explained it; every one is polite to a ghost; one never
knows. . . . And then I was in no wise any longer an earthly
reality. Actually it was as if I had returned to my home in the
person of my own grandfather; forty years ago the naturally
acknowledged owner and master, today out of place in every
respect, disturbing the new order of things. Or rather, the discrepancy was a much greater one. In the consciousness of the
Esthonians a gulf of centuries divided 1920 from 1918. In
1918 Esthonia did not exist as a nation—the Esthonians were
merely the lower class. Now, because of a unique conjunction
of historic events, which made it appear desirable to the victorious powers to erect the small, independent Baltic states as
a bulwark against Bolshevism, a dream which had never been
taken seriously came true.

But why had I for this reason been changed into a ghost?
Here was a true case of the irony of fate. In 1918 we Balts
had called the Germans into the country, because this was the
only way to save it from destruction by the Russians. Thus we
had not only created all the culture which the land possessed
till then; ours, too, is the credit for its survival during the

World War. But we were a thin upper stratum of different race and different language. The trumpet sounded for the uprising of those who had been below. And then the same spirit of Bolshevism, the fear of which had brought about the fulfilment of the dreams of the Esthonians and the Latvians, wrote our death-warrant. And in this case the victorious powers came to the support of that spirit, for its particular view of private rights and private property promised soonest to establish the new states on a credit basis. This spirit of Bolshevism was—and, where it still rules, is—of a force inconceivable to those who have not come in contact with it. It cancelled history as a matter of course. That was possible in Russia, for there the structure which had acquired historic significance had never struck root in the subconsciousness of the majority. That majority believed neither in Roman nor in Germanic law; its subconsciousness did not accept as binding the order of things which the upper classes had fastened on the world; physiologically the masses had remained the same as in the days of Stenka Razin; the Marxian ideology was only a new mode of expression for primordial instincts.* Psychologically, the French Revolution left intact the fundamental laws which had governed the life of old France, for all Frenchmen continued to acknowledge it, if not consciously, then unconsciously; this was what made the subsequent Restoration possible. In Russia there took place a complete *solution de continuité*. There new men rose to power, to whom the rights of those who had lately been the rulers meant as little as the rights of the Pelasgians to the modern Greeks. One may see from this how, in the last analysis, everything depends on actual psychic forces. Rights cannot subsist where they are not acknowledged; property is an illusion where the belief in its rights has disappeared. Then life *really* begins anew.

In spirit the Esthonian revolution was primarily a specialized

* Cf. the detailed exposition of the true meaning of Bolshevism in my book, *The World in the Making*.

expression of the Russian, for at its outbreak the Russians in
the country far outnumbered those to whom Esthonia was their
real homeland; it was this Russian revolution which, in the
broadest sense, cancelled history. Suddenly, after 1918, it was
as though we Balts, natives of the country for seven hundred
years, had never been. And the equivalent of centuries *really*
lay between 1920 and 1918. I felt this from the first moment
of my arrival. The six weeks which I spent after the old
fashion on the hereditary estate were the ghastliest in my life;
I could scarcely sleep for the constant pounding of my heart;
the absence of outward change in my environment made me
feel the inner change all the more violently. And the feeling
was so ghastly primarily because I soon knew that on Baltic
soil this "Russian" revolution was really something senseless.
Had the same fate overtaken me in Russia proper, I should
surely have found it easier to adapt myself to it; for there it
was true destiny. But the Baltic lands belong to the *Western*
sphere of culture. The subconsciousness of their inhabitants, as
a group, had in it as little of the living Russian motif as did
that of the French. The Esthonian and the Latvian states, in
constituting a dam against the Sarmatian flood, were rendering
the same service as the Baltic aristocracies had rendered once
before. To that extent the entire contrast between the Germano-
Balts and the original inhabitants had been artificially en-
hanced. I knew that very soon Esthonia would turn to the
West, not only outwardly, but inwardly, that its Bolshevism
was not an outburst of its true nature, but a disease imported
from without. . . .

A ND yet, as a spirit, I am more thankful just for the tragedy
of my Baltdom than for anything else. Because of it I
have experienced in person something which otherwise could
only be reconstructed, at best, as a faint probability based on
half-mythical traditions. *I have witnessed in person the birth
of a nation.* When I was a child, the Esthonians did not con-

stitute a nation, but a peasantry and a servant class; they were *Gesinde*. This word *Gesinde*—its nearest English phrase is "the servants' hall"—was used among us, characteristically, to denote a peasant home. The language was that of a primitive people; abstract words were almost wholly lacking. There was, instead, an immense range of words to cover the hundreds of nuances between forest and moorland, between field and meadow, between the various species of wild fowl. I was, roughly, a school contemporary of the first trained and educated Esthonians who, finding no outlet for their activities in their homeland, scattered over the entire Russian Empire. Thus, when the Revolution came, there was suddenly revealed in existence a new people capable of self-government; so suddenly, that I made a solemn vow never again to judge reality from appearances. In my boyhood the Baltic countries were, from the political point of view, German, for only the German upper stratum counted. Then they seemed to become Russian. It was during the World War, when millions of Russian soldiers occupied the country, that this aspect reached its climax. But when the Germans occupied the country in 1918, it was as though Esthonia had remained uninterruptedly German. And when the German troops had to leave, in the fall of that year, Esthonia had suddenly become unquestionably Esthonian, and nothing else. Where did the leaders come from? Naturally they were already there, in our midst; but no one noticed them. So completely does everything depend on significance. . . .

Of course, things were done which not only smacked of violence but seemed brought about artificially. A written language had to be produced which should meet all modern requirements; it had to be understood. The first statesmen personally invented one word after another. I have seen the decree issued by a minister of education ordaining that a certain verb was henceforth to be conjugated in a new manner. Yet there was nothing artificial about this event, for the nation caught up these instructions as a matter of course. This was the thing that the oldest myths tell about, expressed in the terms of the new age: some king or other invented the language, created the ideas, transformed hunters into tillers of the soil. . . . It is possible even today; it is not something of the long ago only. What is needed is the conjunction of the white heat of the will-to-birth with that of the power-to-birth, and the story of creation repeats itself in all its primal improbability.

I can speak of Esthonia only from my own experience. But it was much the same in Latvia. And in spite of the one-time historic independence and greatness of the Lithuanians, Lithuania presented an even more extreme picture, in that this nation had long since almost ceased to exist; it had to be not only freed, but in part re-invented. But in the last analysis it was the same in every part of Europe where new nations arose as a consequence of the World War. It is necessary to be clear on this point in order to understand the policy of violence adopted by these states. Tolerance is the normal expression of inner security. Even England has always been liberal only when she has known that nothing threatened her position of victor for many years ahead; she has played the oppressor when she felt herself threatened. Now most of the succession states arose artificially, unprepared, and, in addition, within frontiers which did not correspond to natural boundaries—as is to be expected when countries are staked out in red tape by teachers of mathematics and religion who have to deal with geographic questions and whose first concern is to assert their authority by effecting the self-assurance of Jupiter. Thus for a long time to come their inner state, even in peace, was bound to be one of war. The policies of expropriation, like their attitude toward the minorities, can only be explained thus. The one new state which was inwardly ripe at the moment of its emergence, namely, Finland, did not in any way pursue the same policies. Externally its situation was not very different from that of the Baltic states. Ninety per

cent. Finns, ten per cent. Swedes: no love lost on either side.
But in both the feeling of Finland's destiny and of their common history predominated. Thus, in Finland's case a policy of
radicalism like that of the majority of the succession states was
psychologically out of the question. Outwardly this policy was
everywhere inspired by Russia. Had they not had before their
eyes the example of one class simply destroying the others
with a clear conscience, and coolly confiscating their property—
the same thing last took place under the Spanish Inquisition,
but even there only in individual cases—the Czechs, Roumanians, Serbs, Esthonians, Latvians, etc., would never have
dreamed of treating their fellow countrymen of different race
as they actually did. Assuredly the land question had to find
some new solution; where the old ruling class had become a
mere minority, the old property relations no longer corresponded to the new historic situation. Even cruelties could
not be avoided altogether, for every cancellation of long-
established rights must work hardship. But the particular
cruelties which were of decisive force in this crisis were nothing other than a more or less successful imitation of Bolshevism. The nations which have been guilty of them will some
day be ashamed of them. From the economic point of view the
"reforms" in question already seem to have been carried
everywhere to the *reductio ad absurdum*. And likewise, however unwilling they may be to admit it, the young nations are
everywhere beginning to suspect that it was senseless to try to
elbow out the racial minorities. (In this regard it is precisely
Esthonia who, by granting cultural autonomy to her minorities,
has taken a step toward a better future.) After the fearful
destruction of the World War and after its consequences, the
first premise toward reconstruction everywhere is the co-operation of all the best forces in the common task. Moreover, just
because of the new map of Europe which has incorporated so
many alien races in the body of new and therefore particularly
intolerant nations, the old concept of nationalism is dying out.

The state will inevitably be forced to specialize much more than was the case hitherto; the national element will have to acquire significance independently of the state, something which it never had before.* And then, catastrophes have never meant much in the life of nations. For a time treaties may indeed conceal the true relation of forces; in the long run it must break through. The ruined minorities, wherever they are worth anything, will in the end reach greater heights than ever before. It is a well-known fact that oppression strengthens; were it otherwise, the Czechs, etc., would never have become nations in the modern sense. Oppression has a strengthening effect all the more when minorities which are inwardly strong are torn from their soil; this has been demonstrated by the Jews. From earliest times it was typical precisely of politically powerless groups, that they become rich. Thus, in one way or another, ruined fortunes will soon be rebuilt. But above all, the minorities have a future before them because their destiny compels them to stand for those things which are true to the new age, because their own interests must transform their political backwardness, wherever it exists, into an anticipation of the future. Thus it is just the minorities, whose *rôle* is considered at an end, who are today the true path-finders of the new Europe. The state is losing in importance; it is to the interest of the minorities, and not to that of the majorities, who to this extent are the representatives of reaction, that the former shall make themselves the protagonists of the new relationship between state and nation. By outlawing the minorities, the majority principle has, from the viewpoint of a progressive mankind, been reduced to the absurd: now, if the future is to be better, a new system of rights, still to be created, must be enforced. The issue is this: the individual *as such* must become the protégé of international law, must be recognized as the possessor of inalienable human rights which, in case of

* The best analysis which has so far appeared on the newly emerging relationship between state and nationality is contained in a paper of that name by Gerhard von Mutius in the *Europäische Revue* for September, 1927.

necessity, must be defended for him against his own state. I say the individual as such, not the minority as such, for then the majorities would be logically entitled to the same rights, and everything would remain fundamentally as it was. When such a new system of rights has been instituted, then, and only then, will membership in this or that nation, this or that race, no longer create dangerous frictions. At the very moment when the World War broke out, it became evident that the old concepts and the old norms everywhere stood in need of revision. Everywhere considerable numbers of the ablest residents were found to be not a part of the state in which they lived. Now on the basis of the existing system of laws they could, if they happened to belong to hostile states, be stripped of all their possessions. What a difference between this and the time even of the Crimean War, when the then Governor General of Esthonia, a Herr von Grünewaldt, was afraid that his Czar would be very angry with him because certain English merchants resident in Reval would not be able to move out with all their belongings as comfortably as was befitting! The traditional symbiosis of different nationalities had its origin in the period preceding the triumph of the idea of the pure national state. The World War has shown that, in view of the ever-recurrent danger of war, this idea and the idea of a symbiosis on friendly terms are mutually exclusive. After the conclusion of peace, the resultant incompatibility emerged everywhere in all its colossal grotesqueness. Citizens of the defeated states who had left their fortunes in the victorious countries found them confiscated, as though we were still living in the times of Sulla. Even naturalized citizens of these countries, if they happened to belong to the defeated nationalities, were outlawed— and that with the approval of public opinion the world over. This resulted, on its side, in grotesque counter-effects; precisely at this moment, when the world is becoming unified as never before, when, in order to avoid new conflicts, the proper thing is to find an adjustment of pressure between thickly popu-

lated and thinly populated areas—precisely at this moment the
nations lock their gates more securely than ever before against
immigration, no doubt chiefly that they may not again be
tempted to steal other people's money. And on the other hand
the world is swarming, as never before, with people without
a country and with such as have acquired citizenship wherever
they could. As a matter of fact it seems in certain respects more
practical than before not to be a citizen in the country of one's
residence. There are, moreover, great numbers of persons who
feel instinctively that the day of the significance of the state in
the pre-war sense is over and gone. In 1917, when the collapse
of Russia threatened, I was debating with myself which particular citizenship would best serve me in the years to come;
and the first state that came to my mind was Monaco, because
it had the lowest taxes and because all danger of war seemed
to be out of the question. Unfortunately I was soon apprized
that this exemplary state had made it a principle not to naturalize foreigners. . . .

Indeed, the minorities have a great future before them.
And the reasons are not only empirical-political, but also metaphysical. Beyond a doubt the ruling and privileged classes of
yesterday also carried a heavy burden of guilt; it has never
happened that a class placed in a position of power failed to
abuse it. But now this guilt has been richly atoned. I ignore
those countries and those individual cases where persecution
stopped only with death; the mere fact of overthrow and ruin
means to the man who is typified by high position a thousand
times more than to the little man, and if he can meet the
situation inwardly it means a thousand times more than when
a peasant works himself up. This condition is intensified by the
circumstance that a highly organized soul unconditionally needs
a finer environment. This point is entirely missed by the new
ruling classes in the lands mentioned; just as the Bolshevists,
who had learned personally to regard imprisonment, exile, and
a life of misery in foreign lands as a normal condition were

last to solve the housing problem, so all standards of value which the new rulers applied in compensating the expropriated classes (where such compensation took place at all) were by their very nature defective. Thus the privileged classes of yesterday have more than atoned for their guilt. But now a new privilege beckons to them—*to return good for evil by exerting themselves to the utmost to make injustice impossible for the future*. The ugliness and cruelty which manifests itself in such a high degree in the soul of the newly-risen classes is to a large extent the result of the previous lack of opportunity; spiritual deformities of this kind must be avoided for the future. Oppressed and despised classes must no longer exist on this earth. Indeed, a mission of immediate Messianic import lies before the persecuted minorities.

What applies fundamentally to all minorities applies in the highest degree to the German Balts. The historic *rôle* of this people is in no wise at an end. To begin with, the Esthonians and the Latvians are continuing in every field that which we began; and where no true *solution de continuité* exists, the idea, too, cannot long endure as a living thing. The cultivated forests which constitute the greatest asset of the young state are chiefly of our creation; if Eesti and Latwiya, as members of the Western family of nations, stand as a bulwark against Russia, they are, once again, only continuing the traditional policy of the Baltic aristocracies. As for us, we have absolutely no intention of dying out. That section which has migrated will of course assimilate with the peoples among whom it has found asylum. But a great many have remained behind, and one *émigré* after another is returning. Only one pair of every species was rescued by Noah's ark, and still it seems to me that there are beasts a-plenty on this earth; as far as we are concerned, much more than one couple out of nearly every family remained behind. And, as a group, those who have remained behind, far from being weakened inwardly, seem to have been strengthened. Although they should be

completely ruined, they support more German schools than
ever before; their intellectual life has become more intensive;
wherever they are coming closer to the soil, as in Lithuania and
Latvia, where parts of their estates have been left to them—
but parts so infinitesimal that the life of a country gentleman
is no longer possible—a process of rejuvenation is in the long
run bound to follow: over and over again, cultures blossom
forth in the soil of a peasantry. And then our type is one which
essentially delights in danger; if we had become petrified, this
was due to an all too long security. From now on, the old force
awakens to new life. I know of very few Balts who have fallen
so low that a new rise—if not for themselves, then for their
children—seems improbable. For me this is final proof of the
fact that the spiritual and mental structure of the aristocrat is
higher, in the absolute sense, than that of the *bourgeois*. The
Balts are, in fact, a pure aristocratic type, in this respect most
nearly akin to the Hungarians. Even those who belong to the
bourgeoisie in the matter of class—they are called, in the Baltic
countries, *Literaten*—when compared with the Germans of the
Reich, are, in general, pure ruler-types; with all his feeling for
the commonweal, every Balt feels himself to be primarily
unique. Today, after the loss of their external position as rulers,
this does not manifest itself with the same clarity as hitherto.
But how marvellously manifold the old Baltic life used to be,
founded as it was on the consciousness of uniqueness peculiar to
the aristocrat! In Rayküll I always lived the life of an ancho-
rite. But when I did go out to some festivity, or to visit another
manor, I found all the more joy in the fact that every individual was in the best sense an original; every one was a type
for himself, like the Homeric heroes; as a matter of fact each
man should have been known only by his first name, as in those
days. Because of this consciousness of uniqueness, the Balts were
able to support their fall as no other overthrown ruling class
has done in this age. I will say nothing about the men. But I
would like to hear of a modern equivalent for the following:

When the Germans threatened to march across the Moonsund into Esthonia, all the male members of the aristocracy whom the Bolshevists could lay hands on were packed into cattle-trucks and sent off to Siberia (with two exceptions they returned home later, unbroken in body and spirit); all the women, however, were imprisoned in a building over the stores of mines and torpedoes of the Baltic fleet. A sailor stood on guard with a slow match at hand; the moment the Germans crossed the ice, the building was to be blown up. *Not one* woman of the aristocracy showed the slightest fear; on the contrary, there was a sort of gaiety—we are not going to allow this low pack of murderers to impress us. Which was precisely the reason why these women were very soon set at liberty. Yes, the aristocratic structure of mind and spirit is the highest human product in the absolute sense. The *bourgeois* is the man of security; the aristocrat is the man of danger, of risks. Now a condition of security contradicts the very meaning of life, for all life stands under perpetual sentence of death. To the extent that the peasant is tied down to his earth-destiny, he, too, is not a man of security. But it is only the type of the noble who, in his form, corresponds completely to the meaning of life. This is why we Balts will certainly not go under as long as we do not become *bourgeois*. The new day of aristocracy is dawning everywhere, so much so that there is a great deal of talk about a return to the age which preceded the events of 1789; it is the foregoing which explains it. And actually the new world in the making favours most the sons of the nobility, however ruined their fortunes may be, and favours the proletarians least. The latter threaten to become more *bourgeois* than any *bourgeoisie* has ever been. The decline of France is being prophesied on the grounds of its *rentier* psychology: what was the French *rentier* class, in numbers as well as in intensity, as compared with the social *rentier* class which is springing up in Germany? From the sick-benefit funds to unemployment insurance and old-age pensions, all the latest social legislation aims at one thing—to

breathe the soul of the *rentier* into the workers. It has already
come to the point where any man of forty who has not in one
tricky way or another become a social *rentier* feels himself
déclassé. . . . Should this continue, then Germany, like every
other country with equally good laws, must inevitably perish.
But it cannot continue. The circle has already been completed.
If privileged kings, privileged priests, privileged nobles, became, in spite of their small numbers, unbearable in the long
run, how can we expect a privileged working-class to be put up
with? At a time when the whole world is becoming industrial-
ized and no non-European people has yet seized on the idea
of the social *rentier*, it is clear that Europe will be able to stand
competition only when it will have learned again to "live dangerously." But should this come to pass, then the nobleman will
as a matter of course again become the leader.

A ND what of the Baltic country as a whole, looked at from
the viewpoint of Europe? It is, first of all, a land with a
spirit all its own. I know few countries which, physically, have
such power to mould the spirit of man; as pure landscape only
North America and the Balkans seem to me equally creative.
The latest research has shown that the races which have hitherto
been called Caucasian, or Indo-Germanic, came originally from
my homeland. I gladly believe this. It is certain, in any case,
that the Goths once dwelt there. Even today the Esthonian
language contains Gothic words. Since then races of Finnish,
Germanic, and Slav origin have been in turn superimposed as
rulers (the Latvians, the present masters of Latvia, came into
the country after the Germans; the old inhabitants whom they
already found there were not Latvian). Here, however, the
emphasis does not lie on the question of origin, any more than
it does in the United States, but on that unified particular whole
into which all the blood of the Baltic countries has flowed. The
German of the Reich who has grown up in the Baltic countries
becomes a Balt; so does the Pole, the Swede, the Russian; yes,

even the Jew. Wherever this assimilation did not take place it
was due to the fact that the individuals in question—it was thus
particularly with the Russian official—remained artificially
aloof. No doubt the Balt is not a clearly defined product. The
northern type touches at points the Nordic which has also created the Swede and the inhabitants of St. Petersburg; the
southern and western type, again, touches at points the Pole.
And the German element in the historic upper classes indues
every Balt—of whatever blood, for the dominant strain always
works creatively by suggestion—with a particular German character, independently of speech and training. But even with the
German Balt it is not the German element which makes the
Balt, even though, with few exceptions, he puts the exclusive
emphasis on the German side of him much more than any German does; it is the Baltic element. It is difficult to define this
in the abstract, since we have to do with a border type. Yet
a single glance at the one analogue which may be found in
Europe clears the way to an understanding; I mean the Belgian. It is not only outwardly, but inwardly, too, psychologically, that Belgium presents the picture of a Franco-German
border country. Whether the German predominates, as in the
Fleming, or in the French, as in the Walloon, it is the Belgian
element which is the essence with him. Thus the Balt, too, is
primarily Balt, whether there is more of the German in him
or more of the Pole, whether he is more Swedish (the Esthonian type is much more Swedish than German) or more Russian, whether he lays the racial stress on the German element or
on the Esthonian and Latvian. Every genuinely indigenous inhabitant of the Baltic countries strikes the outsider primarily as
a Balt. In him live side by side, however unconsciously, German
ideals, German cultural tradition, and German ethos, the Scandinavian spirit of independence, the suppleness and swiftness of
the Slav in general, and the vital rootedness and generosity of
the Russian in particular—all of it held together by the specific
spirit of the landscape which once created the primal form of

the Viking. For the Viking was essentially a Balt, a son of the Baltic, delighting in adventure. It is the Viking character in the Balt, then, which also produces the specific limitations of his present-day type. Like the seafaring Norman, he is not richly endowed with soul; he easily makes an impression of dryness and barrenness. He is intelligent, temperamental, witty, but it is only in exceptional cases that his soul is receptive to world-influences in the sense of pathos. If Turanian blood is added as a dominant—as in the case of the Esthonians—the basic traits become those of materialism and matter-of-factness. There are a great many possible and actual shadings, according to the proportions of the elements. But it is the Balt element as such which is, in spite of everything, the basic characteristic. The purest type, of course, emerges in all its clarity, here as elsewhere, only in the most gifted individuals; and these have been wholly, or almost wholly, of German blood. But these Germans, again, are in the same sense different from the Germans of the Reich. Whether it is Harnack or Patkul, Alexander von Oettingen or Karl Ernst von Baer, the surgeon Werner Zöge von Manteuffel, the last Esthonian of traditional greatness of mould, Alexander Keyserling, my grandfather, or the Mongol chieftain Ungern-Sternberg or myself—the basic type was always the same.

Beyond a doubt the present ruling classes in the Baltic states will merge more and more into the traditional basic type. If they diverge from that type, it is much more as members of the lower classes than as the carriers of a specific blood. And that they have it in them, after having conquered in themselves the feeling of subjection and of the *parvenu*, to become ruler-types, is already demonstrated by their outspoken anti-*bourgeois* character. This clearly lies in the *genius loci*. Sweden, too, is anti-*bourgeois*, and so is Russia. But with all that, Sweden is not aristocratic, and Russia is essentially plebeian-minded; if the latter can today stand under the sign of the proletariat dictatorship, this derives from the same circumstance which has always permitted the Russian to talk big about the baseness of his soul. As opposed to this, the Baltic landscape always gives birth to ruler-types.

As Balts the Esthonian and the Latvian will of course be different from the German Balt: it is obvious that the blood-heritage plays some part, and the psychological situation, too. The Esthonians and the Latvians have only adapted themselves to some extent to the spirit of post-war Europe, and consciously deny all tradition, while we German Balts consciously live it. The matter-of-factness of the Esthonian is specifically Turanian: so is his tenacity; it is impossible not to recognize here the psychic kinship with the Hungarian and the Turk. On the other hand the Esthonians have a great deal that is Scandinavian and very little that is specifically German in their psychological structure. Thus the Indo-Germanic Latvians resemble, again, the Slavs. And yet, as every outsider must perceive at the first glance, both races are most nearly akin to the German Balts; they stand in the same relation to these as the French type which has issued from the *tiers état* does to the old aristocracy. And here, to, we are faced by a racial difference of blood. Europe owes her specific character, as distinguished from that of Russia, America, and China, to the fact that its various geographic regions have been conquered and reconquered time and again, so that new ruling classes have continuously been produced; and everywhere in Europe the various classes are fundamentally of different blood. Much can be explained from this circumstance, above all in the history of the last two hundred years, when the religion of equality arose for the first time as a mighty counter-ideology opposed to the existing state of things. If all Frenchmen are, in spite of their differences of blood, essentially French, and all Germans (admittedly with a much lighter degree of unification) essentially German, this is due to the fact that history and physical surroundings conspire to produce a psychic coalescence of the various blood-streams. Now in the Baltic countries it is the physical contours of the land which do more than anything else to make Balts of all the inhabitants; they are of immense formative power. And if there is no common consciousness of history, there is on the other hand a much greater blood-unity than the former upper strata and the former lower strata would like to admit. All the conquerors of the earth, without exception, have had children by the daughters of the land. In earlier times, in contrast to our own, the upper strata left a larger posterity than the lower: in this sense they were literally the fathers of their country: when history opens, we frequently find whole tribes descended from kings. This explains why the greater part of France, down to the south and west, is shot through with the Frankish type—the Franks never migrated into the country in large numbers. To a very large extent the same has, of course, happened in the Baltic countries. To begin with, the Esthonians certainly do not bear less Germanic blood in their veins—be it Swedish or German—than Ugro-Finnish; there is, moreover, an original Gothic base. This blood-unity, and not the diversity of stock, explains in large part the extremes to which the Baltic agrarian revolution ran.

WHAT future can we prophesy for the Baltic states? Unquestionably a very important and significant one. Once again, as often before, a condition of backwardness will prove an advantage. As a matter of fact the phenomenal rise registered of late by Germany is due to the Thirty Years' War, which was originally a tremendous set-back. Because of this, it still possesses a large middle and lower class, rich in potential talents, as the broad basis of the national pyramid; today it has been conclusively proved that democracy sterilizes the lower classes of their talents, while making for the elimination of stocks with hereditary gifts; one has to be immunized against the comfortable life no less than against smallpox, and when the individual rises too rapidly, the preliminary conditions of such an immunization are lacking. In the Baltic countries, until a few years ago, the most valuable types of Nordics remained earthbound in the primitive sense. Today the entire fallacy of the Germanic claim to exclusive worth has been scientifically exposed; it is the *Nordic* type that matters, whether pure or whether crossed with East Baltic blood, and it is to the latter type that the Esthonians and the Latvians, too, belong. But the German ruler class, too, had remained behind on its own particular plane; and to the extent that it led a peculiar and isolated life, to the extent that it lingered on in a pre-modern state, it, too, has retained its vitality unexhausted. Since all influence moves from the upper classes downward, the Esthonians and Latvians are now busily engaged in copying our mistakes. It was our mistake that we interpreted our Germanism in political terms, which under the given circumstances was inadmissible. In the same sense the Esthonians and the Latvians have now made a goal of their Esthonianism and Latvianism; their nationalism has no more meaning-content than ours. Thus the various stocks which inhabit the Baltic countries will for a time live in a state of internal feud. But the true and essential history of my homeland is yet to come. What has taken place on its soil till now is what takes place everywhere immediately after a first conquest. The actual history of Eastern Europe began something like a thousand years after that of Western Europe. This, again, is bound up with the adjacency of Russia, whose real history has perhaps not yet even begun; it is possible that the czaristic period may some day be compared with the pre-Minoan period in its relation to the classic age of Hellas. If we desire to see clearly, we must once again think back to Belgium, that exact western counterpart of the Baltic states. How many historic dramas have played themselves out on that soil! How many races have ruled it! In the end, very late in its history, it developed into an independent state with a character all its own. In the same way the Baltic region, too, is still at the beginning of its development. First came the age of chivalry—of which we German Balts were the protagonists; and now the age of the old, primal stock begins to dawn. But something else is yet to come. Further admixtures will inevitably take place. Wedged in as the country is between Germany, Poland, and Russia, a new unity will inevitably be created in the long run—but a unity of the same type as that of the Baltic orders of knighthood was. Who knows whether these countries will always remain independent? At any moment they may be overrun by Russia, or they may be subjected to some other foreign rule. But if an aristocracy so weak in numbers could not even be conquered, let alone assimilated, how much less can this happen to wider national units? And more and more will the Baltic races stand close together in times of danger, just as the German-Balt youth readily poured out its blood in the hour when the Red armies threatened all that was Baltic with annihilation. Until the new Russia has become consolidated, the Baltic states will live under a perpetual threat. So did Belgium, during a period of centuries. But all the more surely—of this I am convinced—will a new Baltic nation emerge. And when that point has been reached, even those who hate us German Balts today will learn to see in us the first founders of the state. Then the old coats-of-arms will once again be unearthed. Then the old Ritter- und Domkirche of Reval, today the Church of the See, and the monuments of the Orders of Knighthood—among them the wreath of honour of Ritterschaftshauptmann Alexander Keyserling—will no longer be regarded as memorials of an age of foreign domination, but as memorials of an early national history.

Russia, as such, no longer belongs within the real European picture. It stands on the threshold of a new historic life. The *rôle* which it has played for Europe, through its great literature, belongs, from the viewpoint of the present, to a past which is almost as alien, as remote, as the age of Pericles seen from the viewpoint of the latest Greek policy. Tremendous and significant events are yet to come in that country, but in relation to a new, extra-European world, just as in America. But, as I

showed in connection with Spain, Russia does, as a border country, belong to Europe. The latter, through Russia, stretches
out toward the Orient, psychically as well as geographically,
just as it fuses with Africa through Spain. To this extent the
Baltic states have a much greater significance than Belgium,
with which I at first compared them. The latter country is
only the mediator between countries of closely related cultures;
the Baltic states and the Baltic civilization are the inner and
outward mediator between two of the most gigantic cultural
spheres differing from each other essentially. In this *rôle* of
mediator, then, I see the great historic task of the Baltic states.
It was altogether remarkable how, within a very short period
after the revolution, the new Esthonia settled into a condition
which one cannot but call post-Bolshevist—post-Bolshevist not
only by virtue of the radical reforms which were adopted at
first, nor yet by virtue of the conquest of Bolshevism as such,
but because the new state, definitely related to the civilization
of the West, is yet a child of the Bolshevist spirit in contrast to
democratic liberalism; it is therefore the *future* which has
consolidated itself there. Russian influence will always remain
very strong in the Baltic states. It always was. If, before the
war, this was not evident externally, that was due to the strong
opposition to Russia—to which the Baltic states belonged politically—and its policy of Russification. Most people do not realize that enmity creates a community of spirit no less than love
does, and that only the indifferent remains uninfluenced. Today, with the external inhibition removed, Russian influence
can manifest itself only with increasing force. If it cannot be
said of the majority, it can at least be said of the best and most
representative *émigrés* in Germany that they are finding out
more and more how much of the soul of Russia lives in them;
and as to the Esthonians, they actually speak Russian among
themselves, just as the Balts spoke French among themselves
in my grandfather's day. Thus, in the end, there will have to
arise in the Baltic lands a transitional structure between Russia

and Europe, one which, however, has its centre in the West, just as America must remain essentially European in origin, however strongly the primal spirit of the continent may some day come to manifest itself. And Europe *needs* a transitional structure of this kind. Just as Russia had to have a window toward Europe—Peter the Great built it—so Europe needs to-day, more than ever before, a channel of communication with the renascent Orient, and it must be a vital channel, belonging organically to both, and not merely a connective theory. For Russia today represents a future which every man must somehow share, if he wishes at all to become equal to the tasks of the new historic period. It is not only the whole Asiatic continent which is renewing itself through the polarizing centre of Moscow; for the West, too, its significance is tremendous. We have already seen, in connection with Italy, how, in its roots, Fascism is at one with Bolshevism; the closing chapter will show how the spirit of the new America also converges with that of Bolshevism. To this extent Soviet Russia is, among other things, the expression of a unified spirit of the age which is dominating the whole world more and more. But even independently of its present function as a historic symbol, Russia has a great significance for Europe; that influence which it exerted since Dostoievsky continues without interruption and to the same effect. Why is it that the Dostoievsky type, chaotic as it is, possesses such an enormous power of attraction? It is not only because of the state of fluidity which it represents in contrast with the rigidity of many of the older European life-forms—something we have already touched on in connection with Spain—but because in Russia man has anticipated the extreme inner tension belonging to the type which alone seems to be quite adequate to the tasks of an ecumenic civilization. The European of the kind we have known hitherto is too narrow, too provincial, to master it; in this regard he stands in the same relation to the Russian as the Frenchman does to the German and the Anglo-Saxon. And since every forward-look-

ing European feels this unconsciously, Russia will exert a tremendous attractive power, however the conscious mind may
guard against it; it is well to recall here the observations at the
beginning of the chapter on England on the meaning of love between nation and nation. It appears to me that under these historic circumstances the Baltic type encloses within itself extremely important possibilities for the future; thus, unless all
signs fail, a significant future beckons to this little country, the
very existence of which was scarcely suspected before the war—
this assuredly not in the sense of political greatness, but in a
sense which is much more important: as the cradle of significant
individuals. The task of the country as such lies along the same
lines as that of Poland and Roumania; all three body forth the
inwardly fortified frontier of Europe against the Orient. Pol-
and is more virulently Catholic and Occidental than any other
country, because by virtue of her Slavic character she feels with
special force her difference from the Russian spirit. Roumania
asserts with a sort of convulsive insistence her affiliation with
the Latin world (the next chapter will show that what we are
really dealing with is the Greek-Byzantine), because the South
Russian not only lives next door to her, but actually lives within
her soul. The same roots feed the nationalism and Protestantism of the Balts. But, in contradistinction to the Roumanian and the Pole, the Balt does not feel essentially hostile
toward the Russian; he is both sundered from the East and
open to it. In him the Russian lives as kinsman. From the viewpoint of Europe, he is actually the Western European variant
of the Russian, as which he was accepted all over the world
before the outbreak of the war. And this means: despite his
Occidentalism, there lives in him the far-flung nature of the
Russian, the strong Russian tension, but in the form of a traditional culture. Thus it may well be that the Balt will be among
the first to produce out of himself the ecumenic type, the ecumenic type of the East-West variety. And it is for Germany in
particular that he may prove to be a polarization centre of the

utmost conceivable importance; because he belongs to the German sphere of culture, he, more than others, may help the German to burst the bonds of the traditional German narrowness which has become, for the far-flung newly emergent world, nothing more than provincialism.

I have looked very far ahead. Now my spirit flies back to the place of my birth, to the family cemetery of Rayküll. Pure accident led to the choice of the site. Strolling one day with his children through the marshy woods, my grandfather came upon a gigantic, freakish boulder and, as if moved by an inner spirit, said: "Here we shall all lie buried some day." My father, a sufferer from melancholia, touched with foreknowledge of an untimely death, wrote these lines for the same little grove:

> I know, too swift draws near the time
> When I shall meet my doom,
> The fir-trees of a northern clime
> Shall stand about my tomb.*

His tombstone still stands there, probably covered by now with moss and hidden by wild undergrowth. Mine will not stand there, but I think of this without bitterness. No one can rob me of my memories. I am conscious, all the same, of my origin. Today, no less than ever, I belong to my homeland, as far as any wanderer on earth can have this feeling, for it is because I am a Balt, and not a German of the Reich, because I belong inwardly to two worlds, a border-dweller in space as well as in time, a Viking and a child of the steppes, carrying within me both the oldest tradition and the remotest future, that I am able to do the things I am doing. May the younger generation of Balts meditate on this. The pre-war age is gone forever. A new age is dawning. New tasks present themselves, tasks of far-

* Ich weiss es wohl, nur gar zu bald
Werd' ich zugrunde gehen.
Am fernen Nord, im Tannenwald,
Dort wird mein Grabstein stehen.

flung, far-reaching significance. More than ever does every-thing depend upon individual men. Where can the important individual soonest emerge and find the spur to his life-work? In the place where the landscape brings forth the spirit of ex-panse, and where the narrow local limits nevertheless deny him the possibility to live himself out within them. In this already lay the spiritual origin of the Viking.

THE BALKANS

THE BALKANS

WHAT is the significance of the Balkans to us who live in other lands? To what extent are they a reality even to those who know nothing about them? Why is it that the word "Balkanization" is almost always rightly understood and rightly applied? Seen from without, it is thus, and not otherwise, that the problem of the Balkans presents itself. As far as I can see, its symbolic sense may best be apprehended from two starting-points; the first is the generally accepted statement that the Balkans are the powder-magazine of Europe. The second is the fact of a peculiarly elemental and irreconcilable racial enmity.

That the Balkans are the powder-magazine of Europe is obviously due to the second and not to the first-mentioned cause. There is antagonism today between England and France, as there once was between Austria and Russia; as long as it is at all possible, such antagonisms are fought out indirectly on remote foreign frontiers, so that the immediate relationships can continue as if everything were in order. Furthermore, whenever it is possible, a nation prefers to let some one else do the shooting and the dying. In this connection the fact that the Balkans do actually represent overlapping spheres of interest is almost irrelevant. Here one might appropriately say: *Si les Balcans n'existaient pas, il faudrait les inventer.* This explains why a conflagration which begins in the Balkans is more liable than any other to become a world-conflagration. But the Balkans could never do this by themselves. They would never have become the one suitable place for the concentration and provocation of conflicts if there were not in those parts—this brings us to the second of the two principles enunciated at the beginning—such a peculiar elemental enmity between the races that these are momentarily ready to fly at each other's throats; there the state of war appears the only normal one.

How has this come about? The immediate causes are clear.

The peculiar system of government of the Turks allowed every local type to retain its *status quo*. They neither oppressed nations as such, nor did they ever set themselves the building of a new nation as their goal. Thus the various Raja peoples lived on for centuries unmixed and un-unified, retaining, side by side and within the same territory, an original particularism such as exists elsewhere only among savage tribes; the result was that when the nationalist spirit awoke, it found at hand an instrument possessed of a higher electrical potential than could be found anywhere else. In the second place, certain of the Balkan peoples are, and for some time will be, not only obviously but essentially savage. If today the Serbs are still living to some extent in the heroic age (they alone among the Jugo-Slavs come under this heading, the Croats are Slav Austrians), if the Albanian is, as a type, the immortal noble-minded robber —for he is the oldest of the Europeans: his traditional ethos, which in the time of Pyrrhus of Epirus perhaps embodied a spirit similar to that which the League of Nations represents today, is from the modern point of view a true brigand ethos— then the Bulgarians, in spite of their robust peasantry and their industriousness, are in the last analysis a nation of Comitadji; like the Afghan Afridi, like many of the Berber tribes, they find full expression for their friendly and sociable instincts in personal hatreds and personal blood-lust. There a lawyer, a doctor, may become a highwayman overnight, like the North-Indian princes who, educated in England, return to their country and relapse into barbarism at a moment's notice. My personal contacts have been only with Bulgarian writers; the habit which they had of breaking their agreements, and of writing abusive letters, was an aboriginal expression of the Comitadji spirit; the pen became both pistol and stiletto. One need only observe the wild features, the huge, shapeless noses of the Bulgarians—everything about them belongs to the primitive. They are, in actuality, man as seen by the Freudians. The tension between these wild races and the intellectual Greeks, the superior

Turks, and the lyrical Roumanians amply suffices to produce an extremely explosive totality.

But there are other, deeper reasons, beyond these. Why does this state of affairs seem ineradicable in the Balkans? One may recall, in this connection, Shaw's prognostications concerning the Irish in his *Back to Methuselah;* in a few centuries the last of them would be living in the Balkans, for there alone, of all places, would national problems still exist. The will to mutual oppression and mutual extermination, carried to an extreme unknown elsewhere on earth, actually seems essential to the Balkan races. And this elemental will cannot really be explained on the grounds of the blood-strains to be found in the country. From the earliest times the stocks have intermarried in wild unrestraint. There is no doubt that the neo-Greeks are preponderantly of Slav stock, and yet essentially Greek. And as far as Macedonia is concerned, it has been conquered and reconquered, ravaged and raped back and forth, nationalized and denationalized so often that even the Last Judgment will find it difficult to settle once for all the question of its racial identity. And on the other hand Macedonia has produced, over and over again, men of violence and action of extraordinary calibre, whatever they might be by blood; such was Alexander the Great, and such is the *ghazi* Mustapha Kemal. It is then in the Balkans themselves, as a psycho-physical unity, that the chief reason for the condition of the Balkan peoples must lie. And when we think now of the Balkan feuds of ancient Greek times, the feuds which had as their goal nothing less than mutual extermination and which came to an end only when the Turks of that day—i.e. the Romans—suppressed them from above; when we think, further, of the peculiar bitterness with which religious differences were fought out in Constantinople, how the slightest deviations from an accepted text led to murder and assassination, we realize that the Balkans of today are nothing but a caricature of the Balkans of ancient times. *The spirit of the Balkans as such is the spirit of eternal strife.* Inhab-

ited as they are by primitive races, they present the primal picture of the primal struggle between the one and the all. In the
case of the highly gifted and highly educated nations and individuals, this picture emerges as the spirit of the agon. But the
earth-spirit of the Balkans as such is the primal formative
power. What applies to the Baltic provinces applies to the Balkans in the highest degree.

Does it not become clear now why the greatest danger which
threatens Europe is involuntarily called "Balkanization"?
Europe, too, is Balkan in essence. Imagine a Europe as unified,
as levelled down, as America or Russia; its sense would evap-
orate. Europe is essentially small and fragmented, physically as
well as psychically. Its earliest spirit had its birth in the Balkans. For it is not the spiritual heritage of the Greeks which is
in question here, but the fact that it was in the Balkans, in the
field of tensions constituted by city-states at perpetual war with
each other, that there first came into play the specific differentiation which nation after nation has since perpetuated in one
long, consistent line. Europe is exactly as much of a unity as
the old Balkans were. It is the interference-field of the most
powerful and most incompatible tensions in existence today;
the Romano-German to begin with, and then the West-East
tension, the tension between the modern and the antique, down
to the purely empiric tensions between the various national
individualities.

If these tensions interfere upon a high plane, they can be
only a blessing. But what happens if the agon becomes a mutual
struggle to the death between each and all? In that case, Europe
will become a gigantic replica of the modern Balkans. Thus we
Europeans must be grateful for the fact that there exists a
living Balkan world as the grave of the culture of antiquity,
and from this we must learn what to avoid. For the spirit which
came into power with the World War actually threatens to
transform the equivalent of the ancient Balkans into the equivalent of the Balkans of today. To me a poison-gas war between

Europeans—conducted either on the physical or the spiritual plane—is something much more evil than all the ambush murders of the Balkans. And as yet the danger is far from past. Majorities and minorities, friendly neighbours and the like, hate each other hardly less than the Bulgarians and the Serbs. Nor are there any natural reasons why this should not become progressively worse. The more savage Balkan peoples have been overtly or covertly at war for entire decades; nothing seems to stand in the way, not attrition, nor hunger, nor loss of man-power. A primitive life is primarily true to nature. Man must become accustomed to a life of culture, not to trench-life. Mortal danger is normal as well as wholesome. No animal ever knew such security as we enjoyed during the forty years which preceded the World War. This is why no wild animal has ever been known to degenerate. Let no one invoke economic considerations in this connection. These can be deciding factors only where a passionless intelligence dominates. That is why there never has been and never will be a true revolution in Germany. Where a nation abandons revolutionary projects because they do not "pay" (they never do, of course), there an authentic revolution is physiologically impossible. But there is as little physiological ground to expect that considerations of reason should ever interfere with a mad impulse toward self-destruction. Emotions and passions, wherever they dominate, are their own ultimate deciding principles. They dominate, more or less, among all the European peoples, with the exception of the Germans. Thus in Europe, too, the Balkan situation carries within itself the principle of constant intensification.

L ET us now turn to specific Balkan questions. For this purpose I ignore the Serbs, Bulgarians, and Albanians; for the time being, they are primitive warrior and robber races; they inject no personal factor into the total European structure. And the Pan-Slavic idea has become pointless since the Slav peoples have all achieved independence; a new Russian Pan-Slavism

would unquestionably meet with the united opposition of all of
Russia's "blood-brothers."—First as to the Roumanians. The
contention that this people belongs within the Latin sphere of
culture is pure fraud. It certainly does not do so merely by
virtue of the Romance language which it speaks. Everything
depends on the spirit, and in no single respect is this Latin. To
the man of education it comes under the heading of the Byzantine-Greek, and little wonder; for the aristocracy which dominated until recently was almost wholly Greek by origin. The
fact that the Roumanians have more *esprit*, in the French sense,
than any other people outside of France, is explained by the
circumstance that before the rise of Paris, this *esprit* was to be
found most not in Rome, but in Athens and then in Constantinople. If they desire at all costs to be French in spirit—the
Roumanian four hundred would rather be foreign- than Rou-
manian-minded!—the explanation must be sought in that same
power of prestige which made it appear quite natural to the
Turkish conquerors of Constantinople to prostrate themselves
before the holy power of the *basileus* long after the empire of
the Greeks had shrunk to miniature dimensions. The best Roumanian wit is actually Byzantine; in Roumania there has survived until this day the art of the epigram, which since the
times of antiquity has flourished nowhere else on earth. The
lyric style of poetry, which is more important for Roumania
than for any other modern country—of the Roumanians of
note, one out of three, we are told, is a poet of importance—
would have to be classified as an expression of the Slavic variety
of spirit, just like the neo-Greek, were it not that a certain
joyfulness and a certain static quality seems to approximate it,
again, to the German, and even to the Hawaiian. In this, then,
there is something specifically Roumanian, and the attempt to
trace it further back would, as in the case of every unity of
style, be a misunderstanding. In all probability we have to do
here with a living Thracian-Scythian heritage, just as their
modern rugs remind one most of the Scythian models. But the

effect produced by the Roumanian people in the mass is one of complete unity of spirit with the South Russian. I saw nothing in that country, either of men or conditions, which would not have appeared just as authentic on the banks of the Dnieper. They are the same good, gentle, unpractical people, with the same kind of soul. A train in which I was travelling once was snow-bound for twenty-four hours; the entire incident, as well as the experiences which attended it, might just as well have taken place on the Russian steppes. Whenever I think of the Roumanian national dances I am always reminded of the flood areas of the Dnieper (*Plavni*) and, by association, of the Russian description *plavnya dvishenia*—it is the gliding motion of the swan or of the soft waves that pass along the river reeds. And whenever I have had to listen to the lively complaints of all the Roumanians I have ever met on the subject of the wicked Jews, who invade the country in larger and larger hordes, and who cannot be got rid of, either because they are too powerful or because the Roumanians are too good-natured, I am always reminded of the Ukrainian fable by Gogol, which runs as follows: One memorable winter night the Devil came and carried off the Jew; at first there was nothing but rejoicing; before long, however, everything was out of joint, and soon a cry went up from the whole country: How can we live without the Jew? Finally, to the relief of every one, the Devil brought back the abducted Jew.

Now that the event of war has turned Bessarabia over to Roumania and has disinherited the boyars, it is to be expected that with the passing of the years the Roumanian people will take on more and more of the South Russian character. It is true that one thing will forever be lacking to give them the Russian appearance: the inner force. But in South Russia it was only the Cossacks who had this, owing to their admixture of Tartar blood. The first heroes of the national myth were, again, Warangians, i.e. Scandinavians. The Roumanian is absolutely devoid of that temperament which the Russian calls *Dukh*. In

Bucharest, too, I had gipsies play for me as often as possible;
but so devoid are they, in that locality, of passion and temperament, that on a certain joyous night I simply had to snatch up
the conductor's baton in an attempt to put some fresh spirit
into the orchestra. But I only half succeeded; the Roumanian
gipsies, too, are apathetic. The astounding natural richness of
the country cripples both the temperament and the will. *Blago-
datj*—blessedness—is the word which the Russian always uses
when he speaks of the Ukrainian soil. It applies equally to Roumania, both as a physical reality and as a spiritual national
force. If we compare the wildest Roumanian life set down in
writing, the stories of Panaït Istrati, with *Taras Bulba* by
Gogol, we shall see that in spite of all the murder, rape, etc.,
with which it is thickly studded, the effect, when contrasted
with the Cossack life, is one of mildness.

Roumania, then, is a Balkan border country. It could have
become Russian. Instead of that a section of what was once
Russia has become Roumanian, and the new country does not
continue the old Russian cultural tradition. Will it not be the
true mission of Roumania to accomplish what Russia failed in?
Did not the history of the latter, too, begin as a rebirth of the
Byzantine spirit on Slavic soil? The process was arrested when
the centre was shifted from Kiev to Moscow, where the spirit
of Genghis Khan entered the ascendant. His tradition, again, is
being carried on by the Bolshevist movement, in so far as it
organizes powerfully. But does not the Byzantine spirit, for
its part, merit a rebirth? Would not Europe be tremendously
enriched if that tone, which sounded an accompaniment to the
entire Middle Ages, and the echo of which really called forth
the Italian Renaissance, were to sound out anew? It will not do
so in Russia. There the Byzantine element has long been essentially dead, or dissolved into unreality. The bureaucracy was
dead, while education on the one side and the Church on the
other—as far as its Byzantine perpetuation was concerned—
were unreal. It was only in the externals of the liturgy that the

true Byzantine element still continued as a life-force, but this
not for religious reasons, but rather because of the primary
feeling of the Russian for the theatre. In other regards Russian religiosity is purely Russian; it is early Christian, in so far
as early Christianity was primitive and not Byzantine. Now I
do not know how matters are with the religiosity of the Roumanians, but it did not fail to make a profound impression on
me. The princes of the Church impressed me as a living paradox; they present an exterior which in my mind, with its Russian memories, is indissolubly associated with the spirit of
strength and gravity, while in reality they are much rather
abbés of the eighteenth century; concerning a number of them
stories of the most gallant adventures are circulated, with little
enough harm to their reputations. But there is not the slightest
doubt that the Roumanian Church is a living thing. It is there
alone that Greek Orthodoxy has not become petrified. And thus
it is only in Roumania—granted the existence of the necessary
religiosity—that the Byzantine element could achieve rebirth
in the religious sphere. In other spheres it can certainly achieve
this in Roumania alone. In accordance with the historic law of
non-recurrence, rebirths never take place except in new bodies.
Thus it was that the old Hellas returned first as art in the
Renaissance, then as spirit in French classicism, and then finally
as philosophy, embodied in German idealism. In Greece, Hellas
will never arise again. Nor will Byzantium, that entirely new
culture-monad as compared to the old Hellas. I consider the
Byzantine predestined to be reincarnated in the Slavic world.
Wherever this has happened so far, in the mediaeval Bulgarian,
Serb, and Russian civilizations, the phenomenon has been authentic. Yet it was upon a lower cultural level, for the cultural
gulf between these peoples and Byzantium was altogether too
wide. But as against this, the Byzantine civilization might find
rebirth in its highest expression in Roumania. It is not without
significance that until recently, the true rulers of Roumania
were Greek aristocrats. Throughout the period of Turkish dom-

ination, the Byzantine tradition was continued uninterruptedly only in the Moldavian principalities. Cultural influence has the same natural downward flow as water. Just as the Esthonians and the Latvians will continue the spirit of the Baltic barons and not that of the age of the *bourgeoisie,* so all the Roumanian cultural phenomena that I know of are stamped with a Byzantine character. This is true all along the line, from the cuisine—which is almost identical with the Russian, proving that both of them had their origin in Byzantium—to the *esprit* of the country and its poetry.

It is this Byzantinism which the Roumanians themselves misunderstand as "Latinism." Thus, if they have any European mission at all, it should be to awaken the Byzantine spirit to new life. And it goes without saying that this land and this people *could* have a great future. Those who do not believe in the possibility of new races, new cultures, are painfully unimaginative; they are hardly better than the French, who still refuse to believe that the Germany of 1870 has become a definite reality. It is true enough that the old Roumanian upper class is, as a class, played out. Bucharest is fantastically reminiscent of czarist Russia; it is a St. Petersburg in miniature. Just as the latter had to die because it lacked inner strength, so that Roumanian class which hitherto alone was known to the foreign world must also perish. But the peasantry is healthy to the core; it is conservative to the core, like all very old races. And should any one raise, in this connection, the question of lack of system and of honesty, let him bear in mind the following: against the background of the expanse of Asia, exactitude and accuracy in the German sense look just as ridiculous as they actually do to the Russian. In the same way corruption is the normal, or at least the primitive expression of the will to oblige; that is, the human and personal means more than objective considerations. This is one of the reasons why from the viewpoint of the German civil servant, all great ages were corrupt; personalities, human beings, counted then, and human beings are always all-too-human. The extent to which this explains why the man who is honest, and nothing more, lacks all power of attraction, became quite clear to me in Bucharest. A poet told me about the eunuch cabmen who abound in that country; they belong to a special religious sect. They seem to be admirable people, honest and decent beyond all others; *it is possible that castration has something to do with this*. . . . The observation of the poet was not altogether irrelevant. Of late criminals, too, are being "reformed" by sterilization, and even by mere hormone injections; and apparently not without success. We need only take a murderer and pour sufficient ovarian secretion into his veins, and presto! there you have the nursing instinct. . . . Another obstacle on the path of Roumania's advance is the fact that the nation has no turn for industry and commerce. But for this purpose there are the Jews, whom they will never shake off. And the anti-Semitism of the Roumanians which inevitably results from this destiny will do much to keep this people awake and vital, and to strengthen its awakeness and vitality, in the same sense as the energizing effect of the threatening proximity of Russia. Furthermore, Greater Roumania shelters large numbers of Hungarians and Germans. In the long run this will certainly make itself felt, whether through the structural addition of a new aristocracy or by the production of a new national type on the basis of a favourable fusion of blood-strains.

Now as to the Greeks. From the outset two things are to be borne in mind if we are to do this people justice. The first of these considerations applies to the ancient Greeks no less than to the modern. The Greeks are a people born of cold and not of warmth. This applies, of course, to all the Balkan races. What distinguishes the Balkan world radically from the Italian is its rawness. I know of no body of water which can be so cold, affect one so frigidly, as the Black Sea. The winds of the far north beat unobstructed over it across the Russian flatlands.

One cold winter's day I stood on the shore of that sea and watched how the foam of its gigantic waves almost froze on the instant into fantastic ice-formations. I thought of Iphigenia in Tauris, who rose as in a vision before me, almost freezing to death in her Greek attire; I thought at the same time of the ancient Russian myth of the ninth wave out of which seven swordsmen, in complete steel, sprang to the land and thus took possession of Russia's soil; and then I understood how Russia, of all countries, could become Greek and beyond all doubt does belong to the Greek sphere. The Balkan world is as raw and cold as the northern Germanic world. Just as Bucharest produces, in wintertime, much the same effect as Moscow, so Constantinople is cold compared with Naples, and thus even the most southern Greek landscape is cold in comparison with other landscapes of the same latitude. To this corresponds the "shining" quality of the Greek sea with its islands and coastlines. And when the shining gods and men of the mythical ages once inhabited them—pure Nordic types, as we would call them today—it meant something different from the conquest of Sicily by the Normans; *those* Northerners belonged here; those radiant figures were part of this radiant landscape. A picture of things as they may have been in the long ago presented itself to my spirit for a brief moment when I saw the beautiful blond Queen of Roumania against the background of the Roumanian people; she did not appear foreign, but simply more noble. In the same way the Greek nation which remained after having absorbed the race of conquerors was still a people of a raw climate. Even in Corfu, tender and magical, where the world of the Phaeacians still survives as a mood, the Greek impresses one as more akin to the Russian than to the Italian.

Thus the Greek world, wherever it has retained its excellence, is austere and severe. The beauty of ancient Greece was austere and lucid; equally sharp and lucid was the thought of ancient Greece. The Church became severe and austere on Hellenic soil, and until this day the undegenerate country folk have

remained severe and chaste. In accordance with this the counter-
type to the good, typical Greek, the Levantine—and he, too,
has always been there—is a pure, clean-cut swindler. He has
absolutely nothing to make him sympathetic. He has not even
any of the pathos of the eternally massacred and eternally surviving Armenian, that most un-blest among the unhappy old
races. He is very clever, very versatile, yet utterly shallow. He
is cunning, yet utterly devoid of mind in the higher sense. He
is as versatile as Odysseus himself, but without a background.
He is supple, but incredibly tactless withal. He is the pure
swindler-profiteer, and nothing more. And again there stands
out sharply the unity which combines him with the northern
Orthodox Greek world, in contrast to the neighbouring Italian;
the Levantine stands in exactly the same relation to the best
Greek type as the thoroughly shallow *salon* Russian, eternally
chattering French, but eternally insipid, does to the authentic
Russian.

I am convinced that the Greek world was always made up of
both of these types, but at one time on a very high plane.
Odysseus was surely no ordinary swindler. And the Achilles
type has completely died out, in spite of some of the splendid
figures to be found among the Ewzones—the bodyguard of
the last kings; at the very best a Nicias may appear nowadays,
from time to time. Yet on the whole this world always was of
a positivist matter-of-factness, and in this again it touches the
Russian. It would be altogether beside the mark to speak in
this connection of the Dionysian element: Dionysus, who came
from Thrace, had the Russian *Dukh*; he was the orgiastic spirit,
the compensation to lucidity of the mind. It may be that the
Thracians actually were the forefathers of the modern Russians, as they certainly were of the modern Roumanians; Socrates had pure Russian features, and he argued as unendurably
as a Russian student. If we look for soulfulness, lyricism, sweet-
ness, on Hellenic soil, save as an exception to the rule, we are
more apt to find them in modern than in ancient Greece; just

as the neo-Greek literature has a more lyrical ring than that of
Plato, so the folk songs of some of the remote shepherd popu-
lations—Melpo Logotheti, who first collected them, once sang
them to me in Darmstadt—are richer in feeling than anything
ancient Hellas ever produced. This is the good result of the
influx of Slavic blood.

The Greek, then, does not belong to the South but to the
Northeast. Only as the product of that region can he be understood. And now I come to the second consideration which must
be borne in mind, and yet so seldom is; as a people the Greeks
are only a little younger than the Jews and have been living
under their present conditions for only a little shorter period
than the latter. The Graeculus was already scarcely distinguish-
able from the modern Hellene. At the time when Kiev adopted
Christianity, the language was already nearer to the modern
(at least phonetically) than to the classic; and just as today, the
majority has always lived parasite-fashion, or at least as an
alien colonizing body, among foreigners. Indeed, in the Near
East there is hardly less Greek spoken today than two thousand
years ago. And now let us look at the situation through the eyes
of the Greek. Is there not something horrifying in the fact
that this world, so much older than any world which has won
recognition today; that this world which, in contrast with the
Italian, has remained, since classical times, essentially the same;
this world whose children are almost without exception more
gifted than those of any other—*no longer means anything?*
When this side of the question became clear to me for the first
time, I shuddered. It is a real tragedy to be a modern Greek.
Nor is it to be wondered at that the feeling for the discrepancy
between what might and should be and what actually is should
give rise to the strangest compensation-forms. Every Greek
affects to believe that all non-Greeks are barbarians. Twenty
years ago, when I paid my first visit to Hellas, a waiter would
be very reluctant to serve a guest unless the latter had first
shaken hands with him. On one of the Hawaiian islands, inhab-

ited chiefly by Greeks, the hotel-keeper greeted me conceitedly with, "My name is Lycurgus, of Sparta: you know the name, what?" And then he continued, "We are still the foremost people in the world, for we have the brains, and we have the money." The state of mind back of such grotesqueries is tragic rather than laughable; never was there a sharper contrast between actuality and significance. Thinking of the Greeks, I first became fully aware of the real tragedy of the Jewish destiny. Psychologically the Jews are still, throughout, a people of antiquity. That which differentiates the Frenchman radically from the German, creates a great gulf between the Jew and the Northerner. What we call a Christian today is nothing other than the Northerner or the type who has been fixed by the spirit of the North. All antiquity was determined by the *nomos*, the law. And it was not Jesus who abrogated the law—the young barbarian peoples had never known "law" in this sense, and they therefore interpreted Jesus' hostility to the law to suit themselves. To the whole of antiquity the just was the ideal. But men of justice in this sense may be found today only among the Jews. The world of antiquity started with the *polis* and later dissolved directly into the *ecumene*. Thus the Jews have remained till this day a tribe with a peculiar law of their own on the one hand, while on the other hand they are an all-human people. This character of antiquity which belongs to the Jews can even be proved directly by psychoanalysis; C. G. Jung has shown, by a comparison of the dreams of Jews with those of Christians, that at the same level of the subconscious where the Germanic type is still a lake-dweller, the Jew is an Alexandrian. And now with regard to their particular history: living for thousands of years, as the majority of them have done, without a state of their own, without the opportunity to live their own history, it was inevitable that their innate feeling for history should be something different from that of their host peoples. They always rose to great heights only when an age or a state was in process of liquidation. A legend of that period already tells that the Colossus of Rhodes had been cornered by the Jews. From earliest times they drew profit chiefly from the weakness of nations. Furthermore, for thousands of years the majority of them were able to live only as middlemen, and this has compelled them to centre their lives about the universal instrument of communication—money. They were accordingly unable to see anything essential in those things which contained the essence of life for others; this explains the Jewish origin of the modern agrarian revolution. Because this was the only way in which they could sustain themselves, the Jews were at all times compelled to lay the emphasis on what was immediately transferable—intelligence and money. And is it not inevitable that Jews and Christians should see the history of religion—and therefore the entire Christian era—in different perspectives? To orthodox Jews, Jesus and, more than he, Paul, who must be considered the real founder of Christianity, must appear—and, from the Jewish viewpoint, justly—as nothing other than the typical representatives of the traditional Jewish romanticism. As against this, the Christian is interested in Jewish history only to the extent that it was a preparation for the history of Christianity; to him the Jew who has remained orthodox must appear as one unsaved by grace, one petrified in the law. But from the Jewish point of view the very idea of salvation is without meaning. There is thus no possibility whatever of a common understanding. In the best of cases the Christian can understand the Jew; the reverse never happens. Again and again the Jew assures the Christian that he is utterly unaware of the special state of salvation claimed by the latter, for which reason the essential difference between Jew and Christian must be an illusion. As a matter of fact this difference is a supreme reality, for the world which we call Christian today *never was* Jewish; it never knew the Jewish basic experience of the Commandment. Whether it felt itself safe in the womb of nature, as it did in its best pagan phases, or safe in the care of God, as in its best Christian phases, it was always equally alien to the essence of Judaism. For this reason the Jews are right in judging the *goy* today as they judged him in antiquity. . . .

But to return to the Greeks: Is there any hope at all that they can renew themselves? Will they not be for all time burdened with their ancient heritage which has remained a dead memory, and which has never been transposed into a new form? The historic law of non-recurrence generally works itself out with the greatest cruelty in those cases where it has fixed no absolute end. In the case of the Jew this is symbolized by the legend of the Eternal Jew; Jewish motion eventually became motion in a vacuum, a blind, senseless circle. What new, living thing can come from the Greeks? Here a "culture-soul" has lived itself out with utter completeness—with utter completeness because we are dealing here not only with the body of ancient Greece, but also with all Hellenism and Byzantinism. It is in Roumania, if anywhere, that the latter will emerge anew. The others were reborn, to whatever extent they could be, in the classical Renaissance of Europe. And whatever was still capable of development in the Greek world has continued its growth in the body of the super-national Christian Church. That it was the Greek Church which petrified was due to the petrification of Hellenism and not of Christianity. Thus the Hellenes are today in a far more tragic state than even the Jews. If the two nations resemble each other in many respects this is due, apart from the fact that they are the two last nations of pure antiquity, to the similarity of the lives which they have led for thousands of years and to their similar gifts of high intelligence. But the Jews were the carriers of a faith which imparted a meaning to their historic lowliness and unimportance, as well as to their arrested development. The Greeks have nothing of this kind. They are nothing but an ancient race and as such have none but romantic ideals, i.e. ideals rooted in unreality, which as a matter of fact no longer play a real national *rôle*. They are greatly gifted, but without a goal. Here we may feel, more tangibly than anywhere else on earth, the objective reality of that which Spengler calls a "culture-soul," and Frobenius, "Paideuma." For a while a "spirit" graced that framework of aptitudes which, in spite of all infusions of new blood, still subsists on the whole—the descriptions of Thucydides are just as applicable to the mass of modern Greeks— then that spirit withdrew. What continues to live on is without a meaning of its own.

What is to become of the Greeks in the years to come? Let us assume—as will probably be the case—that they will experience none of the mutations or metamorphoses which have ensued so frequently in Italy. Then they will live on as one of the "unhistorical" nations, which is what most of the peoples are. Yet the hope remains that even then they will at least bring forth individuals of all-human importance. To that extent they can, in the future, again play a *rôle* similar to that of the Jews, who, if they do not actually lead in most intellectual fields in every country, do at least produce most of what is second best; it is, indeed, unthinkable that so rich a framework of aptitudes should forever produce nothing of importance. And it is precisely in the new world in the making that Greece can most successfully fulfil this function. In a world which is dominated by the transferable, the high intelligence of the Greeks undoubtedly gives them a great advantage over many others. Here once more their condition resembles that of the Jews. If the out-and-out German smells the "Jew" in every spirit, he is, ideally speaking, not altogether wrong; that which was once specifically Jewish is today the universal spirit of the age. There is a further convergence of the generally human with the specifically Jewish in this, that the emancipated intellectual of our age appears primarily and typically to be either uprooted or without any original roots at all, exactly like the Jew who, originally authentic enough, occupies himself with matters toward which he stands in no living relationship. And finally, it is characteristic of our age that the emphasis is laid, as a general thing, on the intelligence. And only among the Jews has this been the case till now. For thousands of years they have, in fact, accepted the astounding dogma that the ignorant man cannot be pious. But this convergence which we have observed by no means constitutes Judaization, for, were it so, this age of progress and intelligence in which we are living would not be at the same time the age of the most outspoken anti-Semitism. Now what applies everywhere to the Jews by virtue of their intellect, applies in the Near East to the Greeks—except that the latter can point to the advantage of being an authentically rooted nation. It may therefore well be that before long they will once more take the first place among the peoples of the Balkans and of the remainder of the Near East, in the same sense as in Roman times.

Yet who knows? Perhaps, in spite of everything, a true Hellenic renaissance will yet take place. The folk-songs of the Hellenes continue to haunt me. And more than one neo-Greek poem which has come to my attention seems in the same way to be big with national promise. Contrasted with the ancient Greek, this lyricism rings as absolutely new as does the Florentinism of the Middle Ages contrasted with Republican Rome. . . . But however this may be, the first thing that Greece has to do is to overcome the delusion of grandeur which she has nourished till now on memories of antiquity. She must understand that nobody is interested any longer in the land as such, that the antique order of greatness can never be restored. And before this goal can be attained there will have to take place a molecular transposition within the people as a whole. But it is precisely this process which now seems to have been prepared. In what manner? By the repatriation of the Hellenes of Asia Minor! These do not suffer from the traditional delusion of grandeur; they are likewise devoid of the chief vice of the Athenians, their political frothiness. Today they already constitute an important part of the population of Athens; they work—something which the native-born Athenians are often too proud to do; nor are they real Levantines. Perhaps, chiefly through them, a new foundation may be laid in years to come for Greek significance. If Kapodistrias came out of Dalmatia and Venizelos out of Crete, the important Greeks of the future may easily be the descendants of the refugees from Asia Minor.

Now finally as to the Turks: Now that the fez, together with other external distinguishing marks, has disappeared, it is easier to get a true picture of this people. It is only now that we can perceive how close is the blood-relationship with the other stocks of the Near East; only in exceptional cases can it be said of a Turk—if he does not happen to be an Anatolian peasant or the direct descendant of one—that he could be nothing else than a Turk. It becomes similarly clear, at first glance, that in this case the process of modernization not only followed the line of destiny, but was thoroughly normal; the only abnormality was the lateness of its beginning. To him who knows what psychic atmosphere means, it is *a priori* clear that the contact with the life and spirit of the Greeks during a period of seven centuries, and the intimate relationship with Europe during a period of five, produced of necessity a state of psychological unification, a premise absolutely lacking in the case of Japan at the time when the latter began to imitate us. That is why the modernization of the Turks presents absolutely no problem. But all the more does it become clear, against the background of the other Balkan peoples, *who* the Turks are. There is something really unique about Turanian blood when it is seconded by the spiritual formative power of Islam (whatever I have to say about this I have already said in the *Travel Diary*). In spite of all new admixtures of blood, this people is fundamentally identical with the ones which made the great conquering forays. Thus everything that has taken place since the peace of 1919 can be understood only on the basis of their spirit. First, then, the Turks are still essentially nomads. Today they are leaving Constantinople, inwardly, if not outwardly; it is already—one might also say *still*—as if they had never been there; the proper atmosphere of the city is once again—or is still—Byzantine; in other ways it is reminiscent of Rome. To the enduring part of the city the Turks have added only their glorious mosques, but they did this just as Tamburlaine erected his pyramid of skulls in the desert. Everything else was or is either tent or caravanserai, intended to be dismantled. So, at the end of the war, they folded these tents, and pursuing the tactics of their forefathers, withdrew until further notice into their native steppes—today Angora; it was exactly thus that Genghis Khan returned again and again to Karakorum. Thus their rapid modernization is also a sort of military manoeuvre. The Turkish budget, of all budgets, has been balanced; in Turkey there is no inflation; things move there with a tempo which outdoes that of Fascist Italy; what is this but a state of war? That is precisely why, in spite of the bitter material sufferings of the majority of individuals, the country continues to advance. If the number of suicides among the youth, particularly the feminine youth, has reached horrifying proportions, this does not indicate decadence—they are war casualties; where, in the old patriarchal families, wife and children were no expense, today it is materially almost impossible to go on living. But the thing is being done all the same—at the sacrifice of lives. It is only from this point of view that we can at all understand the tremendous achievements of the *ghazi* Mustapha Kemal and his aids, certainly by far the greatest since the founding of the Empire by Bismarck. He turned utter catastrophe into complete victory. The means to this end he found in the hereditary heroism of the Turks, their equally hereditary genius in diplomacy, and their sense of possibilities—equal, in this last, if not superior, to the English. But the *spirit* which made use of these means was that of the great leaders of nomad peoples. Overnight the Ottoman Empire was abandoned in favour of a new Turkish national state. *That* state had never been defeated; it had had no share at all in the World War. It could therefore begin as a new thing; it could defeat the

other powers. Today, in the breast of the Turk, there reigns
only the emotion of victory. But this, too, was possible only
because he is essentially a nomad. Germans in particular are
struck by this complete detachment from the immediate past;
they explain it by Islamic consciousness of fate (Kismet). In
this they err; Islam has created this faculty of detachment only
among the Turks, because among them it strengthened something which already existed. Thus, as far as I know, it is only
among Turks that it is forbidden, in the name of God, to ex-
tinguish a fire. As the Arab does not live in wooden houses
which are predestined to be burned, he is not anything like as
detached. That is what the Turk is—a nomad, in time as well
as in space. Today, after having burnt his tents, he has left the
Ottoman state for that of the Nationalist Turks, has left Stam-
boul for Angora, has left the Middle Ages to enter, after the
World War, the modern age, just as, in the time of his remotest ancestors, he left the winter for the summer pastures.

So much for the nomad character of the Turks. It certainly
represents a much more important element in their make-up
than their Islamism, which only helped in the training of aptitudes which were already there. It is only because this is so
that the world which was conquered by the Turks never really
became Turkish; wherever a culture flourished under the Turks
it was, with the exception of a few special fields—like ceramics
—an Arabian culture, which they let be, as they did everything
which came under their rule. Thus the Islamism of the Turks
only benefited the specific Turkish rulership, a rulership based
on the absolute equality of all men; it did not create it. The
Turks are indeed the purest ruling race known to the history
of Europe and the Near East: they are that in an even purer
sense than the Magyars, in that they are by nature fitted *only* to
rule. Every man who belongs to the ruler type dislikes work
in the sense of the ethos of work—an ethos which lives more
strongly in the Germans of today than in any other people
since the Egyptians. If he can do better than work, this, of

psychologic necessity, makes up for actual laziness; it is this laziness which enables him, out of the instinct of self-preservation, to find ways of getting others to work for him. To this extent even the Englishman is essentially lazy. But the Turk will not—or would not till recently—do any sort of work at all except of the kind which has always been considered aristocratic: land development and war. Nor did he ever take the trouble to think out an administrative machinery which should lighten and ensure his lordly laziness. Until the fall of the sultans, the position of the grand vizier resembled that of the jafar, the right-hand man of Haroun al Raschid.

From the formal point of view, the government was mostly in the hands of favourites. But as a rule these were capable in more than a few ways. The happy choice of favourites was the consequence of the altogether wonderful knowledge of men possessed by the Turks. As a matter of fact the Turkish Empire was always administered exclusively through a knowledge of men—knowledge of men as a thing in itself, as it were. The maintaining of the distance between rulers and people which makes this possible presupposes, once more, an essential ruler type. And this applies most of all to that freedom which must of necessity be granted wherever there is no petty apparatus to carry on the sordid tasks of life. So that the Turk was, as a ruling conqueror, even more tolerant than the Britisher. But he was tolerant on the basis of the Oriental view of life—a man was free as a beggar, a mule-driver, a dervish, but not as a "modern man"—and only to the extent permitted by the security of the despotic régime. This ruler character is so essential to the Turks that in spite of all its circumstantial similarity to Bolshevism—which also expresses itself in the forms of certain representative personalities—it still endures and will undoubtedly continue to endure. The loss of the old faith may indeed exercise an influence in the opposite direction; when men of almost identical blood are, as Greeks, Levantines, and as Turks, rulers, the circumstance must certainly be traced, in part, to the effects of Islamism. But the Turks will remain Moslems *psychologically*, even when they no longer believe Islam has given them their form. It is just for this reason that I am a firm believer in a new Islamic unity,* which will be built up on psychological similarity and identity of tradition, not on religious faith. But above all, the ruler character of the Turks will endure by virtue of the traditional consciousness that they are something higher than the races which they once ruled, and by virtue of their sense of self as born masters. He who is Turkish in the best sense and consequently sees men and things at a distance, to whom gold is not everything, whose sense of self does not depend on his external position, must inevitably feel himself the superior of the familiar and venal Greek, the plebeian Bulgarian, the soft Roumanian, the weak Egyptian, and the unrealistic Arab.

WHAT, under these circumstances, are the future possibilities of Turkey? And what significance can the Turk have in the new world in the making? The national future seems to me clearly adumbrated. If they are not the rulers of other peoples they can, as an essentially nomadic race, have only a small state, in which to live among themselves. This state is now rising on the healthiest conceivable foundations. One should not permit oneself to be misled by certain unpleasant things in Constantinople and even in Angora. The demoralization of women, the abuse of alcohol—these are quite natural reactions after more than a thousand years of restraint. It is to the grandsons of the present-day peasants of Asia Minor, and to them alone, that we must look for the future embodiment of Turkey, and the greatest care is being exercised that they shall grow up under better conditions than their fathers knew. It is equally clear that in spite of a possible lack of talent for industry and technical processes (a *possible* lack—the Turkish chauffeur is by far the best in the world), Turkey is modernizing herself to the necessary extent. She will certainly never

* Cf. my *World in the Making.*

stand at the apex of the modern world; that is not possible for
everybody. But in the long run every one does finally adapt
himself to the spirit of the time. And where the ruling class
is unable to do this, the task must of necessity be turned over
to alien stocks. Just as the Roumanians *must* have their Jews, so
the Turks will in the long run be compelled to import as many
engineers, etc., as their interests demand. Should the Islamic
world be set in motion, it is clear, furthermore, that Turkey
will again be the leader. There is not a single Islamic people
which can measure up to the Turks in the characteristics of the
ruler and the leader. But in the present connection this possibility is of no interest to us. What significance can the new Turkey have for *Europe?*

Her significance can, indeed, be very great. Let us turn first
to the question whether she will play any European *rôle* at all.
It is self-understood that she will do this, and to a greater degree in proportion as the population of the former Roman Empire of the East participates in the life of the Mediterranean
basin not as a passive object but as an active partner. This new
participation is certain. And the Turks, residents here since the
thirteenth century, belong to these parts much more than to
Asia. In any case, then, Turkey will have an active part in the
life of the new Europe. But what can her peculiar *rôle* be? *It
should be the* rôle *she has always played, but this time on the
basis of equal rights to all and not on the basis of oppression.*
This, then, brings me to the most representative general problem of the Balkans, the problem of their physiological democ-
ratism. The structure of all the Balkan peoples is democratic
in that nowhere has the mass lived itself out through identification with the fine flower of the nation. In this regard the Balkans are the exact counterpart of Hungary. Every one feels
himself, by his origin, the equal of every one else; if there
existed, or if there still exists, an aristocratic ruling class it is
looked upon as representing the rule of foreigners. Now the
democratic spirit is capable of taking on the most various forms.
The proletarian can act as the polarizing centre—and the re-

sult is the ugly picture of present-day Russia. Or else an entire people, accustomed to oppression, devoid of the sense of worth, can be both familiar and arrogant: such were the Greeks hitherto. Or else every one feels himself to be, finally, the equal of every one else, as a highwayman: then culture becomes impossible; this applies, until some change takes place, to the Bulgarians. Now the Turks are the extremest believers in equality that have ever existed, but at the same time the extremest gentlemen. Should it not then be their mission to body forth in life, on the plane of the gentleman, that spirit which Bolshevism embodies on the plane of the proletarian and Fascism on the plane of flaming youth? To me the Turks seem really predestined for this end. All over the world the privileges of distinguished birth have forever disappeared; among the Turks even more than among the British, distinction is the tacitly granted claim of every man. In Turkey, therefore, that basic danger of democracy, universal envy as the decisive life-force, threatens less than anywhere else. It is for this reason that the Turks gladly acknowledge the leadership of the better man. And they are helped, again, by their extraordinary inborn knowledge of men to find those who are really better; thus it will be easier for them to achieve a solution of the problem of a rational hierarchy. And finally, they are even today essentially warriors and to that extent hard; they are devoid of all sentimentality. Thus they will enter more freely than many another people the new iron age. . . . The new Turkey can, indeed, fulfil a great European task. He who does not believe this forgets two things: first, that southeastern Europe, which was once a dominant force, may very easily become again one of the most important regions; second—and most important—that the prewar prestige of the European and the Christian is gone.

L ET us now turn back to the Balkans as a whole. They present a structure of the highest possible tensions. Roumanians, Greeks, Turks, are *toto genere* of the most diverse substance, and the Bulgarians and Serbs are, again, totally different from them. And yet the Balkans constitute a unity, and always have done so. Always has one part sought to conquer the rest. They have, correspondingly, been ruled from out of the most diverse centres. No equilibrium of the independent parts has yet shown itself to be enduring, let alone final. And it is more than improbable that, within an appreciable length of time, the dynamic state will yield to the static. The whole of Europe, gravitating in the Franco-German field of force, may achieve a peace-union like that of Switzerland much sooner than the Balkan region. It may, of course, come to pass that just as the Ottoman established and maintained for centuries an artificial state of peace, so the external influences of the Powers will for a long time to come keep the Balkans as they are today. But I do not, I cannot, believe that any device will ever pacify the Balkans to the degree which the chancelleries of the great Powers believe they have already attained. A real enduring state of peace has never been brought about except as the expression of the ripeness achieved on the further side of a period of *Sturm und Drang*. And who would care to maintain that this period is really over by now? The Balkan races, all of them, are young. Even now the Roumanians are building themselves up into that nation which they will some day be. The Turks have only just begun to think entirely in terms of self. The Slavs of the Balkans still stand upon the very threshold of civilization. The Greeks alone emerge as a people essentially old. But they, too, may perhaps achieve rejuvenation. Let things turn out as they may, it is more than improbable that the Balkans will forever remain what they are today. All indications point to the promise that sooner or later the eastern Mediterranean will again acquire an independent historic significance. Too many nations are finding rejuvenation on its shores. In the face of this fact the last traditional suzerains of this region, France and England, are, as such, growing old. This is organic destiny, from which definite conclusions may be drawn if only because the awakening of young peoples to individual independence inevitably takes place in opposition to the traditional tutelage, however able the latter may be. Of late Italy has begun to strain toward expansion into the Near East. But in the long run she is bound to fail in this, first, because the age of colonization is past; second, because there is no greater contrast than that between the Italian and the Balkan worlds. So great is this contrast that even the marvellously unified Roman Empire split in two as soon as it touched Constantinople. It may certainly come to pass that Italy will make temporary conquests. They will mean nothing permanent. In the long run this new conquest by foreigners will only redound to the benefit of the independence of the eastern Mediterranean, in that it will awaken in the nations involved a stronger consciousness of their particular characters. In any case I personally believe in an awakening of the eastern Mediterranean region to new historic independence. It must ensue, if only as an aftermath of the emancipation of Asia. This will impart to the Balkans a significance of a new sort, which would be, at the same time, a rebirth of their ancient significance: that of cultural middleman in the Mediterranean world between East and West.

EUROPE

EUROPE

Does not the motto of this book, the word of the Apostle to the Gentiles, "For all have sinned and come short of the glory of God," show itself now to be more than justified? After the first quick draft I thought the book out carefully, chapter by chapter; I have not the impression that I have not been just, utterly just, to every people. Every people has its good points. But not a single one has a divine right to haughtiness. Above all, every nation which looks down upon the others in a delusion of grandeur, believing itself to embody the human ideal, simply makes itself ridiculous. If anything applies in a general way, it is this, that everywhere the advantages are compensated by correlative disadvantages. I am thinking of the mutual vilification which has become the common practice since the World War; is not a good, hearty laugh the mildest reply to France's claim to be the teacher of mankind— for that is the meaning of the classic word *magistrature*; to the claim of Germany to be the doctor of mankind—for it is only thus that we can interpret the phrase that the world shall be healed in the spirit of Germany; to the claim of Switzerland to embody the political ideal, to England's claim to carry the white man's burden for all, and so on? There is much that can be said against Alfred Adler's idea of what man essentially is, but the nations which exalt themselves above all others are in the last analysis purely and simply Adlerian cases and, as such, deserve to be pitied; their boastfulness really indicates an inferiority complex. It is true that a disciple of Freud argued recently that Alexander the Great conquered the whole world only to abreact his Oedipus complex; Freudian cases may indeed exist among nations, too. But instances of Jung's theories, in which a dream of greatness and beauty anticipates the reality, have never come to my notice. For nations have no "self" to be integrated. If the psychology of the masses is so much more primitive than that of every individual, the explanation

349

lies, simply enough, in this, that in the mass only the empiric psychological elements, i.e. the mere instruments of the metaphysical, of the truly human, come into play. If the individual loses himself in the mass, he loses, in the same proportion, in worth. Nations are more or less favourable means for self-realization. More than this they are not and never can be.

We may, on the other hand, deduce from these considerations what constitutes a justifiable national pride. Dostoievsky tells us that for every man his race points his particular way to God. Every man is tied down to the empiric instrument of realization of his people; this gives direction to every ideal and sets bounds to it; to this extent the idea of every particular people represents the exponent of the direction in which every one of its sons should strive. In consequence the aim of every people should be self-determination and the completest fulfilment of all its possibilities, for only in a state of psychoanalytic normality can it guarantee to the national self the complete expression of its possibilities. Oppressed peoples are always spiritually ugly; only in exceptional cases are very poor ones inwardly free. But the perception of the same truth also sets bounds to a sensible effort at national self-uplift. Not only the oppressed, but the oppressors, too, suffer spiritual harm. Relationships which are too wide, no less than those which are too narrow, are dangerous; every emphasis on the pole of the "I" without a correlative emphasis on the pole of the "you" creates a pathological complex. In this lies the deepest cause of most national tragedies.

Thus the excrescences of nationalism can be rightly evaluated only as symptoms of disease. But here, at the same ideological spot, the limits of sensible psychoanalytic examination are revealed in the national as well as in the individual connection. If the analyzable is not the ultimate factor—for a closer examination of this question I refer the reader to the psychoanalytic chapter in *Wiedergeburt*—the temporary inadequacies of the

national disposition, too, are not ultimate factors. For the same
state of things obtains in the nation as in the individual; actually it is the inadequate which stands for and awakens productivity. This explains why peoples of a problematic or sinner's
psychology have meant and mean more for the progress of
mankind than peoples of perfection. The Jews are the most
inadequate people in the world, and the advantages of the Hellenes were overcompensated by tremendous faults. And today
the Germans and the Russians signify more than the British and
the French. The all-human significance of even the two latter
peoples derives from the time when they still had no claim to
self-righteousness. That matters stand absolutely thus, and not
otherwise, is shown with particular clarity by the case of Scandinavia. This culture-sphere, too, was for a short time of all-
human significance in the highest historic sense; namely, when
for the first time in the modern West the woman of this sphere
became conscious of her own problems. But now, when every
girl passes through her Ibsen stage as through an embryonic
phase, this significance is lost.

But if we now lift ourselves to the highest point of vantage
which earth-bound man can attain, we are compelled to say:
how can the perfection of the nations, as such, possibly be regarded as the ultimate goal? This life is only a means to a
higher end; were it otherwise, no pessimism could be black
enough. The unconquerable tragedy of life is the premise to
all spirit- and sense-realization. Every purely earthly goal is
reduced to absurdity by the mere fact of its evanescence. This
alone should make clear the fundamental irrationality of any
static ideal and, with it, of the claim to exemplary perfection
made by a people which in any sense believes itself to have
reached its ultimate goal. Obviously no even halfway great individual ever believed that he himself—and still less his people
—had reached the goal. But most European peoples of our
time either believe, like Pharisees, that they have reached it,

or else they hope to reach it in the immediate future. That is why my first task was to make all of them as ridiculous as I could, or at least to set forth the relativity of their importance. As long as they think as greatly of themselves as they do today, there is no salvation for them. And the fact is that they are all of them more than imperfect. In not a single case does the reality even remotely correspond to the national opinion.

This, I believe, is the first deduction to be drawn from our journey through Europe. The second deduction is more cheerful. We may console ourselves in the knowledge that nowhere on earth is there a richer multiplicity than this of our little peninsula to the Asiatic continent; not even in India, in spite of its kaleidoscopic variety. It is only from the viewpoint of the *Jahrmarkt von Plundersweil* that India is more manifold, and not in the sense of metaphysical substance; this is already proved by the physiological monism of all Hindoos. It is just that metaphysical substance which, in the case of Europe, is so marvellously different from people to people. It is true that one must look closely in order to become aware of it. On the eve of my world-journey I wrote the following: "Europe can no longer enhance me. This world has become too intimate to me to compel my soul into new formations. And then, in and for itself, it is also too limited." I could write thus because at that time the planet as a whole was my normal environment. Since the war I have been compelled to confine myself to Europe. And then the same thing happened to me as during the war-years on my Esthonian estate; where it had once been my wont to complain about the limited choice of walks, I discovered a new one every month. And just as I found, within the narrow confines of these walks, more singularities than on my distant travels, so, in the European scene, I have become aware of nuances more numerous than all the great differences I observed in my world-journey. But under all circumstances a microscopic view always offers more entertainment than a telescopic. How can one possibly make merry over the starry heavens? Every glimpse into the ways of men—and particularly so if intimate matters are at issue—opens a full world of amusement to the observer.

But our review of Europe leads us to a third conclusion. And this confirms the statement in the *Travel Diary* which follows immediately on the sentence last quoted: "All Europe is essentially of one spirit." For did we not, in one instance after another, involuntarily reach the stage where we examined the various nations and countries in their relation to each other, and not simply the one against the background of the other? Again and again we discovered in the thing that is, a *mission;* but a mission obviously premises a pre-existing higher unity. Again and again the title of this book * was confirmed; this anatomization of Europe does actually mean the spectro-analysis of a body presenting a unified exterior. This book would therefore remain incomplete if the examination of the component parts were not followed by a description of the whole. And that not as a *résumé,* but in the sense, precisely, that the various elements revealed by the spectrum belong as necessary component parts within the unified body.

To what extent is there such a thing as "Europe"—a thing which undoubtedly did not exist a short time ago except in the geographic sense? To the extent that the wider range of relationships which has recently begun to emerge within the body of mankind can compel new differentiations. And we are dealing here with inner relationships, moulded by psychological factors. No purely external unity has ever possessed stability. All previous attempts at the unification of Europe, such as were made more or less consciously by Julius Caesar, Charlemagne, and Napoleon, failed because the differences between the various European peoples meant more at that time than what they had in common. Moreover, they really had very little in common at that time. From the point of view of life-

* In German, "The Spectroanalysis of Europe."—*Translator's note.*

experience, the distance between Paris and Cologne was, even in the time of Napoleon, almost as great as the distance today between Sidney and Berlin; the psychic organism, no less than the physical, remoulds itself, in its range and limitations, in correspondence with external environment. At that time, then, the Berliner differed from the Parisian more than he does today from the Australian. Today space, as a significant factor, has been conquered. Science has made a general mutual understanding possible. Because of the shift of emphasis in the structure of the soul from the untransferable to the transferable (cf. the exposition of these views in *The World in the Making*), the ecumenic state is becoming a reality. And this brings with it a new, far-flung unity. But this by no means implies uniformity; on the contrary, to the extent that it is a living unity it compels new differentiations out of itself, just as every multicellular organism appears, by contrast with the unicellular, to be differentiated in a new sense. Today we know that even the latter, for all its tininess, is highly differentiated; so were the tribes and clans in their early days. But the greater organism is, precisely, articulated in a new and different sense. Thus it is an error to conclude that the conquest of space and of the barriers to mutual understanding must lead to deeper resemblances; that it is an error has already been shown by experience. Since 1914 France and England have lived to a high degree in a state of symbiosis, and never were the two nations more different, or more keenly conscious of their diversity. Thus the contact of the Orient with European civilization has served, precisely, to evoke Asiatic nationalism. But, to repeat, every pre-existing unity implies a new kind of differentiation as compared with the unity which preceded it. Just as the clan once meant more than the nation—indeed, up to the time of the French Revolution the latter did not exist at all, in the modern sense—so, on the basis of the inner ecumenic state, new living unities are being integrated. *And one of these unities is Europe.* Europe is not being created by the pan-European or

any other movement; on the contrary, that movement, like
every other movement of the same intent, is possible only because it represents a living and creative tendency. Europe is
emerging as a unity because, faced at closer range by an overwhelming non-European humanity, the things which the Europeans have in common are becoming more significant than those
which divide them, and thus new factors are beginning to predominate over the old ones in the common consciousness. It
was, then, this primary consciousness of the European which
enabled us to judge every individual nation from the point of
view of its mission; if a primary consciousness of the European does exist, a judgment of this sort becomes just as natural as a definition of the particular properties of the lungs
and the liver in the physical organism.

A living "Europe" is therefore arising today as a branch
of the all-human ecumene. It already exists as a psychological
reality in all leading spirits. The specific subconscious, which
is conditioned by its own peculiar history and which has the
last word to say on a man's attitude toward the external world,
is beginning to work itself out in the conscious. It is beginning
to do this because man is a creature of differentiations and develops in one way or another in accordance with his relationship
to the "not-self." Hitherto the difference between the French
and German being could be regarded as a primary significance.
Today it is outweighed by the consciousness of that difference
from the Russian being, and above all from the Asiatic, which
is common to them both; and this will become increasingly true
in proportion as the moods and ill humours of the World War
die out. And in the same way this consciousness is becoming
increasingly accentuated by their contrast with the New World.
Only a little while ago the educated North American was as
a matter of course still one of us. Today America, or at least its
younger generation, embodies a new world in the literal sense.
The primal spirit of the American soil and the spirit of the
negro are already disputing the supremacy with the spirit which

has immigrated from Europe, and whatever the outcome be, the final synthesis will be specifically American; it will perhaps be as different from the European as the Greek culture was from the Minoan, Phoenician, and Egyptian cultures in which it had its roots.* However strongly the consciousness of an Occidental commonweal may have predominated in spite of everything till now, one thing is certain; given the present complex of psychological relationships, the consciousness of differences is bound to dominate. If, from the cultural point of view, the Americans must first of all become younger and younger, until an authentic American cultural soul is created, we, on the other hand, will inevitably feel older and older in relation to them. It is becoming ever less and less a question of the Americanizing of Europe—if this word has any meaning at all, it must signify something deeper than the mere adoption of more rational economic methods. Before long we will become frantic pure-Europeans. With a few individual exceptions, we will understand each other not better, but worse than

* Cf. the extremely interesting statements by C. G. Jung in his paper, "The Earth-Conditioning of the Psyche," at the 1927 session of the School of Wisdom, printed in *Leuchter* 1927 (*Mensch und Erde*). I quote: "The first thing that attracted my attention among the Americans was the profound influence of the negro, a psychological influence, of course, without admixture of blood. The expression of the emotions in the American, his laughter before everything else, may best be studied in the society columns of the American newspapers; that inimitable Rooseveltian laughter is found in its primal form among the American negroes. That peculiar walk, loose-limbed, those swaying hips, observed so frequently among American women, are of negro origin. American music draws its chief inspiration from the negro; the dance is the negro dance. The expressions of the religious emotions, the revival meetings, the Holy Rollers and other abnormalities, are strongly influenced by the negro—and the famous naïveté of the American, in its charming as well as in its more unpleasant forms, can be easily compared with the childlikeness of the negro. The extraordinarily lively temperament of the average American, which shows itself not only at baseball games, but more particularly in an astonishing passion for verbosity (the most instructive example is the boundless and interminable torrent of words in the American newspapers) can hardly be traced back to a Germanic ancestry; it resembles much more the "chattering" of the negro village. The almost total absence of intimacy and the overwhelming mass sociability of the Americans reminds one of the primitive life of the open huts and the complete identification of the individual with all his tribal relatives. I had the feeling that in all American houses all the doors are always open, just as in the American country towns the gardens are without hedges. Everything seems to be part of the street. . . . In the hero fantasies of the American the *Indian character* plays a leading *rôle*. The American concept of sport goes far

before. And, however paradoxical it may sound, this will take place precisely because "understanding," as such, will play in the future a *rôle* of ever-increasing importance. The more stupid a man is, the more things he accepts as self-evident. Wonder is the privilege of the wise. Thus the more we understand, the more we must be struck by what is not understandable. And actually no man can understand another whose subconscious is too divergent from his own. Not only the variations in the soul-structure, but the historic age of the soul, too, creates unbridgeable differences.

But on the other hand the same causes are leading to a keener perception of similarities. Thus the inhabitants of Europe are steadily becoming conscious of the fact that above the individual nations and cultures of Europe broods a new, living reality, that of the *European*. Accordingly, the French, the German, etc., is becoming different from what he has been hitherto; the basis of his relationship to the whole has shifted.

beyond the good nature of the European. Only the Indian initiation ceremonies can compete, for brutality and cruelty, with the rigorous athletic training of the American. The mass achievement of American sport is for that reason astonishing. In everything that involves the American will, the Indian comes to the fore; in his extraordinary concentration on a given goal, in the obstinacy of his persistence, in his unfaltering endurance of the severest difficulties, all the legendary virtues of the Indian come into play. . . . I have observed that among my American patients the hero-figure also has the Indian religious aspect. The most important figure in the Indian religious ritual is the shaman, the doctor and exorciser of spirits. The first American discovery in this field—one which has also become important for Europe—was spiritualism; the second was Christian Science and other forms of mental healing. Christian Science is an exorcistic ritual; the demons of sickness are denied to be existent, the proper formulas are chanted over the rebellious body, and the Christian religion, which represents a high cultural level, is used for magic cures. The poverty of spiritual content is appalling, but Christian Science is alive; it possesses a thoroughly earth-rooted power and has worked those wonders which we would look for in vain in the official churches. *Thus the American presents a curious picture: a European with the manners of a negro and the soul of an Indian.* He is sharing the destiny of all usurpers of an alien soil; certain Australian aborigines assert that it is impossible to conquer an alien soil, for alien ancestral spirits live in that alien soil, and thus the new-born children of the conqueror will incarnate alien ancestral spirits. This contains a great psychological truth. The conquered alien country assimilates the conqueror. Unlike the Latin conquerors of Central and South American, the North Americans have maintained the European level with the sternest Puritanism; but this could not prevent the soul of their Indian foes from becoming their own. It is everywhere within the power of virgin earth to bring down at least the unconscious of the conqueror to the level of the autochthonous inhabitants."

And this shift is mirrored in his consciousness, and from this, again, reaches out creatively into the emergent reality.

To which class does the reality belong which is involved in the case of the European? For we are concerned here with him alone, and not with the unity of an ecumenic humanity. Will he represent a new race? A new nation? Oh, no! It will be a new *unity of style*. It is unity of style, and nothing else, which can at all create living commonweals. Seen as a whole, the biologic material has always been the same. The nations and the cultures which emerged from it depended solely on whether a spirit—and what spirit—animated it from time to time. It is exactly the same as in the art of the painter. Colours and forms and the laws that govern them are accessible to every man, but a Rembrandt creates something *unique* by means of them. A significant national being stands and falls by the same character of uniqueness. Thousands and thousands of peoples, all of them built up of the same or a similar primal material, have wandered the earth. But few of them have acquired real form, and among these only the fewest have asserted themselves permanently. These last were in every case peoples which stood in the same relation to the others as the work of a Rembrandt to that of an inferior painter. Even the former do, of course, embody a special style; it is impossible to live without having some sort of style. The phrase of Buffon, *le style c'est l'homme même,* applies to every realm of life in that the style embodies the last, irreducible synthesis of the rational and the non-rational which is the ultimate essence of everything alive.* But in style there is the great and the small, the convincing and the unconvincing; there is the transferable and the untransferable.† A national type endures only when it embodies an all-human value and is to that

* Cf. the detailed exposition of the train of ideas outlined here in the chapter *Jesus der Magier* in *Menschen als Sinnbilder,* and the chapter *Geisteskindschaft* in *Wiedergeburt.*
† On this latter problem I refer the reader to my study *Die begrenzte Zahl bedeutsamer Kulturformen* in *Philosophie als Kunst.*

extent intelligible to all, and when this value is not a miniature value, revealing itself only under the magnifying-glass, but when it radiates light and is visible from afar. Because this is so, the present-day French do not mourn the denationalization of their Gallic forefathers, but, on the contrary, take pride in it. And thus it is only those races which embodied a high unity of style which live on as gens in the human heritage. These are, in the first line, the Egyptians, the Jews, the Greeks, Romans, Hindoos, and Chinese. They continue to live *personally*, just as the gen does in the new life-unity of the single cell. That is why we learn the ancient languages—as the Hindoos do Sanskrit—in order that we may measure up to modern life; this study serves to vitalize one's *own* living heritage. A nation without a soul of its own, i.e. without a style of its own, is merely brute material.

The changes and wanderings of the nations that have been predominating forces on earth are therefore in reality the changes and the wanderings of styles, not of races. Since the time of Adam the latter reproduce themselves as primal raw material; they take their form from the spirit which rules for the time being. There can be no doubt that the latter is, in its manifestation, more or less bound up with a specific blood. Nevertheless it is quite incorrect to put the main emphasis on this bond. What is there in common between the Englishman and the present-day American of pure Anglo-Saxon blood? Psychologically they differ much more than the Frenchman and the German. Thus the East European Jew of Khazar descent is none the less thoroughly Jewish. And wherever the wandering Germanic peoples have settled, they have dissolved out among the native races which they first conquered. The nature-element which is really a determinant force, is the landscape, in the paideumatic sense.* Specific souls (not spirits—the

* A detailed exposition of the concept Paideuma, of which I have made frequent use, will be found in the book of that name, by Leo Frobenius, which appeared in the series *Erlebte Erdteile,* issued by the Frankfurter Sozietäts-druckerei.

spirit can never be explained in terms of earth) * do seem beyond all doubt to be bound up with specific landscapes, whatever the reason may be. And the synthesis of the two can in itself become so powerful a factor that the question of the blood-components hardly enters at all. The present-day Greeks are still thoroughly Greek, even though the last remainder of the old Hellenic blood has almost ceased to flow in their veins. The French readily naturalize every foreigner because they know themselves to be strong enough to assimilate everybody. But what Paideuma, or culture-soul, or psychic atmosphere, means in the last analysis, we do not know. By contrast unity of style, through which these inapprehensible elements everywhere manifest themselves, becomes, wherever it exists, an objective concept.

Style makes the nation just as it does the individual. Do not the observations in this book constitute one single demonstration of this truth? Everywhere it was the psychological which was shown to be the first and last factor. All differences were shown in the last analysis to rest on differences of *adjustment* —but adjustment is nothing other than artistic form. The German judges everything on the basis of the *thing*, the Italian on the basis of the *man*; in the case of the Englishman the emphasis is laid on the subconscious; in the case of the Frenchman it lies on the most brightly lit plane of his workaday consciousness. And the determinant form, the unity of style, need by no means be "national." Asked whether he is an Englishman, one of the principal characters in Shaw's *St. Joan* answers indignantly, "I am a gentleman." Thus, even during the World War, when Russian·reservists were asked of what nationality they were, they answered, "We are Orthodox Christians." Every prince inwardly feels himself to stand above the nations, every aristocrat feels a closer kinship with members of his class in other nations than with his own countrymen of an-

* Cf. my lectures *Der Erdbeherrschende Geist* and *Der Mensch aus kosmischer Schau* in *Leuchter*, 1927 (*Mensch und Erde*).

other class. The man who becomes a monk consciously looses himself from all natural bonds. Thus the Internationale of Social Democracy—and still more the Internationale which is centred in Moscow—is creating a real unity which is, nevertheless, not national. Indeed, when I analyze my own self-consciousness, what do I find myself to be? First and foremost, I am myself; second, an aristocrat; third, a Keyserling; fourth, a Westerner; fifth, a European; sixth, a Balt; seventh, a German; eighth, a Russian; ninth, a Frenchman—yes, a Frenchman, for the years during which France was my teacher have influenced my ego deeply. My case is perhaps abnormal, because actually I feel myself identical only with my spiritual essence, and see in my corporeal being only the raw primary material. But I believe myself for that reason to be the more able to measure the importance of blood. All impulsional power is unquestionably conditioned by the blood. It is because of this that the races, as biological entities, change so little in the course of the millennia—the lives of most men are decided by primitive instincts as surely as are those of animals. But as contrasted with this, the *spirit* of a nation is qualitatively different. The most fanatical Pan-German would never assert that the Teutones and Cimbres were representatives of the "German spirit," nor could he deny that the racially pure Jew, Gundolf, is today one of his most typical representatives. The connection is effected by means of the "collective subconscious" of Jung. Yet that connection is never indissoluble. A people can lose its spirit in exactly the same way as the individual gives up his in dying —except that the people continues to live on as a biological entity. It is to the spirit, then, that cultural value, and indeed all value, must be referred. We must, of course, concede to the blood whatever belongs to it; since the union of tradition and physical descent constitutes the real hereditary factor in the case of man,* and since blood alone fixes man indissolubly to

* Cf. the detailed treatment of this fact in the chapter, "The Meaning of the Ecumenic State," in *The World in the Making.*

the earthly processes, it is useless to look for the perpetuation
of a spirit without the medium of blood; even in the cloister
it takes place thus, though in special form. But the emphasis
lies always and everywhere on the spirit. And the one exponent
of spirit is style.

For this reason there can be no question of the equal value
of peoples *qua* peoples. Peoples, as peoples, have no value
whatsoever; they are only primal raw material. The only thing
that matters is whether they have a special style, and, if so,
what value this style has. This serves to explain a number of
things. Why is it proper to speak, in connection with Europe,
of only two spirits (*Geist*), the French and the German? Because it is only with the French and the Germans that the emphasis lies on the mind. Let the other nations be as independent as they will: the fact is that as soon as they shift to the plane
of mind, they become provinces either of France or of Germany. As against this, England possesses an ethos of great attractive power, a model social culture, and a highly transferable
outward civilization. The style of Russia springs from the tension between her spirituality and her nearness to nature, that of
the Spaniard from the tension between the primal consciousness
of the flesh and extreme *tenue*. Thus, if we wish to understand
things rightly, we must, in spite of all current prejudice, examine the present in exactly the same way as we look at history.
Thousands and thousands of peoples have disappeared, and we
do not mourn the loss. And this is perfectly proper, for under
all circumstances the human race continues to exist; and in the
same way culture, wherever it exists, survives the life and
death of the various racial stocks. But now the question arises:
What can and will the birth of Europeanism signify? What
changes will it bring about? What is its mission in the world?
Can the free will of man help it to become something good?
It is to these questions that we must turn at the close of this
book.

We have already seen that the European, and with him Europe, is emerging inevitably. He is emerging as a specific product of differentiation out of an already existent all-human unity, itself the product of spiritual experience. He is emerging from a consciousness of difference *vis-à-vis* that which lies to the East and that which lies to the West of Europe; and that consciousness of difference causes the common consciousness of all Europeans to outweigh the consciousness of those things which divide them. Now, if our spirit journey through Europe has taught us anything at all, it has taught us this: we are dealing, in the case of Europe, with an astoundingly manifold, astoundingly riven structure; the Balkans constitute its truest prototype. That is why there can be no question of the unification of Europe in the sense of an effacement of all differences, as a desirable goal. To seek its unification on the Russian or the American plan is, on the theoretical side, to misunderstand it completely; on the practical side it is—to desire its destruction. Should things go well, there will ensue a new unity on a higher plane, a unity which the nations, continuing in all their old force, will themselves build up. Should things go badly, Europe must fall into complete ruin. This process, whether it takes a turn for the good or for the bad, finds an historic analogy which it would be difficult to take too seriously—the domain of Islamic leadership in the Near East. Islam has never effaced national and cultural differences. And yet, as long as their religion was a living thing, all Moslems have felt themselves to be brothers; and in this *rôle* they have possessed a specific and very powerful character. But wherever the national element lost its ultimate significance in the Near East, without having been replaced by some other positive force, there emerged a pure Levantinism, i.e. the most extreme characterlessness the world has ever known. Nothing is more instructive in this connection than the comparison between two inhabitants of Constantinople, both of whom seem to represent the same degree of racial fusion, but one of whom is a

Turk and the other not. The former is essentially a master, essentially character; the latter, a characterless swindler. A corresponding danger unquestionably threatens Europe and can be averted only if there emerges a consciousness of the higher unity of living Europeanism, leading to a new, specific unity of style. For national seclusion in the earlier sense is perhaps still possible politically, but not psychologically.

This leads to a conclusion which, at first glance, is altogether astonishing: *It is for Europe's sake that the internationalist idea must not conquer Europe.* The profoundest reasons for this circumstance have been definitely implied by the introductory remarks to this chapter. Nations are nothing more than raw material for the self-realization of what is individual and unique. If the latter is to manifest its unique metaphysical substance, the emphasis, on this earth, must also be laid on the empirically unique. That, in the first line, is the empiric individuality. But on the plane of the species, of the type, which every one also embodies personally, it is the national group; it was in this sense that Dostoievsky could teach that for every man his own nation embodies his personal road to God. But here everything depends on the right placing of the emphasis. The man who interprets his uniqueness in terms of a vulgar egotism loses his soul instead of gaining it, for he centres himself in the not-self. This truth has an even stronger application when he makes use of his national feeling not as a function of his personal uniqueness, but as a function of his relationship to his "fellow man": all relationships within the field of external values is an external relationship. Now the man who emphasizes the international, i.e. an abstract relationship toward *all* men, must diffuse and lose himself completely in externality, for there is no such thing as an international humanity. Now in the new world in the making the international idea is inconceivably powerful. When the transferable completely dominates the untransferable, when the limitations of space have become illusory, when all concepts of law, all science, all business interests demand an international understanding, the corresponding Internationales become not merely realities, but logical necessities. But if the representatives of these Internationales wish to keep their souls whole, they must see to it that they represent them only as officials, as civil servants. It is in this respect that the Jews can serve as exemplars. From the very beginning the Jews have been internationalists, yet on the basis of an extremely accentuated Jewish national consciousness. Jewish internationalism does *not* signify the same thing as the internationalism of other peoples; it is simply the expression of the interested desire on the part of the parasitic body for the disappearance of all obstructive limitations in the host body.* The Jews cannot recognize the earth-rooted nations as ultimate values; they must desire the dissolution of all rigid forms, the erasure of all boundaries, until the last distinction, that between Jew and *goy*, has been reached. This is the explanation of

* There are, furthermore, reasons based on a profound life-philosophy, which in turn has its roots in the uttermost depths of national life. With regard to this last point, the following remarks will have to suffice here; Jewish ethics operate exclusively with absolute values; their immediate demand is for the founding of the Kingdom of God, a kingdom of absolute justice. The Jew is constitutionally incapable of understanding moral relativity. In the ethos of the Northerner, and particularly of the Englishman, he sees the essentially un-earnest; to him our norms are rules of the game and nothing more. (Maurice Samuel, the Zionist, has made this so clear in his book, *You Gentiles* [Harcourt, Brace and Co.], that for a closer examination of the question I refer the reader to him.) This kingdom of play he desires instinctively to destroy, in the name of God. It is in this cause, and not in any spirit of vengeance for secular oppression—no people has revolted less against that, since for thousands of years it has been the natural environment of the Jew—that we must seek the explanation of the Jewish origin of most subversive theories as well as of most of their ablest representatives and realizers; every natural force is destructive in its effects when it works outside of the framework of relationships. In this, too, we shall find the root of that which has always nourished practical anti-Semitism. The spirit of the Old Testament is that of purest ethos, incredibly one-sided. But all spirit when viewed practically is primarily ethos, for in this resides its capacity for initiative. If it works with all the forces of the soul and of the blood within the framework of relationships, it constructs; if it works outside the framework of relationships it destroys. The well-known disruptive element in the Jewish spirit derives from the fact there is a discrepancy between what his ethos means to the Jew, and what the same ethos means to his host peoples. To this ethos the Jews owe their survival unimpaired for thousands of years. But on those who are alien to the Jewish kind, the effect produced by that ethos is destructive, for not only does it fail to correspond to their spirit; in many of the profoundest respects it is actually directed against them.

Jewish revolutionism, in itself a paradox in this, the most conservative of all peoples that have ever existed. But their internationalism is nothing but the exponent, in terms of their life-
philosophy, of an extremely strong and emphasized feeling for
national being. That is why it does not harm the authentic Jew.
We must at this point examine the Jewish question in somewhat
closer detail, for on the basis of that question we shall soonest
grasp the meaning of the difference between super-nationalism
and internationalism. From the viewpoint of the other races,
and in his relation to them, the Jew is a functional parasitic
type; this effect has been produced by his curious history.
Everywhere, during the mediaeval era, which was an age of
manorial economy, the Jews were the sole commercial and
money men. Then, when the age of intellectual progress came,
and with it the concept of fluid assets; and when, later, the international element in commerce began to dominate as a result
of the improvement in transportation, the Jews were lifted on a
tide which was particularly favourable to their inborn nature
and served to intensify it. That intensification will proceed
apace, for the tide is still rising. Precisely now when, as a result of the general loss of substance in a national scheme of
economy, everything depends on international relations; precisely now, when the man of inward internationalism is quickest to grasp the situation instinctively; precisely now, when the
new era of violence introduced by the World War and the
treaty of Versailles, with the correlative necessity for the weak
to accept the inevitable, gives precedence to the type which is
accustomed to reckoning with superior powers and to profiting
by its position—precisely now is it ridiculous to expect the
finish of the Jews. On the contrary, as long as they remain
Jews and consciously cleave to their national identity, they will
consolidate, in an increasing degree, into *the* international nation. And since there certainly exist international values which
need to be represented, the Jews will perhaps once more play
a purely beneficent *rôle*. But only to the extent that they re-

main, on the other hand, Jews. As soon as they abandon their
Judaism, they are bound to deteriorate as internationalists, too,
as so many liberal Jews are already doing. For the non-Jew,
on the other hand, internationalism cannot possibly become a
goal in the good sense. Every man must before all else cleave
to his nation, just as the Jews are doing to an extreme degree.
And whosoever is not a parasite, but a host body, must find his
faith in this—the unity of land and people.

THE international idea, then, must not triumph. This, however paradoxical it may sound, is the first premise to be
accepted if the new Europe is not to be still-born. As against
this, however, and again for Europe's sake, the supernational
must triumph over the national, for it is only thus that Europe
can sustain itself as a whole against the super-powers of the
East and West; it is the supernational idea, in the sense of a
Europeanism just as affirmative and just as strong in consciousness of uniqueness as any unique individual ever was in his
individual capacity and in his capacity as a member of a nation.
How far this is possible has been demonstrated by the example
of Islam, cited above. And at all times new syntheses, such as
have never existed before, can arise as the foundations to the
consciousness of uniqueness; the nation, as such, is still little
more than a hundred years old; before it there was Christendom, there was the commonweal of the nobility, the clan,
the class—there was no such thing as a nation. Now if the living European evolves into a type, another apparent paradox
will ensue; there will be an increase, and not a decrease, of the
national emphasis in the relation of people to people. I have
indicated on several occasions that the new age presents a synthesis of extreme universalism and of equally extreme particularism; it is in Europe that this will emerge with the greatest clarity. I advert again to India, the only other section of
the world which is equally variegated; there we seem to be
dealing with an accidental agglomeration, for there the basic

note is sounded by the non-rational. In rational Europe one variety seems to condition the other; it is an essentially differentiated organic structure. If, then, *vis-à-vis* the East and West, Europe becomes conscious of its self as an exclusive unity of style, the same must apply in equal measure to the unities of style which compose it. And this brings us to the more exact definition of Europe as distinguished from all other collective structures in the new world in the making; it should be noted clearly that I speak not of what "should" be, but of what *is* irresistibly taking place. The nations are, *as a simple matter of fact,* becoming more and more accentuated. Their consciousness of uniqueness is, *as a simple matter of fact,* becoming keener. How far the international spirit is failing to change the course of things is demonstrated by every case which comes up before Geneva, and by the increasing unimportance of the liberal press. There ensues from this a general state of tension of a higher degree than has ever been known before. In consequence all Epimethean minds are in daily fear of a new outbreak of the World War. But that can never happen again, *for by now these tensions are, in the last analysis, subject to the principle of solidarity and not to the principle of the struggle for existence.*

The situation is what it is because in the depths of the subconscious, Europeanism has already come to life. For this reason the era of post-war nationalism is one of such mutual fructification as has never been known before. We have only to think of the tremendous influence exerted on the whole of Europe by Russian emigration, i.e. by that part of the Russian intelligentsia which has remained European: or of the intellectual exchange between the best spirits of France and Germany, more intensive today, a decade after the war, than ever before. We have only to think of the newly emerging European importance of Spain, meaning thereby a general receptivity toward her spirit on the part of all men who count for anything, or of the leavening effect on all Europe of the neo-

Italian national idea, or of the fructifying impulses which
come even from Hungary and Turkey, or of the reluctant but
none the less unceasing spiritual Continentalizing of England:
if all this does not signify a commonweal, there never was one.
For a true commonweal is always a state of tension, analogous
to that of love and marriage. The unique element of productivity in the post-war forms of commonweal which are in
the making resides in this: *that in all places and in all respects
it is just the exclusivity of one's own kind which is seen to be
of importance for others;* nationalism, which has functioned
hitherto under the principle of the struggle for existence, is
now becoming a function of the principle of solidarity. Thus
a shift is taking place in all relationships. The glorification of
one's own country at the expense of the others, once accepted
as the eleventh commandment, has suddenly become an absurdity. We suddenly understand again what Dr. Johnson
meant by his harsh dictum, "Patriotism is the last refuge of a
desperate scoundrel," and what Grillparzer meant by his statement that the way of humanity lies through nationalism to
bestiality. It is becoming a primary spiritual experience that
the various nations *supplement* each other. And those within
whose souls the future state of Europe has already become a
reality read and hear the tirades which exalt any one nation
above the others with feelings like those awakened by an account of Assyrian slave tortures. This book has, I hope, made
it clear in what sense the national differences derive in the first
instance from differences of adjustment. It must further have
been made clear that every specific adjustment excludes, by its
very nature, certain specific possibilities. It is not possible to envisage everything from every point of vantage. From the
point of view of the Britisher, the German is limited; so is the
Frenchman from the point of view of the German; so is every
nation from the point of view of any other. But in exactly the
same way every nation has its advantages from the point of
view of every other nation. And all of them are mutually

complementary within the framework of the higher synthesis of the European world. But is the "European" after all the highest type of man? There will surely arise, before long, a corresponding type of supernationalism which will for the time be as virulent as any nationalism ever was; this would then be the European equivalent of American Messianism. But of course the European, too, is not the ideal man; I have already defined his limitations *vis-à-vis* the Orient in my *Travel Diary*. *But on the other hand he is more than any previous inhabitant of Europe because he is of wider scope.* All superiority depends on the integration of those values, which on their own plane are exclusive, into a higher unity.

T HE European *is* more than any previous inhabitant of Europe. This carries us over from *inevitable* development as a function of fate toward *possible* development as a function of free will. I have dealt in detail with the fundamental aspects of this problem in *The World in the Making*. Here I need only touch on the definition of the specifically European aspects. *Under what conditions* will the European become a higher being than any previous native of our part of the earth? *When every nation, as a special and separate entity, will learn to confirm every other nation as the complement to itself within the framework of Europe.* Then, and only then. Then, and only then, will the idea of competition in the same fields of achievement, that unhappy idea which bears the chief guilt for Europe's attempt at suicide, yield place to a new division of labour among the nations. For then only will the psychological premises of that division of labour become an organic reality, a molecular transposition of the self-consciousness such that the emphasis of the love toward one's own people shall rest on those things which the people alone can accomplish, or can accomplish better than any other. This will of its own accord transform what until now was the principle of vanity, of envy, of backwardness, the static principle, into a forward-looking principle; every one will then recognize his own nation to be what it has always been to the great man: *his task*. Then, as every national representative will feel, the proper thing will be to make of every nation the best, the very best, which its possibilities permit. And that no longer for the sake of exclusive self-glorification, but for the sake of a higher unity—not at the expense of the others, but for the best interests of all. When this has been done, the national consciousness which has existed hitherto will have been transcended from within.

What shall the nations set themselves, from now on, as the highest national tasks? The answer is unequivocal: to re-create the nations which have existed until now into better nations. It is not altogether likely that entirely new nations will arise in Europe. It may well be that nations which have remained backward will some day, as if overnight, find themselves in the very vanguard; Walter Scott still knew the Scots as half barbarians, and today they measure up better than any other section of the population of the British empire to the tasks of our age; thus more than one young people, deriving its first form from the spirit of the new age, may well outgrow many an old one which is too heavily weighted down with its past. But since, in the case of Europe, we are dealing with an essentially old continent—similar in that regard to India and China—and since its consciousness of difference *vis-à-vis* America and Russia is based primarily on this fact, we may hardly expect any revolutionary changes. But the nations which already exist can become better, those which have aged can receive an impulse toward rejuvenation, the unformed ones can still emerge with a style. Today almost all of the nations present a less happy picture than in previous times. In the majority of cases the high-water mark of achievement already lies in the distant past; in the case of the old cultural strata we see everywhere a distinct process of degeneration; by far the greater part of the newly emerging classes are nothing better than raw material.

But the same thing has always happened in the past, in view of the finiteness of all hereditary lines, and the same thing will forever happen again in the future. Contrariwise, however, a people can always renew itself phoenix-wise, and either create out of itself a new, higher unity of style or else enter into such. Most people fail to see how close is the kinship, in this respect, between the nation and family. The truth is that every family of a definite type is a real nation. The nation has one appearance or another according to the family types which predominate in it. All the varieties of human beings have developed from one root, or at most from a few roots, exactly as, in time, the wolf developed into the Pomeranian and the pugdog. And since families die out in time, since certain types perpetuate themselves while others do not, the nations alter in accordance with the type which predominates at a given moment. Only in exceptional cases do the present-day French resemble outwardly those whom Clouet portrayed; it is only in exceptional cases that the best traditional English type emerges among the younger generation of old cultured families. In this way the nations are constantly exposed to an automatic process of change. Wherever an inborn force, animated by a living style, works itself out in differentiations, this process leads to something better. In the same way it leads to something worse when variations become petrified or decay. But in any case the possibility of progress disappears whenever all tensions are resolved. All realizations of values premise earthly tension as a medium. The people of India became spiritually great when a state of tension between the invaders from the north and the original inhabitants had become stabilized. The same was true of Hellas. The invading ruling type was, as may be seen from its statuary, purely Nordic; and it was unintellectual, devoid of problems, as the Swede still is today. But from that very mixture proceeded the amazing Hellenic intellectuality, and long before psychoanalysis was ever heard of, the Hellenes themselves correctly indicated it to be the product of the tension between

the Apollonian and Dionysian elements. In the same sense
England reached her highest level with the stabilization of a
peculiarly successful admixture of the Romanized Norman
element with the pure Germanic. And the German, finally,
possesses all-human significance not as a Nordic, but as an
essentially intellectual being, as which he has finally become
stabilized, on the basis of a highly complicated Celtic-Ger-
manic-Slav admixture. The primal type of German has long
since ceased to be Siegfried; in its modern form it is—Strese-
mann. All German intellectuals resembled him; even the
Goethe type, which, as a matter of fact, is classified as Dinaric,
is more akin to him than to the Scandinavian.

If today the European seems less considerable than he has
been in the past, and if the European situation is, on the other
hand, creating new possibilities out of itself, it becomes clear
that what has become worse may in actual fact become better.
It is well, from this point of view, that the new closeness of
European relationships is so favourable to exogamy. Nothing
could be more advantageous for all the European nations than
an influx of Scandinavian blood. Intermarriages between Catholics and Protestants in Germany are in every case a blessing
to the country, for the German Catholic is at all times the
bearer of an older cultural tradition, while the Protestant,
per contra, is the stronger and freer force. A real blessing for
the lower classes is the introduction into them of a cultural
blood, either through illegitimacy or else through the descent
of women into their ranks. Indeed, who can tell whether even
the addition of Jewish blood, as long as it does not lead to the
death of the race, would not show itself, in time, to be of advantage? It would certainly mean a refinement of intelligence
and sensitiveness. However, we still lack in Germany sufficient
data to be able to judge what the effect of Jewish blood is in
the long run. But it has scarcely been of any harm to Spain.
There Jewish blood flows in the veins of nearly every one, for
in the time of the Catholic kings a very high percentage of

burghers and aristocrats were Jews; these were converted by violence, and during the first period the question of race did not arise. What strengthens my conviction that there is a high proportion of Jewish blood in the Spanish world is the Spanish *castizo,* that extreme emphasis laid, in later times, on the blood; that would scarcely have happened if impurity of blood had not been the rule. Who knows, indeed, whether even negro blood harms in the long run? The woolly hair so frequently observed in Italians surely goes back to the negro slaves of Roman times. Both Pushkin and Alexandre Dumas had negro grandfathers. And as regards the blood of the yellow races, the founder of the Pan-European movement is a half Japanese. No; there is nothing to be said *a priori* against mixed marriages, for all so-called pure bloods now existing go back, at some point, to a stabilized fusion of blood-streams.

But above all, we must remember that in the long run every tension—the prerequisite to every realization of values—equalizes out, and then the time has come to create something new. And this brings us to the essential problem of the European world, the problem of its special style. *The living European is something other than the Frenchman, Englishman, German, considered as his own last resort, in the same way that a painting by Rembrandt is something different from a painting by Meissonier. And it follows from this that not only the total synthesis of the man, but his component elements, too, must, in the case of the European, be other than what they have been in the nations hitherto.* Every change in the total organism is mirrored in the change in every cell; every new totality of condition creates, out of itself, new component parts. And the old ones actually die out; we should never have witnessed such frantic efforts at self-reanimation in phenomena ranging from old Prussian monarchism to the Wotan cult, from the idea of the French Revolution to the Caesarian idea of the natural boundaries of the Latin world, if all these outlived forces were not close to their natural death. As a matter of fact ecumenic man can be neither old Prussian nor Hessian, neither a Frenchman of the Poincaré type nor a John Bull. The wideness of his scope excludes, by its very nature, many formations. The same miracle occurs here as in every organic metamorphosis, from embryonic development to hereditary transmission. Certain formations vanish altogether. Others are transmitted as invisible, others, again, as visible gens. At the beginning of this chapter we saw how ancient India, Egypt, China, Judaea, Hellas, Rome, and the Middle Ages all live on, unmingled, in the body of mankind. In *Jesus der Magier* and in *Geisteskindshaft,* I showed how all great spirits live on *personally,* in the same sense, whether they are consciously remembered or not. To this extent the Christian demand for a personal relationship to Jesus stands as the one productive relationship to every great spirit. Now in exactly the same sense the authentic units of culture which now exist in Europe will, if they are of independent and general worth, continue to live on in the new unity of style. But only if they are such; all mere provincialism, and above all, of course, all formlessness, will disappear completely. And this *ought* to be so; the old can be replaced by something better, and nothing will be lost of man either as a biological entity or as a child of God.

This brings us back to the question of blood fusions. Evidently every unity of style is, as such, a purely spiritual unity. And wherever it exists, it is the primal unity; indeed, the infusion of a new meaning creates a new set of facts; new meaning even revitalizes in the purely physical sense; this was the effect produced by Christianity and by Islamism in the Mediterranean basin; it is the effect produced today in the world of the East by the spirit of the West. But if a new unity of style is to emerge, then the old formations must also fuse together on their own plane; there must even ensue a physical rejuvenation. This, then, is the reason why no new culture was ever born except in connection with a new fusion of bloods. There is a connection between physical and spiritual rejuvenation; on the one hand every new spiritual influence, as such, rejuvenates; on the other hand receptivity to the new spirit-impulse depends on physiological relaxation, so that the peoples which take over the new impulses are always new; for as a matter of fact this is already the case when new strata of the population rise to power, or when different stocks belonging to the same faith intermarry. The rejuvenation of a people without a favourable infusion of new blood is impossible for the same reasons which cause deterioration of the stock in endogamic families. A rejuvenation of this kind is needed now more than ever before since the time of the Wandering of the Nations. So new does the world in the making appear by contrast with the world that was, so deeply do the changes reach into the most intimate cellular structure, that the old crystallizations can only be barriers today. And the crisis has been preparing on this plane, too, for a long time. It is no mere accident that Jewish blood flowed in the veins of such an extraordinary number of the representative spirits of the last half-century; the mixed type of the American could not have exercised such a general attractive power had it not made possible the manifestation of something new, single-tracked, positive, true to the spirit of the times; for some time past almost every superior intelligence among the English has been traceable to Irish or at least Scotch ancestry. The same or similar phenomena will emerge more and more clearly in the near future. In my opinion France's best safeguard for the future resides, in this sense, in the large numbers of Russian emigrants who have entered the country; Russian blood works as a solvent everywhere; the present soul-structure of the French, rigid as it is, needs one thing more than anything else—relaxation. And thus the German, too, must change in many respects, if he wishes, as a people, to achieve European standing. He must become finer, more differentiated as a soul; he must train himself to a higher sense of form, achieve a higher degree of inward discipline and bearing. The German must become, as a national type, that which the great individual German was: *something more than a mere German.* He must become that which once emerged as the political formlessness of a Holy Roman Empire of German nationality. Is there a single great German in whom the Latin form does not play a necessary part? Take away from Goethe his classical education and his love of the classics, and he ceases to exist. The same applies today to Stefan George. The same applies to Frederick II., the Hohenstaufen, to Frederick the Great, to Bismarck, the first master, at the court of Napoleon III., of the French *esprit.* The same has applied throughout to the entire German aristocracy; their norms were and are of general Latin origin, for the German by his nature lacks the sense of form. In Hölderlin, again, Hellenism lived personally; in Nietzsche it was the Latin and the Slav worlds, and the same is true of Leibnitz. Indeed, the German spirit in its highest expression has always been more than German; it has always represented a super-national tension. It is therefore more native to the German than to any other European people to develop the European type out of himself. Whatever possibilities he has for a great future in the post-war world reside in this.

IN dealing with the individual nations I have indicated enough to enable any representative of them, with insight of his own, to discover for himself how far he should work with his own people. Wherever possible this was done with humour, so as to avoid any harmful inner reaction. And the Spanish motto *insistir nunca* is particularly applicable to nations. I will therefore say nothing more on this problem. And as regards any advice on the question of intermarriages, it would be rash to preach anything specific at this point. As I have already demonstrated in the chapter "On the Right Choice of Mates" in *The Book of Marriage,* only the right instinct, guided by insight, can be relied on permanently to create aright. In closing I will only seek to show to what extent *Europe as a whole* must effect an inner transposition, in what things it must look for its true task in order that it may remain a positive factor in the development of mankind.

The material superiority of Europe is of course at an end. As contrasted with the new world it has become very weak, very small. Its power in the East will also end before long. It may be that the industrial centre of this planet will shift over to Asia. Invention is difficult, but even the ape can imitate. Before long all our technical ability will be common human property. Before long, if we continue to plume ourselves on our achievements, we Europeans will be stared at just as Cornelius Nepos would be if he suddenly appeared in our midst with a general claim to the world's worship; we have become our own classics. Thus our prestige, the mightiest of all factors for power, has disappeared. But above all, it was the social achievements of the last few decades which undermined our material power. I have said whatever is necessary on this point in the Baltic chapter. *Under these circumstances the mere self-preservation of Europe compels it to adjust itself to what it can do best, to what no one can take away from it. And that is its intellectuality.**

Europe's entire significance has always been based on that; he who does not know this does not rightly understand the concept of "spirit." It is not a question of intellect, logic, principles, and the like; spirit is in a general way the principle of meaning in man, the basic cause of all creation, all form, all initiative, all transference, and, subjectively, all understanding. The two fundamental categories within the framework of which it expresses itself are those which have been called, since the time of the Greeks, the logos and the ethos. All European significance rests upon logos and ethos. Of purely ethical significance were the Jews who, while not a European people, have participated to the deepest extent in the training of the Euro-

* There is no exact word for *Geistigkeit,* which is here rendered alternately by "intellectuality" and "spirituality." It is used here to indicate the predominance of what the Greeks called the logos principle.—*Translator's note.*

pean spirit, and are today as necessary a part of us as certain specific parasites are to the intestinal tract. The logos and the ethos of Christianity—and not its *eros*—are the primal sources of its historic power. It was in the logos and the ethos, in different distributions of emphasis, that the "meaning" of the Greek and Roman civilizations lay. With the Germanic races there emerged into the world what was primarily a new, higher ethos. With the Renaissance and the Reformation the emphasis shifted again toward the pole of the logos. But whatever the circumstances, everything depended, in Europe, on the spirit. In the case of Europe it is an indefensible prejudice to place even the slightest emphasis on the *eros*. It is taken for granted that that principle, too, was at work. But if its presence was exaggerated with such emphasis, it was by virtue of what Leonardo has pointed out in his dictum: *Dove si grida, non è vera scienza*. Every Hindoo, every Chinaman, every Arab, lives more love than a European. There is, of course, a limitation imposed by this surplusage of the logical and the ethical; but in the main that cannot be altered, and the European must learn to accept it. But the importance of the European lies primarily in the positive element, which emerges in correspondence to the negative element in this situation. It is limitation which everywhere produces the master. We should not be called upon to be the bearers of spirituality, the logos principle, on earth, we should not be God's hands, as I have put it in the *Travel Diary*, if, for us, the exclusive emphasis did not lie on mind. Greek form still lies at the base of Near Eastern art; the Jewish ethos still lies at the base of whatever ethos is at work throughout the world. All science is of European origin. And as regards Christianity, its power to expand and transform derives from the fact that it embodies understanding directed toward practical use. There are, in Asia, religions which are equally deep, if not deeper; but the principle of the earth-conquering spirit does not live in them. In and for itself spirit is indeed—as I have pointed out in the Adyar chapter of the *Travel Diary*—without earthly power; the most tremendous spirituality can achieve nothing if he toward whom it turns will not come forward to meet it—we have but to think of the legend of the second thief on the cross. Now in Europe the spirit is essentially earth-conquering. Because of this it can be an effective historic force. This results from the fact that the European presents a specific synthesis of spirit, soul, and body; because of this synthesis, and by virtue of the law of correspondence between meaning and expression, the ultimate essence of spirit becomes effective on earth.

Thus the significance of Europe has always derived from its *Geistigkeit*. The nations in whom the emphasis lay elsewhere never acquired all-human significance. If Europe has from time to time also acquired external power, it was not a primary expression of the European spirit, but the consequence of its practical application—just as great fortunes are built up on the basis of inventions produced by some unworldly scientist in pursuit of purely intellectual interests. And today the significance of Europe is based on its spirituality to a degree unknown before. *For that is the one thing in which it is still unique.* It is at the same time the one thing which is, precisely at this moment, susceptible of the most tremendous intensification. Any earthly sense-realization must have empiric tensions as its premise. In Europe these tensions are becoming intensified to an unheard-of degree. The inner relationship of our continent to the new West as well as to the new East is one of extreme tension. The consequence of the closeness in space between the various European peoples has again been the creation of extreme tensions. To this may be added the external need of Europe to assert itself through superiority of mind. Thus Europe may be about to enter, at this very moment, upon the era of its greatest intellectualization. Now even the European peoples which are not intellectual in and for themselves can share in its achievements. Tension, as such, creates new abilities, and those who cannot lead in the work can still help it on better than any non-European. But the chief reason why Europe's greatest prospects lie in this one direction derives from the fact that the spirit can rule only where the entire emphasis is laid on the unique and its value. All values are personal. Just as Christ proclaimed and taught the infinite worth of the human soul, just as all ethics have their unique meaning in the free will of man, just as all creative originality derives from the unique, and just as there is no other form of understanding than personal understanding, so the rule of the spirit on earth stands or falls by whether or not the emphasis is laid on the individual, and on him only. Today this condition obtains only in the case of the European. That which is called the genius of the Nordic race—intellectually it is beyond question less gifted than many southern races—derives solely from the fact that the Northerner is by nature an individualist. Thus his blood has everywhere helped the principle of uniqueness, the real creative element, to come into its own. But whatever the facts may be in regard to the Nordic question, this remains true: today Europe alone, of whatever blood it be, represents the principle of uniqueness.*

This, then, should give us a concrete definition of what Europe's task is to consist in during the coming era. It should consist in the representation of the principle of individualism. It is diametrically opposed to what is accepted by world reformers who have lost their balance as a result of the experiences of the World War. Europe's future does *not* lie in the triumph of socialism. I am the last man in the world to deny the tremendous value of the socialist idea, and least of all as it is embodied in the idea of historic materialism. Every day my heart is wrung when I see how many more children of inferior worth—not only in the physical, but also in the spiritual and moral sense—grow up among poor families than in the finer homes; this is unquestionably due to material conditions.

* Cf. the detailed deduction of this decisive truth in my *Wiedergeburt* and in the lecture *Der Mensch aus kosmischer Schau* in *Leuchter,* 1927.

Were it not so, the illegitimate children which are born into the lower classes, and there are millions of them, would resemble their high-born fathers; were it not so, it would not be accepted as a matter of course that these should remain in the social stratum of their mothers. And *per contra* the numerous illegitimate children who bear the great name of one who is not their father would not so naturally be accepted into the stratum of their so-called fathers. I have always been amazed by the candour with which "faithful subjects" speak of the "real" descent of their rulers, without being influenced thereby in their legitimism. Historic materialism is to a very great extent in the right, and it indicates, in my eyes, the lowest kind of heartlessness and a radically evil will, to deny it. The wave of socialism which is now spreading over the whole of our planet is, even though it should level down all the heights, an immediate blessing. When we have at last reached the stage when we are able to create material values, when there is no longer a way of inheriting Nibelung treasures bearing no interest, we should and must reach a point where the state of material well-being becomes normal with every man. And actually no sacrifice is too heavy for the attainment of this end. When we remember how horrible the conditions were among the lower classes only a short time ago, and still are in non-European countries, when we remember, further, that at least seventy per cent. of the spiritual and moral degradation of which they are accused can be traced to their material circumstances, every effort must be exerted to raise the general level. Above all we must put an end to wage-slavery, which consists in placing labour and merchandise on the same level. It is because everything depends primarily on this question of raising the general level that, from the social point of view, there can be points of contact between the spiritual Gandhi and Lenin. But that which might be the gospel for Russia and India can no longer be such for Europe. Europe brought the socialist idea into the world. It has made a reality of it, or will before long, to the extent that this can be done without destroying the European tradition of culture. Therefore, if Europe still has life-force, it cannot remain standing at this point. And it has life-force—more than ever before. It is becoming rejuvenated and will become more and more rejuvenated as the inner transformation of its component parts proceeds. It will therefore set itself new and higher aims. Socialism is necessary in order to broaden the basis for a higher formulation of problems. To stand fixed there belongs only to the nations which are still crude. In and for itself, individualism stands as much above socialism as Christ's doctrine of the infinite value of the human soul does above the contemptuous attitude of antiquity toward the slave. Thus the task of Europe is not anti-socialistic; it lies beyond socialism. And all the greatness of its possibilities for the future rests on this fact.

L ET us now return to the point where it became clear that every human monad derives its qualities and its position from its specific relation to the whole. We stated there that Europe is constituting itself anew inevitably, as the result of its position of contrast to America and the East. Now what do we see in America? There, in spite of all the elbow-room in the field of material achievement, the individual is simply ceasing to exist; all development is moving in the direction of standardization; manners and morals within each stratum of society are becoming so uniform that the only parallel to them must be sought in the army corps. If the principle of equality was justified at first on the ground that it was the only method which enabled such various groups to live together, it is today eating into the inmost nature of the inhabitants. The ideal of the same life, the same emotions, for all, is steadily becoming a reality. Today the principle of American individualism applies only in the commercial field, in that every one may do what his intelligence and his power permit him. Freedom of thought is disappearing with terrifying rapidity. It is only in exceptional cases that the element of individuality is recognized as a value. Intellectual interests as such play hardly any part in the life at large; all intellectual values are weighed by their practical application and by their application to the collective benefit. Thus everybody wants to be like everybody else. Each college claims to be more "democratic" than the others, meaning thereby that it is more hostile than the others to originality and superiority. The man in the street is becoming more and more the ideal. Thus the majority principle leads to a tyranny more powerful than any which has ever existed before. For it is this tyranny which makes for the happiness of the man in the street, all the more as it enforces a sort of optimism which, however it may fail to represent the true state of affairs, is for that reason the more effective—like prohibited alcohol. For the immediate future this can only become worse from year to year. First, the American soul is becoming primitive again. And then, sooner or later, those social strata which today have no power, will some day acquire it. The tension between the old colonial culture and that of a young life which is becoming conscious of itself must become more and more accentuated, for the first already bears the aspects of senility; and the more accentuated the tension, the greater the threat of a radical change. In any case America is moving further and further away from Europe. I do not indeed question her more distant future; there will arise on that side of the ocean a new, original culture, deriving psychologically not only from European, but also from Indian and African roots. It will bespeak the spirit of the continent, and will probably be not intellectual, but religious, social, and practical, as that of the Incas was. And the death of the colonial culture will have to be an indispensable preliminary to the rise of this other. America is bound to become primitive at first, for the normal adult can only grow out of the child. Later on the blending of the primal spirits of Europe, America, and Africa in the new landscape may very likely create tensions as productive as those created by similar processes in India and Hellas. Personally I expect much from America's remoter future; it is certain to me that the prophecy in the *Travel Diary* will some day find fulfilment. But America must first sink back into primitiveness, must exhaust all her energy in physiological achievements. This is the way of all youth; America's present-day objectless idealism only mirrors in a large way the experience through which every stripling passes. The period between the *Mayflower* and the World War, with Washington's Constitution, will some day be regarded as the equivalent of what the Golden Age meant for Greece. But what is good for America may be ruinous for the rest of the world. America has now seized the material power, which under all circumstances brings with it the greatest prestige. Thus America's primitiveness, healthy as it is in itself, may so long be mistaken for progress as to mean the beginning of a great night of spiritual darkness for the whole of this planet. . . .

And now as regards Russia. The first thing to be done is to indicate briefly the numerous points of coincidence between America and Bolshevist Russia. The life-philosophy of Russia, too, is today materialistic and anti-metaphysical. The sex emancipation which is the aim of young feminine America differs in no essential from the ideals and achievements of Russian womanhood. In exactly the same way American caste ethics are beginning more and more to resemble Russian class ethics, and American justice is growing more and more like Russian class justice; American intolerance toward everything un-American is also beginning to resemble the intolerance of the Russians. The same applies to the machine-like equalization which derives from the same reasons in both countries. The lower the original social stratum, the more does the collective become the ideal. In America, as in Russia, and in the same sense as in Russia, the individual is sinking back into the undifferentiated mass. But Russia is, for the rest, something specific, and it is just this specific element which creates the tension with

Europe. Russia has admittedly taken collective man, in contradistinction to the self-determining individuality, as her aim.
In that country it is admittedly hoped (we may recall here the
quotation in the chapter on Italy) to replace personality, hitherto an unavoidable evil, by an apparatus. He who does not
know Russia himself, i.e. does not understand her soul, should
read and absorb René Fülöp-Miller's *Bolshevism,* which will
some day come to be regarded as the classic book on the Leninis-
tic phase; it certainly does not do justice to the positive element
in the new Russia, but it is for that reason the more just in its
treatment of what Russia signifies to Europe. Bolshevism as a
national movement—which is, of course, something totally different from what is intended by its doctrinaire leaders—can
be understood only on the basis of that serfdom which continues to work in the subconscious; it promises the Kingdom of
Heaven to the nameless masses. And as things go, the ideal of
the future bears the closest resemblance to the very thing which
it is fighting. The ideal of the Russian worker reminds one
most of all of conditions on a Roman trireme, where the slaves,
changing shifts at stated hours, pulled at the oars in time to
the hammer-beats of the overseer. And since Bolshevism is
preparing a paradise for those in whose souls the old serfdom
still survives, there is nothing to be amazed at in the Machine-
God which it is trying to substitute for the Christian God. For
the poor wretch, eating is actually the most sacred thing; for
him materialism is the most suitable religion. If this is only
now becoming evident, it is because only now are those material means known which can lift up the general level of conditions. But with all this I do not retract a single word of what
I have said in *The World in the Making* concerning the positive side of Bolshevism. There is not the slightest doubt that
Bolshevism *is* today the gospel for the masses of the Orient,
for what the latter need most at the present moment is material progress; nor is there any doubt that the leading Bolshevists are genuine idealists. Among the ruling strata there doubt-

less reigns an authentic idealism and a fresh new life. The symbolic significance of Moscow for the Orient, as a sign for a better future, cannot be questioned. Still, I have nothing but contempt for the European who, for these reasons, is ready to forget that millions of the very people who were spreading our spirit, the European spirit, in Russia, have been slaughtered in the foulest manner; and equally contemptible to me is the German who, when reminded of this, says, with a superior smile: "Revolutions are not made with gloved hands." This is the sort of thing which is said by a man who is personally too much of a coward to defy even a policeman. I think with the same contempt of the European who acquiesces lightly in the proposition that for Bolshevism there is only a class ethics: whatever benefits the so-called workers is good; one may do absolutely anything to all the others. This point of view is lower than that of any known tribe of savages; it is, unequivocally, the ethics of the criminal. It is *not* of one spirit with the Catholic Inquisition, for the latter honestly believed that by burning the body it would save the soul of the heretic, while the Cheka is merely there to safeguard the material advantage of a definite class. The Satan that rules here is not Lucifer, but that same Devil who was portrayed by Dostoievsky, a shabby city intellectual with the soul of a lackey. The ethics of the new Russia can be understood, and to that extent forgiven, only by reference to the spirit of Russian sectarianism. Lenin used to say, "It does not matter if three-quarters of the human race disappears, if only the remaining quarter is communistic." In so far as Lenin was a great man, this meant religious fanaticism. It is indeed of decisive importance to perceive—and this again has been made clear for us by Fülöp-Miller—that Bolshevism is of one spirit with all authentic Russian sects. All of them wish to realize the Kingdom of Heaven *on earth;* they all stand in opposition to the Church primarily because the latter, in its promises of salvation, was not sufficiently positive and earthly. Thus the entire Russian *intelligentsia* has at all times

been utilitarian; we may remember Tolstoi's expression that
a single pair of boots is more important than all of Shakespeare.
Thus the earthliness of Bolshevism is, before everything else,
typically Russian. Its idealism and fanaticism have the same
meaning as the idealism and fanaticism of any Russian sect.
If the Bolshevist despises the *bourgeois,* if he regards freedom
as a *bourgeois* prejudice and sees nothing wrong in the butch-
ering of heretics, it has the same sense as the condemnation of
the ruling Church, to take a large matter, or the condemnation
of cigarette-smoking, to take a small one, or the self-lacera-
tion and the self-immolation of real fanatics, like the Dukho-
bors and the Chlysty.

Now things will surely not remain in their present state in
Russia. That will be seen to by the very system of education;
if children are taught frank disobedience, the consequence is
bound to be that the next generation, or the one after, will be
just as rebellious against authority as the present generation
is submissive to it. In this, then, Russia will become similar
to America, a future which was in fact foretold before the
World War by all who knew the country; here is seen the
reverse of the incline on the other side of the Atlantic. In
just the same way the "animal" which today rules Russia will
some day, in correspondence with the polarity dominating the
Russian soul, if it does not yield up its place to the "God," at
least give Him a place in the sun. In this the Eurasians must
be seen as the *heredes designati* of the Bolshevists as spiritual
leaders. But Russia will remain Asiatic even then; her European days are over. And above all she will remain collectivist.
Communism was, in one form or another, the ideal of every
Russian. As owner he never felt himself to be in the right;
if fortune favoured him in any way, his conscience always
troubled him. That is why, for a long, long time to come, the
emphasis will rest, in Russia, on the dull masses. And since
these are still barbaric, with the instincts of the primal herd,

there cannot soon arise a new Russian culture. Is it not quite clear now that Europe, with everything that is of value in it, stands in the same contrast to Russia as to America? It will be so for a long time to come. The Russian is more primitive than the American seems likely ever to become. I am certain of a great future for Russia; nay, of one of the very greatest in every respect. Within this marvellously gifted people, rich in soul and vital power, one of the most important cultures of mankind will yet blossom forth. But that great, radiant future which I foresee can dawn only after centuries. Until that time chaos is inevitable.

In the more immediate future America must in any case predominate externally as reality and symbol, and Russia at least as the latter. Why? Because in an age of general barbarization it is the primitive which best bespeaks the spirit of the time. We are now definitely in the age of the chauffeur and the negro dance. Something further should be added on the question of social progress. Every life-phenomenon is of multiple significance. That of the dominating social idea also has the meaning that the individual soul is sinking back into the primordial group soul. The American ideal of service, which is thought to be the highest ideal of Christian civilization, coincides, psychologically, with the norm of every negroid tribe. It is a fearful indication of German demoralization, occasioned by the defeat, that representatives of the German spirit who in other respects deserve to be taken seriously should see in Henry Ford the exponent of a superior ethos; nay, even the ethos of nobility. The ideal of service does not extend further than the ideal of social utility; it knows nothing concerning what is unique. A high standard of living, and not the salvation of the soul, is its highest aim. Thus mere production becomes an end in itself, an absurdity which on the practical side is already becoming patent from the fact that more and more Americans are living on their future income, so that the present is being sold into deeper and deeper debt-slavery to the future—which from the viewpoint of the soul signifies the same bondage as that of the Jews in Egypt, save that the happiness which such bondage offers to the earthly consciousness is deadly in its effects on the higher and deeper development of man; in this respect America actually does appear to be Satanic in spirit. And it is in exactly the same way a dreadful indication of demoralization and despiritualization that a philosophy like that of Alfred Adler (it should be carefully distinguished from his psychotherapeutic and pedagogic method), which lays the emphasis on "one's fellow man," i.e. on a concept of relationship, should not be considered a threat against humanity.* What Adler seeks as a creator of values, what America represents as a reality, is, from the point of view of the soul, identical with the ideal of Bolshevist collectivism. Man must once again sink back into the group. Undoubtedly this process of regression does mean rejuvenation, quite apart from the fact that in external technical respects it introduces an absolute advance; I repeat that I do not question this latter point at all. But what faces us primarily to the east and west of Europe is, none the less, a return to the matrix of primitivity. This explains, in the last analysis, both the American and the Russian hostility to values; the dimension of values is the dimension of uniqueness. This, then, imposes upon Europe not only a different form of being, but the existence of a mission different from those of the other sections of the world. *Indeed, Europe's mission today is the greatest which has ever been presented to it. To Europe, and to Europe alone, has the task been entrusted to guard the sacred fire of the spirit from extinction during the long night of the spirit which now lies before mankind.* For if the majority of mankind, in its search for rejuvenation, sinks back into the group soul, it means a dark age for spirit, mind, and soul.

* Cf. also my study, *Vom falschen Gemeinschaftsideal,* in Section XIV of my *Weg zur Vollendung.*

Europe's ability to fulfil this task resides in the fact that its entry into the new world in the making—and its entry alone among all the regions—is taking place without a *solution de continuité*. Science and technical development are authentic children of Europe's spirit; their acceptance therefore implies no revolution in the psychic structure. Thus, for us, socialism merely signifies one consequence, among others, of Christianity; it goes back directly to the deepest spiritual roots. Accordingly not only the European *élite*, but the European masses, too, are fundamentally immune to both Americanism and Bolshevism. In Europe no movement of consequence can ever again repudiate spirit for the sake of matter. It is psychologically in advance of the rest of the world. America must become primitive because only now, after a long period of occupation by alien spirits—the rule of Puritanism was actually the military rule of the conqueror—will her primal spirit become the determinant force, and it is a spirit no less primitive than the Russian. The youth of the latter country is strikingly evident. The East and the Far East, again, must—as I have proved in detail in *The World in the Making*—first pass through a phase of materialism. And even where they remain spiritual, their particular sort of spirituality no longer corresponds to modern conditions; the traditional Hindoo saint is no longer the model. From the point of view of psychological differentiation he is not the equal of the European; his consciousness is still in large measure a collective consciousness. What the times call for is the realization, on the basis of strictly *personal* initiative, and on the basis of an express *consciousness of uniqueness*, of those very values which India is still realizing in terms of an undifferentiated group consciousness.

This brings us back to the problem of the basic form of Europe as a totality. The meaning of Europe lies in its individualism; more so, in this present age of triumphant collectivism, than ever before. Now what European would not, by contrast with the American and the Russian, seem an individualist? The Spaniard is an individualist as a man of flesh and blood, the Frenchman as a social, the Britisher as a political being; the German is an individualist as a man of inward spiritual experience, the Italian as a personality pure and simple. But until today none of them was quite consciously the individualist; this alone explains the grotesque fact that Europe could become the breeding-ground for collectivist tendencies. But now the state of affairs is such that if Europe can assert itself at all, it is only to the extent that it places the conscious emphasis on its element of individuality. For only then can it place the emphasis on the qualitative. No value can be produced on the basis of quantity. But quite apart from the question of value, to place any emphasis at all on that which America, Russia, and the awakened East primarily represent, or are better gifted for, indicates a fatal psychological and political misunderstanding. In the new, more compactly interrelated world of humanity, each monad possesses significance only by virtue of its uniqueness. Thus every accentuation of socialism, democracy, and prosperity means, for Europe, the accentuation of its inferior functions; it would be just as if the German were to take the greatest pride not in Goethe, but in the drill sergeant—even though the latter should be in the first rank of his kind. It is obvious that in Europe, too, whatever can be socialized will be socialized; that falls in the same category as reliable train-service. It is equally clear that whatever can be Americanized will be Americanized; that falls in the same category as well-organized department stores. But no European can any longer boast of such functions. That sort of thing can be done by chimpanzees, too,—at least potentially. In Europe the emphasis must be laid solely and singly on the qualitative, and thus on the individualistic and unique. For at the stage of consciousness which the vanguard of humanity has attained today, the realization of values can take place only on the basis of the individual and the unique, through purely personal re-

INDEX

Abd-el-Krim, 91
Adler, Alfred, 349, 390
Alfieri, Vittorio, 153
Alphonso XIII., 83
Alsace-Lorraine, 267
America, standardisation, 210; cultural changes, 355, 356 n.; development, 383; new culture foretold, 384; compared with Bolshevist Russia, 385
Ammers-Küller, Jo van, 263
Amsterdam, 258
Anglomania, 13
Annunzio, Gabriele d', 163, 164
Austria, 145-150

Badrutt, Hans, 228
Balkanisation threatens Europe, 322
Balkans, The, 319-346; problem of, as powder-magazine of Europe: racial enmity, 319; peoples essentially savage, 320; intermarriage of stocks: feuds of Greek times, 321; interference-field of European tensions, 322; structure of peoples democratic, 343; unity of, 345; future significance, 345. *See also* Greeks: Roumanians: Turks
Baltic States, 293-316; spirit of Bolshevism, 294; *rôle* of the German Balts, 302, 306; intellectual life: aristocracy, 303; physical influence, 305, 308; Viking character of the Balt: ruling classes, 307; future, 309; Nordic types, 310; significance: *rôle* of mediator: Russian influence, 312; future of Baltic type, 314; belong to German sphere of culture, 315. *See also* Esthonia.
Balzac, Honoré de, 58, 64
Baumer, Gertrude, 263
Beckendorff, Count, 97
Bedouins, 76
Belgium, French element: character, 265; culture, 266, 269; Flemish art, 266; development, 310; *rôle* of mediator, 312
Bethmann-Hollweg, 100

Bismarck, Otto von, 120
Bjerre, Poul, 277
Bolshevism, 171, 174, 178, 217-218, 294, 312, 385
Bourget, Paul, 193
Boy Scout movement, 31
Buffon, 358
Bulgarians, a nation of Comitadji, 320
Byzantine spirit, rebirth, 326
Byzantine-Greek culture in Balkans, 324

Castile, 75
Cervantes, Miguel de, 84
Charles XII., of Sweden, 274
Chicherin, George Valentinovich, 163
Clauss, L. F., quoted, 70
Cologne, 268
Constantinople, religious conflicts, 321; character, 338
Culture Italienne, excerpt, 176
Czechs, 147

Darmstadt, 278
Dionysius, 331
Don Quixote, 77
Dostoievsky, Feodor M., 146, 313, 350, 364, 387
Dumas, Alexandre, 374
Dutch, The, culture of ugliness, 254; culture, 255; crudeness, 257; Latin form of culture, 258; puritanism, 261; women, 262

Eesti, 302
England, 13-38; instinct: intuition of the English, 15; intellect, 16; political tendencies, 17; ideals, 18; animal type, 20; instinct for power, 21; understanding of fellow-man, 23; social character, 29; sport spirit, 30; intellectuals, 33; religiosity, 34; future, 35
Esthonia, 293; revolution, 293; birth of a nation, 295; grants cultural autonomy to her minorities, 298; aristocracy, 304; language, 305;